$18 —

D1213984

Foreword by INNAIAH NARISETTI

the
TRUTH
about the
GITA

A CLOSER LOOK AT
HINDU SCRIPTURE

V. R. NARLA

 Prometheus Books

59 John Glenn Drive
Amherst, New York 14228–2119

Published 2010 by Prometheus Books

Inquiries should be addressed to
Prometheus Books
59 John Glenn Drive
Amherst, New York 14228–2119
VOICE: 716–691–0133
FAX: 716–691–0137
WWW.PROMETHEUSBOOKS.COM

14 13 12 11 10   5 4 3 2 1

Library of Congress Cataloging-in-Publication Data

Venkateswara Rao, Narla, 1908–1985.
    The truth about the Gita : a closer look at Hindu scripture / by V. R. Narla.
        p.   cm.
    Originally published: Hyderabad, India : Narla Institute of New Thought, 1988.
    Includes bibliographical references.
    ISBN 978–1–61614–183–7 (pbk.)
    1. Bhagavadgita—Criticism, interpretation, etc. I. Title.

BL1138.66.V47 2010
294.5'924046—dc22

                                                                2010012923

Printed in the United States of America

Contents

The Bhagavad Gita, the Hindu Bible

The Bhagavad Gita, popularly known as the Gita, is considered one of the three principal holy texts of Hinduism along with the Vedas and the Upanishads, though strictly speaking it is not one of its scriptures. *Bhagavad Gita* means "Celestial Song of God" or "Song Celestial." It was a dialogue between a dispirited warrior, Arjuna, and his charioteer, Lord Krishna, on the battlefield of Kurukshetra in one of the two major epics of India, the *Mahabharata* (the other is the *Ramayana*). This dialogue, which extends over seven hundred verses divided into eighteen chapters, was not originally present in the *Mahabharata* but was added to it at a later date. Originally written to combat Buddhism, the Gita not only has become very popular over the years but also has ascended to spiritual heights that are afforded to only the Vedas and the Upanishads in ancient Hindu literature.

Like many other religious Indian texts, neither the author of the Bhagavad Gita nor the exact dates of its composition are known, but based on the references to the Upanishads and Buddhism in it, the Bhagavad Gita is believed to have been written post-Buddha by several authors over a period of a couple of centuries in the pre-Christian era, probably 400–200 BCE.

The *Mahabharata*, probably part historical but mostly mytholog-ical, is a very long epic, almost eight times longer than Homer's *Odyssey* and *Iliad* combined, and it deals with the family feud of cousins Kurus and Pandavas. Eventually the cousins went to war, and it was at this point in the story of the *Mahabharata* that the Bhagavad Gita was inserted.

The Hindu religion is perhaps unique among world's religions in that it prohibits almost 85 percent of its followers from reading its own scriptures. That is because the invading Aryans were so racist that they never considered the subjugated native Indians as equal to them or as deserving of respect. Therefore, they developed a strict, hierarchical caste system arranged from top to bottom as follows: Brahmans (the invading Aryans), Kshatriyas (warriors), Vysyas (farmers, herders, and merchants), and Sudras (servants and slaves; *sudra* means "decadent"). Placement in a caste is determined by birth. According to Hindu scrip-tures, Brahmans, the highest caste, are born from the mouth of Brahma, the lord of creation; Kshatriyas from the chest; Vysyas from the thighs; and Sudras from the feet. Not satisfied with that degrada-tion of lower castes, the writers of the Bhagavad Gita went further and proclaimed that women (of any caste) were born from wombs of sin. All the women (50 percent the population), including those belonging to the Brahman caste, and both men and women belonging to the Sudra caste (about 35 percent of the population) were prohibited by the Hindu religion from reading the Vedas and other scriptures and from having any education at all. Only Kshaytriyas (warriors) were given a modicum of respect among the native Indians because of the political power they wielded and the wealth they amassed.

Worse still, below the Sudras, they created a new class of outcasts or untouchables sometime later. These people had no caste at all. They performed the most menial of jobs, such as dealing with dead bodies and cleaning toilets. Higher-caste people were told that if they touched one of the casteless, they would be contaminated and would need to go through cleansing rituals.

As Narla, the author of the present work, wrote on another occa-sion, the Hindu religion, which saw a god in a fish, in a tortoise, and even in a boar, treated some humans worse than the quadrupeds and reptiles. Their treatment in Hindu society was much much worse than that of Jews in Nazi Germany and black people under the apartheid regime of South Africa. They instituted the most barbaric civil law, called *Manu Smriti*, against the Sudras and the untouchables. There is no other religion in the world that is as shamelessly and openly racist as Hinduism.

Dr. B. R. Ambedkar, one of the leaders of the untouchables, a great intellectual and humanist thinker, and the architect of the Constitution of free India, once commented not only that there was inequality in Hinduism but also that inequality was the official doctrine of Hinduism. He said that Hinduism was nothing short of racism, fascism, and Nazism combined.

Free speculation foreshadowed in the Upanishads and the impact of the teachings of thinkers like Kanada, Kapila, and others led to the six *darshans* (schools of thought) of ancient India. These six darshans were actually of differing origins and purposes and were divided into three groups of two complementary schools of thought: Nyaya and Vaisesika, Sankhya and Yoga, and Mimansa and Vedanta. Of these systems, Sankhya and Purva Mimansa strongly refute the theory of God. Sankhya is full of subtle arguments that reject the possibility of there being an all-powerful creator and controller of the world. The only God-fearing candidate among these schools of thought is Utthara Mimansa, of which the philosopher Sankara's (also known as Sankaracharya) Advaita or Vedantic philosophy is an offshoot.

As a reaction against the inequalities and rigidities of Hinduism, a new religion called Buddhism, based on the teachings of prince-turned-sage Siddhartha Gautama (popularly known as Gautama Buddha or Buddha), arose sometime between the sixth and fourth century BCE.

Buddha accepted both the materialistic-atomic theory of Vaiseshika and the rationalistic-mechanistic conception of Sankhya. Buddha repeatedly advised his followers to doubt, inquire, and be honestly convinced before accepting his ideas. Buddha opposed the division of society into four castes. His repeated saying that all four castes are equally pure is rather embarrassing and uncomfortable for the higher castes of Hinduism. The Hindu caste system was undermined by the egalitarian character of Buddhism. The new philosophy of revolution caught the imagination of the Indians and soon spread all over India. Within four centuries after the death of the Buddha, Brahmanism was eclipsed; its dogmas, tenets, and traditions were ridiculed. Repeatedly challenging the supremacy of Brahmanism, the Buddhist revolution, by removing strangling restrictions, brought the Indian people spiritual freedom, social emancipation, and economic prosperity. People were happy. Even the most maligned of the castes, Sudras, became rulers in parts of the country. Brahmanism had fallen on bad days, Hinduism had faced its first challenge, and Brahman superiority and livelihood were threatened.

Buddha disputed the authority of Brahmanical scriptures and vigorously denounced the sacrificial rites and rituals of the Vedic religion. Even though he doubted the existence of the soul or the Supreme Being or *paramatma* (ultimate soul or God), he studiously maintained silence about soul and God and believed in the theory of Karma and rebirth, which is contrary to the theory on which his teachings were based. This caused confusion among his followers. The Sankhya school of thought logically leads to the negation of the soul, reincarnation, and God. In the ensuing confusion, his followers continued to follow Vedic rituals on the occasions of births and deaths. This became a fatal flaw in Buddhism. Deviations from the strict materialist conception and rationalist doctrines in the teachings of Buddha proved to be a fatal weakness of his philosophy and led to dissensions in the Buddhist order, thereby affording a needed opportunity to the defeated and demoralized Brahmans. Brahmans who were waiting for an opportunity grabbed this loophole and tried to undermine Buddhism by creating doubts in the minds of Buddhists with their composition of the Bhagavad Gita dialogues.

Though Buddha was an agnostic and never claimed to be a god, the majority of his followers began to revere him as such after his death. The concept and symbol of God in the Hindu religion were very complex and too speculative until that time. To counter the influence of

Buddha, Hindus needed to create a clearly defined, easy-to-worship god like Buddha to its followers. For a variety of reasons, Lord Krishna, a popular ruler of the times because of his well-known heroic, Machiavellian, and romantic deeds, was the obvious choice; and he was redefined as the reincarnation of the god Vishnu to counter the prince-turned-sage Buddha (who was also later made another incarnation of Vishnu in Hindu literature). In the Bhagavad Gita, Lord Krisha was made to utter that he was God, the creator of the universe; that he created the caste hierarchy to promote *dharma* (peace and harmony) in this world; and that he would come back to earth whenever the Hindu dharma is threatened. It was the most pivotal choice ever made to humanize the concept of God in the Hindu religion.

Facing his cousins, uncles, great uncles, and teachers on the battlefield, Arjuna refuses to fight; his objections represent the position of Buddhism and Krishna's responses correspond with the interests of the Brahmans and the ideology of Hinduism. Krishna's arguments offer a strong support to traditional Hinduism intended to preserve the caste system while also accommodating the popular and unthreatening features of Buddhism.

Later spreading the message of the Gita, Hindu fanatics, with the help of some cruel Hindu kings, so ruthlessly persecuted Buddhists that all were either slain, exiled, or made to change their faith. Some historians think that those converts were relegated to the untouchables. Thousands and thousands of Buddhist stupas and chaityas were demolished, and some of them were converted to Hindu temples. There is scarcely a case on record where a religious persecution was so successfully carried out as that by which Buddhism was driven out of India. The Hindus who were justifiably angry that their temples were destroyed by invading Muslim rulers never expressed any regret to what their ancestors did to the Buddhists.

Written by different authors at different times on the one hand and trying to combine the two vastly conflicting schools of thought of Sankhya and Vedanta on the other, the Bhagavad Gita is full of contradictions—both at the fundamental level and at the highest level of philosophical discourse. What is said in one chapter is contradicted in the very next chapter. Moreover, Sanskrit has a limited vocabulary, so the same word has many different meanings. All this leads to conflicting interpretations depending on the proclivities of commentators. There are now more than four thousand different interpretations and translations of the Gita in different international and Indian languages. For example, Gandhi thought that the Gita was supporting his viewpoint, and he quoted the Gita in support of his nonviolence; whereas his assassin, Godse, also quoted the Gita in support of his abominable act.

Prior to the revivalist Hindu philosopher Sankara's commentary in the eighth century, there were not many commentatries on the Gita. Even after Sankara, not many Hindu scholars took such commentaries seriously until recently. Because of the need for native political leadership in nineteenth century to create an image of an essentially spiritualistic India, as opposed to the materialistic West, Sankara's Advaita philosophy was elevated as the pinnacle of Indian philosophical achievement and the Bhagavad Gita practically became the Hindu Bible.

In fact, one might ask, what is the need for another book on the Gita when thousands of books were already published on the Gita? Most of them are uncritical eulogies of the Gita. As far as we know, prior to V. R. Narla there was only one critical study on the Gita and, sadly, that is out of print: Prem Nath Bazaz, *The Role of the Bhagavad Gita in Indian History* (New Delhi: Sterling Publishers, 1975).

The author of the present work, Narla Venkateswara Rao, popularly known as V. R. Narla to the English-reading public, was a giant among Indian journalists. Besides being an original thinker, a creative writer, a rationalist, and a secular humanist to the core, he was also an eminent sociologist. He was always free, fearless, and merciless in his comments and criticism. He was not afraid to speak the truth, however unpalatable it might be.

He read and digested a lot. His personal collection of over twenty-four thousand books were donated to Dr. B. R. Ambedkar Open University, Hyderabad, India, posthumously.

Narla's book *The Truth about the Gita* reveals his vast learning acquired by a long, critical study and perseverance and his brilliant critical faculties. He analyzed in depth the historical, social, and philosophical context in which Gita was originally written and the pernicious effect it had on Indian society.

As Narla eloquently points out, the Bhagavad Gita is neither moral nor progressive; it is the antithesis of everything that is progressive and desirable in this world, and it indeed is the bible of bondage and slavery. It is anti–human rights and anti–human values. It is a sad day if Indians are still under the delusion that it is their salvation. The sooner we recognize the Gita for what it is, the better for India and the world.

Innaiah Narisetti
Aramalla Purnachandra

PREFACE

I n the pages of this book I have hit hard at some great men, Indian and foreign, who hailed the Bhagavad Gita not only as a great religious classic but also as an infallible guide to philosophy and ethics, to science and sociology, and to much else. I offer no apology for what I did. However great they may be, they are deficient in one vital respect: they lack a modern mind.

What is a modern mind? It is a mind that is allergic to faith, that despises superstition, abhors dogma, hates all cant and hypocrisy. It is a mind that thinks rationally and scientifically and that rejects everything that fails to stand the test of reason. It is a mind that is free, innovative, and daring; a mind that seeks to unravel the still unknown truths about itself, about life in general, and about the vast cosmos of which our earth is a tiny little speck of dust.

And at the center of a really modern mind, there sits, not God, but man. That man is not bound by race, religion, nationality, class, or caste; indeed, there is nothing about him that is narrow, arrogant, mean, or selfish. He concerns himself with this world and not with the next. He does not believe in life after death but in generations yet unborn. If someone turns up and says, "I am your maker," he tells him, "Begone! I am my own maker. In fact, I am still very much in the process of making myself. In my infancy, out of my fear and ignorance, I created myriads of gods and goddesses along with an equal number of heavens and hells. Now I abolish them all."

To such a man with such a mind, the Gita must necessarily appear to be crude and primitive, and replete with half-truths, self-contradictions, baseless assertions, and insufferable braggadocio. As D. D. Kosambi has rightly said, the Gita's "divine but rather scrambled message with its command of expository Sanskrit is characteristically Indian in attempting to reconcile the irreconcilable, in its power of gulping down sharp contradictions painlessly."

Of all my books, the writing of this one has given me a feeling of fulfillment. There was a time when I was hoping that with the dawn of freedom we will awaken into a new life. But to my utter sorrow I find that what we are actually having is a tidal wave of revivalism. We are now far more credulous, superstitious, orthodox, and hypocritical than we were prior to 1947. Our freedom is more an illusion than a reality. When the mind is in chains, how can there be any freedom? Despite our democratic institutions and other symbols of political freedom, we are not even politically free in the real and full sense of the term.

How to explain this? By hindsight I have slowly come to realize that our nationalist movement, right from its inception, had its roots in revivalism. The Bhagavad Gita was the source of inspiration for such diverse types of national leaders as Bankim Chandra Chatterji, Vivekananda, Bipinchandra Pal, Lajpat Rai, Arabinda Ghosh, Bal Gangadhar Tilak, Annie Besant, and Gandhi. It was the supreme gospel of even Nathuram Godse, who assasinated Gandhi. Need we, then, wonder why we have entered a new dark age after our independence? Indeed, even the day, hour, and minute for assuming that independence was fixed after studying the course of the stars and planets in the heavens! As I got older and lonelier—I am now seventy-six—all this weighed heavily on my heart. Can I at this late stage of my life do my mite to stem the rising tide of revivalism?

This book is proof enough that I could. And it is that which gives me a feeling of fulfillment.

What now remains to be done is to thank the many friends who helped me in writing this book. I am specially grateful to Dr. Y. Venkateswara Rao, Dr. D. Anjaneyulu, and Dr. P. S. N. Murti who read its typescript for me and offered many valuable suggestions. However, they are in no way responsible for the opinions expressed in the course of the book; they are wholly mine.

Finally, I want to make an appeal to the younger generation. The world is changing rapidly, and from decade to decade the speed of that change is accelerating phenomenally. During the past eighty years alone there has been more change, much of it for good and almost as much for evil, than during the past eight thousand years of civilization. Either we keep in step with that change and strive to arrest any drift toward disaster (and most of all, a drift toward a global war), or we perish. In this mighty task, the responsibility of the younger generation is vital. Unless it breaks loose from the old habits of thought fostered by the Gita and the rest of the scriptures of the world and evolves new concepts and new values, intelligent life, perhaps all life, will disappear from the face of our planet, which is our mother, our cradle, our hope, and our future.

INTRODUCTION

A more apt title for this book would have been "The Myth of the Gita." For all that is traditionally said about it is open to serious doubt. Was a great war really fought on the plain now hallowed as Kurukshetra? In case it was fought, did every principality in the India of the day, and some even beyond India, join one side or the other? What was the date of the war? Was there a Krishna Vasudeva who elected to be charioteer of Arjuna? Did Arjuna, said to be the single-handed victor of many battles, lose his nerve when he saw the mighty army of Duryodhana arrayed against the smaller one of his own? Granting that he was, in fact, shaken by the thought of having to kill his kith and kin to gain a kingdom, could a pep talk by Krishna prepare his mind for the terrible carnage that followed? And did the two vast armies, poised for battle, stand still while the question-and-answer session between Arjuna and Krishna went on for the better part of a day?

Another important question that faces us is this: in case the Bhagavad Gita, the Song Celestial, was actually sung by Krishna on the battlefield of Kurukshetra, how did it come down to us? The full text of the Gita, says the *Mahabharata*, was reported at the end of the day by Sanjaya to the old and blind Dhritarashtra sitting miles away in his palace at Hastinapura.[1] Not only did Sanjaya report every word that dropped from the blessed lips of Krishna, but he also described the setting of the divine discourse without missing the slightest gesture by the head or hand or the very lifting of an eyebrow. Unseen by anyone, unhurt by any weapon, he moved freely from one side of the battle front to the other. Day or night made no difference to him. He knew no fatigue and worked round the clock. He read the innermost thoughts of everyone as though he had an open book before him.

Naturally this leads us to yet another question. How did Sanjaya manage to do what sounds so incredible? How could he put the inventions of the present scientific and technological age, such as radio, television, and video, to shame? The traditionalists will, of course, retort that even to pose such a question is silly. They will tell you that the sages of that bygone age were only a notch below the gods and they had the power to grant any boon, and Vyasa was a supreme lord of boons. And so, when Dhritarashtra, the congenitally blind Kuru king keenly wanting to follow the fortunes of the war, prayed that Sanjaya, his crony, be given the boon of seeing and hearing and knowing everything, Vyasa gave it readily. Obviously, these miraculous powers were given only for the duration of the war. For we do not know of Sanjaya having used them ever afterward. Furthermore, there was a point when those powers let him down. On the last day of the war, Satyaki spotted him and might have put him to the sword but for the timely intervention of Vyasa.[2]

Brushing aside the traditionalists who put a pious gloss over ugly facts, it should be bluntly stated here that Dhritarashtra, thus favored by Vyasa, was Vyasa's illegitimate son. Can a holy man like Vyasa be guilty of lechery? Yes, he was. And he was himself the natural son of Satyavati, the offspring of her premarital sex with Parasara, a great sage. And in his turn, the greater sage, Vyasa, was the father of four illegitimate sons in all.

Frankly, the age of the *Mahabharata* was the permissive age *par excellence*. In that age drinking and deceiving were customary. Cattle lifting and the abduction of prospective brides were widely prevalent. Fratricide and genocide were not uncommon. To ensure royal succession and to avoid sure passage to hell, the birth of a son even outside wedlock was actively promoted. Indeed, it was at the instance of Satyavati, the queen-mother, that Vyasa impregnated her two royal daughters-in-law, Ambika and Ambalika. Their dissolute husband died prematurely without leaving a son to continue the Bharata dynasty. As we will presently see, this was no solitary example of progeny by proxy in that particular dynasty, nor for that matter, in that particular age.

Despite the fact that Vyasa, according to traditionalists, was almost a demigod, he was not much of a success as progenitor. Dhritarashtra, the son whom he begot by Ambika, was blind; Pandu, the son whom he next begot by Ambalika, was pale and sickly. Only in his third go was he able to produce a normal, healthy, and intelligent boy, called Vidura. And yet Vidura's right of succession to the throne was never so much as thought of. For his mother was the Sudra maid (which in effect meant the slave) of Ambika. Disliking the very sight of Vyasa, Ambika (though urged by her mother-in-law) refused to sleep with him for a second time and sent in her maid. Obviously Vyasa had a happy time with her, for the outcome of his encounter with her in bed was happy. Besides these three sons, he had a fourth one by the name Suka. One day, it is said, Vyasa was rubbing two dry sticks against each other to produce the sacred fire. While on the job, he chanced to see a buxom wench from the large harem of Indra, the lord of heaven. It made him so libidinous that he spilled his seed all over the holy sticks in his hand. Lo and behold! That very moment Suka was born to excel, in some respects, both his father and grandfather in greatness.

If we now turn to the next generation and its principal heroes, we find that all the five Pandavas were illegitimate children. The mother of the first three was Kunti,[3] and each of them had a different father; the mother of the next two, who were twins, was Madri, and they had a set of two fathers. Like Satyavati, Kunti also had premarital sex, and the son born out of that affair was Karna. Unlike Satyavati, however, Kunti did not own up her first-born but abandoned him as soon as he was born. Putting the gloss of supernaturalism over such licentiousness and making gods party to such lechery, as we find it done in the *Mahabharata*, is to degrade gods to the level of lechers!

So widespread was the permissiveness of the age that sexual loose-
ness, bordering on depravity, was not at all confined to the Bharata
dynasty. It was, as hinted earlier, very much present in other dynasties as
well. Kamsa was the son of King Ugrasena of Madhura and the maternal
uncle of Krishna; he owed his birth to the rape of the queen by a danava,
that is, by a non-Aryan. The birth story of Drupada, the Panchala king,
is odious. Still more odious is the story of the birth of his two children
Draupadi and Dhrishtadyumna. His intense desire for progeny led him
to solicit the help of two sages who were brothers. Both of them were
natural sons like Vyasa. Perhaps due to that very reason they almost
matched Vyasa in their miraculous powers. The younger of the two
refused to help Drupada at any price, but the elder agreed to take up the
assignment on the condition that he be given a hundred thousand cows
as his fee. Toward the end of the sacrifice initiated to produce a son, the
officiating sage (that is, the elder one) invited the queen to sleep with
him. As she was having her period, she had to ask him to wait for a few
days. But as the auspicious hour would not wait, the sage produced there
and then Draupadi and Dhrishtadyumna. The two of them emerged
from the sacrificial fires not as babies but as a fully grown maiden and a
robust young man, the maiden bedecked like a princess, and the young
man fitted with a coronet and armor like a prince. While the maiden was
black, the young man looked ugly, almost hideous. The former was so
black that her given name was Krishna ("the black one"). Despite her
dark color, she was stunningly beautiful, and her hand was much sought
after. Ultimately she became the polyandrous wife of the five Pandava
brothers.

To traditionalists, all this may be another proof of the miraculous
power of sacrifices; but to a modern man with a liberated mind, this can
only be the skullduggery that was being widely practiced by the so-called
sages. It is quite likely that the illegitimate children of an illegitimate
sage were palmed off on a willing Drupada as gifts from heaven.

Indeed, it looked as though it was the age of illegitimacy. For we
find, apart from many royal princes, the two leading teachers of
archery of the age (both of them from the priest caste) were also illegitimate; the reference here is to Drona and Kripa. Of course, their

questionable origins are hidden, as usual, behind the smoke screen of sanctimony. Can anyone who cares for naked truth deny that fornication in its grossest form was a part of the more important of the Vedic sacrifices?[4]

There is, I submit, ample justification for referring here at some length to what is frankly putrid stuff. For our traditionalists extol the *Mahabharata* day in and day out as the fifth Veda. They tell us that it is the longest epic in world literature, indeed, an encyclopedia of all knowledge, a veritable treasure house of history and polity, of sociology and philosophy, of religion and ethics, and of much else. They even tell us that what is not found in its pages is not worth knowing. To counter their balderdash, it needs to be said that the *Mahabharata* is also Vyasa's thesaurus of vice.

Without any apology for drifting too far from Kurukshetra and the chariot of Arjuna stationed on no-man's-land to serve for the time being as a pulpit for Krishna, let us now return to the sermon he delivered in the form of the Gita. When Sanjaya, the war correspondent of yore, was giving his graphic oral report to Dhritarashtra that evening, was anyone recording it on electronic tape for the use of posterity? No. But was not Vyasa there to work wonders? He had a prodigious brain unmatched even by the latest computer. With its help, he edited the four Vedas, composed the *Mahabharata*, authored all the eighteen major Puranas, wrote the Brahma Sutra, and did a lot more. To him, reproducing the text of the Gita, which is after all a tiny fragment of the mighty and weighty *Mahabharata*, was child's play. And he did that many years after the Kurukshetra War. Along with the rest of that epic, he taught the Gita to four of his disciples, besides his son. One of the four was Vaisampayana, and like his guru, he also had a computer brain. When Janamejaya, the great-grandson of Arjuna, performed a great sacrifice to extirpate the Naga clan,* Vaisampayana recited for the edification of the great assembly at the sacrifice the whole of the *Mahabharata*, including the Gita. On that occasion Souti Ugrasravas was present and he, in his turn, recited it from first to last for the bene-

---

*Obviously for everything they had a sacrifice with a stipulated fee for the priests in gold, cows, and slave girls.

fit of Sounaka and a host of other sages who performed a twelve-year sacrifice in the Naimisa Forest. It is not on record as to who took up the role of recital after Souti.[5]

However that may be, the point is that between the original teaching of the Gita by Krishna and its recital by Souti at least a century must have elapsed. For after the Kurukshetra War, Yudhisthira ruled for thirty-six years; Parikshit, his successor, ruled for sixty years.[6] It is not known exactly when Janamejaya launched his genocide of the Nagas as a measure of revenge for their assassination of his father, Parikshit. Nor is it known definitely how many years later Sounaka initiated his sacrifice[7] in the Naimisa Forest. But of one thing there can be no doubt. The time lag between Krishna's teaching of the Gita and its recital by Souti cannot be taken as less than a century. Not one but several centuries must have elapsed from the time of Souti to the time of the final redaction of the Gita to writing. If we have to give credence to traditionalists, that gap is to be reckoned not in centuries but in millennia. Over such a wide gap in time did the text of the Gita as taught by Krishna retain its original size or its original shape or the scope of its message?

It can, of course, be argued by the traditionalists that the Vedas were reduced to writing after a much longer gap than the Gita and yet even the nuances of its pronunciation retain their original purity. But the Gita is no Veda and even now its scriptural authority is not universally accepted. In fact, none seems to have taken the Gita very seriously before Adi Sankaracharya, who lived in the eighth century CE and wrote a commentary on it as a part of his campaign to destroy Buddhism. Not to speak of others, neither the Arya Samajists nor the Brahmo Samajists attach much value to the Gita. And so any analogy sought to be drawn between the purity of the text of the Vedas and of the Gita can hardly be relevant.

The improbable setting in which the Gita is said to have been taught and the dubious way in which it is supposed to have been handed down to us are good enough reasons to convince a rational mind that it is a myth. What Alexander Pope said of rumors is amply true of the Gita:

The flying rumours gathered as they roll'd,
Scarce any tale as sooner heard than told;
And all who told it added something new,
And all who heard it made enlargements too.[8]

Having first read the Gita when I was a fresher at college, and that was more than half a century ago, and having given very many years to the study of innumerable commentaries on it, I am convinced that all that is said about the Gita, including its authorship, its time and place of composition, its transmission from generation to generation, its importance as compendium of a unified and profound system of philosophy with relevance for all people and all times, in a word, everything that is sedulously propagated about it, is a myth. In that case, why did I not entitle my book "The Myth of the Gita"? My only reason is the hope that with a comparatively mild title I may not turn the devotees of the Gita against me even without reading me. To be sure, I have no illusions that I can convert them to my view, but even if a few out of their mighty ranks come to realize the hollowness of the tall claims made on behalf of the Gita, mine will not, I believe, be a wasted effort.

A DOUBTFUL WAR

"The word *Mahabharata*," wrote Edward Washburn Hopkins, "is used by Panini, but only as an adjective which might be applied to anything great, connected with the Bharathas, a hero or town, as well as a war or poem."[1] There can be no doubt that the *Mahabharata* is a great poem regarding the Bharathas. As we have it today, it is "about eight times the size of the *Iliad* and the *Odyssey* put together."[2] But can it also be taken to mean a great war that was fought on the plain of Kurukshetra between the Bharathas, that is, between the Kurus and Pandus? There are very many reasons to hold that no such war was fought, and they can be written down serially:

(1) While the Kurus are well known to the Vedic literature, the Pandus are not. As was pointed out by Hopkins, who made a special study of the *Mahabharata*, they do not find a place even in the Brahmanas and Sudras.[3] This was specially emphasised by Max Muller. He said:

> The names of the Kurus and Bharathas are common in Vedic literature, but the names of the Pandavas have never been met with. It has been observed that even in Panini's grammar the name Pandu or Pandava does not occur, while the Kurus and Bharathas are fre-

quently mentioned, particularly in rules treating of the formation of patronymics and similar words.[4]

This means that even during the lifetime of Panini, that is, during the middle of the fifth century BCE,[5] the Pandavas were unknown.

(2) When the Rig-Veda takes notice of a local and tribal war fought between Sudas, the king of the Bharatas, and a confederacy of ten kings on the banks of Parushani (the modern Ravi),[6] surely a war on a national scale, indeed, on an international scale as the *Mahabharata* would have us believe, could not have been left unrecorded in the whole corpus of the Vedic literature. To quote Max Muller again:

> The war between the Kurus and the Pandavas, which forms the principal subject of the *Mahabharata*, is unknown to the Veda.[7]

(3) Kurukshetra is frequently mentioned in the Vedic literature as a holy place but never as a battlefield.[8]

(4) Vyasa and Vaisampayana figure in the Taittiriya Aranyaka but not as the first two authors of the *Mahabharata*.[9]

(5) In the Kathaka Samhita there is a specific reference to a Kuru king named Dhritarashtra, but that reference is not in the context of the Kurukshetra War; it pertains to a ritual dispute between Dhritarashtra and his priest.[10]

(6) Parikshit is praised in the Atharva Veda as the ruler of a prosperous kingdom; Janamejaya is lauded in the Sathapatha Brahmana as a performer of sacrifices and a lavish giver of gifts to priests. But neither is specifically mentioned as a descendent of Arjuna.[11]

(7) In the *Mahabharata* Arjuna is the natural son of Indra, but in the Satapatha Brahmana, he is Indra himself.[12]

(8) An *akshauhini* (an army corps) consists of 21,870 chariots, 21,870 elephants, 65,610 horses and 109,350 foot soldiers.[13] It is said that as many as eighteen akshauhinis were assembled on the plain of Kurukshetra, eleven by the Kurus and seven by the Pandus. The assembly of such a mammoth force is not easy even today, and impossible in the ancient times. Moreover, no single battlefield can hold such a gigantic force. [14]

(9) The total number of horses in the Kurukshetra War works out to be 1,180,980. And yet, strangely we do not hear of any major cavalry engagement. Now, the number of foot soldiers is of the order of almost two million. In spite of it, the role of infantry in the war is nebulous. But references to single combats are plenty. It is, therefore, quite reasonable to presume that the war, if it was fought, comprised mostly single combats, as it was the general practice among all primitive peoples.[15]

(10) On a very liberal estimate the total number of participants in the war could not have been more than four million (in arriving at this figure two men for each chariot and two for each elephant are allowed). And yet, the total number of the dead exceeded 1,660 million.[16] So we have to presume that each combatant died more than four hundred times!

(11) In the age in which the Kurukshetra War is said to have been fought, the weaponry was crude, and no great war can be fought with crude weaponry. In this context, it should be noted that even the Harappans with a higher civilization used as their weaponry only stones and slings, clumsy axes, and arrowheads made of copper, bronze, and stone.

(12) Iron weapons, which are essential for a major war, could not have played any significant part in the Kurukshetra War. Iron came into general use in India only after the sixth century BCE, and it was definitely unknown before the eleventh century BCE.[17]

(13) Magadha was held to be non-Aryan and hence an impure region till a fairly late date. So, too, was all land that lies to the south of the Vindhyas. Because of this, neither Magadha nor any of the South Indian kingdoms could have, as it is claimed, taken part in the Kurukshetra War.

(14) When communications were primitive, transport of large armies from distant places in India and abroad would have posed insurmountable obstacles.

(15) It is simply absurd to say, as it is done in the *Mahabharata*, that Bhagadatta, the king of Pragjyothisha (Assam) played an important role in the Kurukshetra War.[18] He does not figure in the Vedic literature, either the earlier one or the later. Even Panini of the fifth century BCE shows no knowledge of him.

(16) A more absurd thing is to say that the Yavanas, the Sakas and the Pahlavas fought on the side of the Kurus. None of these peoples had any active role in Indian history before, say, the fifth century BCE.

Many more points can be adduced to doubt the historicity of the Kurukshetra War. But I will make just one more: (17) The army assembled for the war, it is stated, consisted of eighteen akshauhnis; the duration of the war was eighteen days; of the active combatants, the survivors after the war on the side of the Pandavas were six, that is, one-third of eighteen, and three on the side of the Kurus, that is, one-sixth of eighteen; Yudhishtira ruled for thirty-six years, that is twice eighteen; Krishna died thirty-six years after the Kurukshetra War, that is, again, twice eighteen; the epic that records the war has eighteen cantos and even the chapters of the Gita are eighteen. This cannot be something fortuitous. Some superstitious fellow, who was a believer in numerology and had a hand in the redraft of the *Mahabharata*, must have contrived this silly nonsense.

In view of these and other considerations, not a few men of eminence questioned the historicity of the Kurukshetra War.

I will refer to only some of them. R. G. Bhandarkar, one of the earliest historians of modern India, much respected for his sound scholarship and sober judgement, had no doubt in his mind that not only the *Mahabharata* but also the *Ramayana* and the Puranas (mythologies) were not historical works.[19] Time and again he bemoaned why modern education was not instilling into us the modern spirit, the spirit that questions everything and puts everything to the test of reason before accepting it as truth.

Another historian and a junior contemporary of Bhandarkar, R. C. Dutt, went a step further; he stated that "the incidents of the war in the *Mahabharata* were undoubtedly mythical." He also thought that "the five Pandava brothers and their common wife were myths."[20] Dutt may not have been a specialist in history as Bhandarkar was. But he had the distinction of translating the Rig-Veda into Bengali, defying the hue and cry raised against him by the orthodox folk as to how a Sudra dare go anywhere near the Vedas. And his abridged translations of the *Mahabharata* and the *Ramayana* into English are still rated highly. So, Dutt should have spoken with knowledge and conviction when he dismissed the Kurukshetra War and the Pandavas and their joint wife as fictitious.

Much earlier than either Dutt or Bhandarkar, Rammohan Roy had drawn pointed attention to one of the opening verses of the *Mahabharata*. In that verse Vyasa calls his epic "a work of imagination."[21] After having acquainted himself thoroughly with the scriptures of all the major religions of the world, and having initiated a new branch of study which has since come to be known as "comparative religion," Roy placed no value on the Gita. In his voluminous writings on religion he ignored it almost totally.

Unlike Roy, Gandhi valued the Gita greatly. "[The] Gita," he said, "has been a mother to me ever since I became first acquainted with it in 1889."[22] Even so, he had serious doubts about the historicity of the *Mahabharata*. He thought that the battle which formed, so to say, the backdrop to the Gita was none other than the battle that goes on all the time in every individual between the forces of good and evil.

Years earlier to Gandhi, Vivekananda took exactly the same stand. He said:

There is enough ground of doubt as regards the historicity of Arjuna and others, and it is this: Shatapatha Brahmana is a very ancient book. In it are mentioned somewhere or other all the names of those who were the performers of the Ashvamedha Yajna, but in those places there is not only no mention, but no hint even, of the names of Arjuna and others, though it speaks of Janamejaya, the son of Parikshit, who was grandson of Arjuna.[23]

Yet in the *Mahabharata* and other books it is stated that Yudhisthira, Arjuna, and others celebrated the Ashvamedha sacrifice.

Despite all this, Vivekananda thought, like Gandhi, that the mythical nature of the *Mahabharata* does not take away the value of the epic as a whole or of its most important section, the Gita. It is a stand that cannot be accepted without demur. Surely, if Arjuna was mythical, his alter ego, Krishna, cannot be a historical personage either. And if both were mythical, how could one discourse to the other? And if some nameless author or authors fabricated the Gita and interpolated it into the *Mahabharata*, how can it be called the Song Celestial or the Divine Lay?

Traditionalists—they are always with us in their serried ranks, and their ranks consist not only of the illiterate but also of the highly learned, including many scientists and philosophers—well, our traditionalists may dismiss Dutt and Bhandarkar as historians of yesteryear; they may maintain that while Roy and Vivekananda and Gandhi might have made history, each in his own way, they were no historians. But can they deny the standing or stature of that multifaceted genius, D. D. Kosambi, as a historian? A mathematician of international repute, he applied scientific methods to the study of Indian coins. He brought to bear the Marxist approach on Indian history. Though our professional historians did their best, first to ignore him, and then to ridicule him, toward the closing stages of his life—and more so after his death at the age of fifty-eight—he came to be recognized as a trendsetter. Apart from his keen perceptions, his capacity to combine many disciplines, and his power to understand the workings of historical forces in shaping the life and thought of a people, he was a man of intellectual integrity. He stated his convictions clearly, sincerely, boldly. Before I finish, I will have occasion to quote from his writings quite often. For the time being, let us hear what he said about our epics:

> From our material it is still impossible to say where the great theme-battles of the two epics *Ramayana* and *Mahabharata* were fought, let alone when—if indeed they represent any historical events at all.[24]

Returning to the subject some years later, he had no more lingering doubts and referred to the Kurukshetra War as "this fictitious great war."[25]

Now we may turn our attention to a couple of living historians, D. C. Sirkar and H. D. Sankalia. To be sure, the former is primarily a specialist in epigraphy and the latter in archaelogy. But neither subject can be mastered without a firm grounding in history. Both of them are fully convinced that in case the Kurukshetra War really took place, it was no more than a family or tribal feud. Some of the points that I made in the opening part of this chapter are based on their writings; those who are interested can refer to their contributions to the co-operative study entitled Mahabharata: *Myth and Reality*, edited by S. P. Gupta and K. S. Ramachandran.[26]

Personally, this study has left me a sad man. For it is clearly indicative of the crushing weight of tradition—*silly tradition, dead tradition*—on the Hindu mind. Out of its forty-one contributors, not even half a dozen show any capacity to think boldly, rationally, origi-nally. And one or two of them have such a fuddled mind as to argue in all seriousness that what millions and millions of people believed for thousands of years as true cannot be fictitious. By the same token, we have to accept the widly prevalent belief over the ages that the eclipses of the sun and the moon are caused by those two impish demons, Rahu and Ketu.

Are our minds so conditioned by our puerile Puranas that we can be fooled by any fantastic nonsense? Is there something basically wrong with our national psyche? I am pretty sure that most of the con-tributors to Mahabharata: *Myth and Reality* fast during an eclipse and take a bath at its end, feeling joyous that by their piety they saved the sun or the moon from mortal danger. It is significant that the subtitle of their cooperative study is not "Myth or Reality" but "Myth and Reality." It is a clear proof that they were born as believers, grew up as believers, and one day will die as believers. They are incapable of doubting, of questioning, and of putting anything to the acid test of reason. In their view, to doubt any old belief is to be an infidel, to ques-tion it is to be guilty of sacrilege, to seek to put it to the test of reason is to condemn oneself to a long term in hell. It is mostly these folk who are in charge of our universities, our national laboratories, our tech-nological institutions, and to our shame, even our government at every level. I know that these are strong words, perhaps harsh words, but they are, I submit, not uncalled for in view of the credulity, bordering on imbecility, that is so much in evidence in every sphere of our national life today.

FALSE SIGNPOSTS

There is only one firm date in the history of ancient India, and that is the year of Alexander's invasion (327–326 BCE). The reason for it is quite simple. Indian time is cyclical. Prabhava, Vibhava, and so on, come around once every sixty years. No year in that cycle of sixty can, therefore, be pinpointed on the scale of linear time.

To be sure, there is a Vikrama Era. There is also a Salivahana or Saka Era. But none can be too sure about the starting point of either. The Vikrama Era, for instance, is said to have begun in 58–57 BCE. Who is this Vikrama after whom the era is named? What is the great deed, the historic event, that it commemorates? There is no clear answer to these questions. He cannot be the Vikramaditya who won a mighty victory over the Hunas in the fifth century CE. For the era starts almost six hundred years prior to that victory. He cannot be Pushyamitra, who assasinated the last Mauryan emperor and founded the Sunga dynasty. For the date of that assassination falls in the last quarter of the second century BCE. He cannot be Kanishka, the most famous emperor of the Kushana dynasty, the reason for it being that he flourished not during the middle of the first century BCE but about a century later. Nor can he be Goutamiputra Satakarni of the Satavahana dynasty. He did, no doubt, crush the Sakas in a heroic battle, but that battle took place in or around 124–125 CE. Furthermore, the inscriptions, brimful of his panegyrics, do not mention "Vikramaditya" as one of his titles. So, when each of those to whom the credit of starting the Vikrama Era is given by one historian or the other is ruled out, there remains Azes, the Parthian who established a large and prosperous kingdom in the Punjab and Sind by about 60 BCE. And he did initiate an era. But he named it after himself, the most sensible thing to do. In Prakrit his era is called the Aya Era or Aja Era; in no language, be it Prakrit or Sanskrit or Pahlavi, is it called the Vikrama Era.

In their desperate bid to solve the unsolvable riddle of the Vikrama Era some of our historians maintain that originally it was known as the Krita Era or the Malva Era in honor of some Malva king or general who defeated the Sakas somewhere, sometime, somehow. At this point I may record the reaction of D. D. Kosambi to this futile debate. Referring to the *Vikrama Volume*,[1] published from Ujjain to commemorate the completion of the first two millennia of the Vikram Era, he wrote:

> The two-thousandth anniversary of Vikram was celebrated with due pomp in 1943, though neither the press agents nor the luminaries publicized were able to shed any light on the problem. The memorial volumes [in English and Hindi] issued on the occasion prove only the futility of such research. None of the mutually contradictory essays in such volumes proves anything beyond the will to believe.[2]

Regarding the other, that is, the Salivahana Era or Saka Era, which, it is said, starts in 78 CE, there is an equally unresolved controversy. When the chronology of ancient India is so uncertain, so hazy, even when we come down to historical times, is it not useless to try to fix a period for the persons and events mentioned in our two epics, the *Ramayana* and the *Mahabharata*, and the thirty-six Puranas, major and minor? Though called epics, the *Ramayana* and the *Mahab-*

harata are, in fact, Puranas only. It is not only useless but, if I may be pardoned a strong expression, utterly idiotic. And yet, that very thing is done in all seriousness.

Whoever started the farce—yes, it is nothing else—was given a fillip by F. E. Pargiter. He was a British ICS officer who rose to be a judge of the Calcutta High Court. Having mastered Sanskrit, he first translated the Markandeya Purana into English. Next he collected the more important of the dynastic lists carried by the Puranas, rendered them into English and published them in book form with a long introduction. The title of his book is also rather long, and it reads: *The Purana Text of the Dynasties of the Kali Age.*[3] A little later he set down the results of his study of these lists in a book entitled *Ancient Indian Historical Tradition.*[4] All the history, dependable history as different from conjectural history, that he could extract from the Puranas is just about a thimbleful. Small wonder, despite their claim to be *itihasas* (current histories) the Puranas are myths and mythologies. They begin with the creation of the cosmos, its dissolution, and its renewal; next they talk of Manu, the Hindu Adam, and his wives and his progeny. Then they give the lists of the kings of different dynasties, past, present, and future. In between these things they emphasize the virtues of the principle of inequality between men, the principle institutionalized in the caste system. They expatiate on the risk of the world going to pieces unless the primacy and the privileges of the priest class are fully protected by the king. And they end up by laying down stringent rules that should govern a man's life from birth to death, and even beyond death, for they tell him how to find his way to heaven, and once there, how to make a beeline for the gorgeous bedroom of a gorgeous Rambha or a Menaka or a Tilottama or a Varudhini or—well, he has a wide choice.

From out of this piffle how much history can be gathered? Nothing or practically nothing. What is worse, it has a highly deleterious effect on our moral fiber. If this is taken to be a reckless, almost a rabid indictment, my submission is that it is late by twenty-five hundred years. What Valmiki and Vyasa are to us, Homer and Hesiod are to the Greeks. Both of them came under heavy attack by Plato, or more correctly, Plato speaking through Socrates. When your gods and heroes are gamblers and drunkards, when they lie and boast, when they are lustful and indulge in fornication, when they are mean, cowardly, and vengeful, in short, when they are given to every weakness and vice, will they not, asked Plato, encourage everybody to find excuses for his own weaknesses and vices? Unless one is familiar with the writings of Homer and Hesiod, what all Plato said in condemnation of Greek myths and mythologies cannot be properly appreciated; hence direct quotations from him are being avoided. Those who are interested can turn to the third book of Plato's *Republic*. The best translation I know of is by Jowett.[5]

Now, in some respects, Xenophanes was more caustic than Plato in his condemnation of Homer and Hesiod. An out-and-out rationalist and materialist, he poured vitriol on mythological gods and condemned the anthropomorphism belief that animals can have feelings like humans without any reservation.[6] Euripides, the playwright, also attacked the myths and mythologies in his own original, subtle, and effective way. And yet, here in India we have poets, playwrights, and philosophers who go into ecstasies over the *Ramayana*, the *Mahabharata* and the thirty-six Puranas and the stuff and nonsense they purvey. However, it is not always an act of foolishness. For hidden behind it, there is a well-planned motive, a long-range plan. It is to arrest the growing forces of freedom, democracy, and equality and to continue in a camouflaged form the old order of society based on "the gradations and degradations" of the caste system. It is significant that C. Rajagopalachari, K. M. Munshi, and other highly astute politicians turned into active protagonists of the Hindu epics and Puranas in post-Independence India.

Though all myths and mythologies, to whichever nation they may belong, are intrinsically nasty, ours are easily the worst from a moral point of view. Furthermore, they are most undependable as sources of history. On this last point, I may quote the eminent Indologist and historian, A. L. Basham. He wrote:

The names of many of the heroes of the *Mahabharata* may genuinely be those of contemporary chieftains, but we must regretfully record that the story is of less use to the historian than the *Iliad*, or most of the Norse and Irish saga literature. . . . It is futile to try to reconstruct the political and social history of India in the tenth century [BCE] from the *Mahabharata* as it would be to write the history of Britain immediately after the evacuation of the Romans from Malory's *Morte d'Arthur*.[7]

Our Pargiters and Pradhans cannot dismiss out of hand the point made by Basham. And so, we see that Sita Nath Pradhan himself had to admit the very many difficulties posed by the Puranas as sources of history. He bemoaned:

The Puranas profess to give us the ancient history of Aryan India. . . . In this . . . business, the Puranas sometimes naturally conflict; sometimes the same Purana makes, though rarely, different statements in different places; very often they corrupt the names of persons; sometimes one dynasty is merged or interwoven into or tacked onto another owing to the corrupt reading that have [sic] crept in, the result being a preposterously long line of kings; sometimes collateral successions are described as lineal; sometimes the orders of succession reversed; sometimes the dynasties are lengthened owing to various kinds of corrupt readings; even a synchronism has been found misplaced owing to a similarity of names; divergent synchronisms have been recorded.[8]

This did not, however, deter Pradhan from using the Puranas to frame a chronology for the history of ancient India. He was a brave man indeed!

Pargiter himself was no less aware how exasperating the problems posed by the Puranas could be to a historian. Without boring you or myself by giving a lengthy quotation, like the one I gave from Pradhan, I will point out that Pargiter had to tackle eighty Janamejayas; a hundred Nagas, Haihayas, Dhritarashtras, and Brahmadattas; two hundred Bhimas and Bhishmas; and one thousand Sasabindus! And this is only a partial list.[9]

This mad confusion would surely make every Pargiter swear under his breath. After wrestling with the Puranas and their dynastic lists for a lifetime, out of sheer irritation, if not desperation, Pargiter himself once exploded violently and said that the Brahmans who wrote the Puranas could see "no valid distinction between history and mythology and naturally there was a tendency to confuse the two, to mythologize history and to give mythology an historical garb. We can thus see why there was a total lack of historical sense among the Brahmans who composed the Brahmanical literature."[10]

Well, I have, I hope, said enough to convince any open-minded man that the Puranas are false signposts for ancient Indian history. Yet, those very Puranas are followed to decide when the Kurukshetra War took place. How the thing is done will be sketched briefly in my next chapter.

DUEL WITH DATES

The concept of a Kali Age is at once crude and primitive. It goes against anthropology, against archaeology, against common sense itself. In humankind's history, there are only three ages thus far; they are the age of savagery, the age of barbarism, and the age of civilization. Like the earlier two ages, the last one also has its different phases. Neither the age nor its different phases end abruptly; giving place to the new, they merge imperceptibly into each other. Often they exist side by side. Though a fascinating subject, it is not pertinent to the present context. I will therefore confine myself to saying that the belief in the recurring cycle of the four ages, Krita, Treta, Dwapara, and Kali, with progressive decline in righteousness (dharma), peace, and prosperity is either crankish or knavish, or both. Yet, attempts to fix the chronology of the prehistory of India begin almost always with a discussion as to when exactly the Kali Age has stepped in.

If that is decided, says the orthodox school, the date of the Kurukshetra War will be decided automatically. On this point, C. V. Vaidya was most unambiguous. "The orthodox opinion," he observed, "is that the war took place in 3101 BCE,* calculating on the basis of the gen-

---

*Others push it back by one year 3102 BCE.

erally accepted belief in India that in 1899 CE, five thousand years
had elapsed since the beginning of the Kali Age." And he announced
regally: "We agree with this orthodox opinion."[1] The orthodox, here as
elsewhere, now as always, believe that the higher they raise their voice,
the louder they bang the table, the truer the beliefs they profess will be.
And they do get away with it, and that is the tragedy of India. Our
nation seems to provide the most fertile soil for the growth of
credulity, irrationality, and superstition.

A part of this state of mind is to maintain that the Krita–Kali
cycle of time is specially designed by God in his greatness for his
chosen land, Hindustan, and for his people, the Hindus. It does not
apply, the old guard shouts in unison, to the rest of the world.[2] This,
in effect, means that we have nothing to do, absolutely nothing, with
the rest of the world and its people and its life. Need we, then, wonder
why for a thousand years or more, Hinduism put its foot down firmly
on foreign travel? Need we be pained why we have come to live like a
snail in its own shell?

Now to return to Vaidya and the orthodox school, pastoral nomads
who rode in horse-drawn chariots and adopted the axe with a shaft
hole as their principal weapon of war, the nomads known to history as
Aryans, were at the start of the Kali Age still either in their original
home or just beginning to disperse in different directions. They were
to take almost another fifteen hundred years to make their first entry
into the Sindh Valley. For reaching the Ganga-Yamuna basin, they
must have taken a further period of five hundred years. How, then,
could a war between well-settled Aryan tribes have taken place in the
neighborhood of what is now Delhi in 3102 or 3101 BCE? To the
orthodox folk, it is an absurd question. To silence you, they have a
hundred and one cogent and powerful arguments. The highest of them
in cogency and power is the one advanced by that worthy Abinas
Chandra Das, and it asserts that the "original cradle" of the Aryans was
India itself, or more specially, the Sapta Sindhu region. Crawling out
of that "cradle," they reached the four corners of the world to shed the
light of their glorious culture. To elaborate his discoveries, to expatiate
on his theories, Das wrote two fat volumes, fat like the Vedic bulls.

They are *Rigvedic India* and *Rigvedic Culture*.[3] His discoveries and theories are so jejune that they do not deserve even a derisive smile. Yet they were gobbled up by many, including a so-called historian of Vijayawada writer. I wonder whether this is chauvinism at its highest point or cussedness at its lowest level.

Leaving Das and his admirers in their "Aryan cradle," let us take up just one argument that is advanced in support of the traditional date for the start of Kali Age. In addition to literary evidence, there is, we are told, irrefutable inscriptional evidence to prove that the Kali Age did begin in 3102 BCE. Yes, there is inscriptional evidence, but it has one little snag in it. The earliest of such inscriptions is the Aihole inscription of Pulakesin II of the Western Chalukya dynasty.[4] It is dated 634 CE. How on earth can any inscription that comes 3,736 years after an event be taken as evidence of that event? It is a thing that only an orthodox mind can comprehend.

Another piece of no less irrefutable evidence is flaunted in our face. It is a calculation made by Aryabhatta, according to whom the Kali Age started in 3102 BCE.[5] But Aryabhatta lived in the fifth century CE, that is, about thirty-six hundred years after the event to which he testified on the basis of his astronomical calculations of dubious value. The validity of this evidence is, again, a thing that only an orthodox mind can appreciate.

The other calculations based on the Puranic lists of kings and their reigns are so widely divergent as to leave us bewildered. To fix the date of the beginning of the Kali Age, the dynastic lists, originally given by the Bhavishya Purana and later copied by the Matsya, Vayu, Brahmanda, and some other Puranas are relied upon.[6] The Bhavishya rests on a big lie, a colossal pretense. It claims to peer into the future and to record the kingdoms that would rise and fall, the dynasties that would rule and fade out, and the history that would unroll in ages to come. On the mistrustful basis of the dynastic lists of that fraudulent Purana and the rest of the lying lot, efforts are made to work out the average length of the reign of each king, and using it as a unit, to travel backward in time to the start of the Kali Age.

Because the dynastic lists in the Puranas vary as regards the number of kings, and as the total period of the reign of each dynasty also varies from Purana to Purana, the average, as is to be expected, necessarily varies. And it varies from fourteen to twenty-five years. To give a few instances at random, according to Pargiter, the average for reign at a "fair" and "liberal" estimate is eighteen years;[7] according to Vaidya, it is twenty years;[8] according to Basham, nineteen years;[9] according to P. T. Srinivasa Iyengar, twenty years for a reign is "a very low figure . . . if the length be raised to twenty-five," it will "not at all be an extravagant figure";[10] according to Vincent Smith, it is just a wee bit above twenty-five, that is, 25.2 years;[11] according to A. D. Pusalkar, it is rightly nineteen years, but as it is good to err on the side of caution, it can be reduced to eighteen years;[12] according to P. L. Bhargava, the average is two years more, that is, twenty years;[13] according to two of the early Indologists, A. F. R. Hoernle and J. F. Fleet, as the lists of the Puranic dynasties are too long, it is advisable to fix the average at no more than fifteen years;[14] according to A. S. Altekar, on the basis of the very learned and the very laborious calculation he made in 1939, the average is 16.5 years, and on the basis of an equally learned and laborious calculation he made in 1959, it is only 14.5 years;[15] according to B. B. Vide Lal, it is fourteen years;[16] according to Sita Nath Pradhan—well, if you are tired of this rigmarole, I am. And so I stop here.

There are three points that are specially to be noted regarding these calculations and conclusions. First, except very rarely no two historians or Indologists or other specialists agree about the average length of a reign, for the material they rely on is mostly faulty, if not fraudulent. Second, when we are dealing with dynastic lists that are very long, a difference of even five in the average length of a reign, can make a difference of many centuries in the final figure we arrive at. Third, we cannot be too sure as to which dynasty followed which, and how many kings actually figured in a dynasty.

To make myself clear I will summarize as best as I can an exercise in fixing chronology taken from Pargiter. It is fairly certain that Chandragupta Maurya started his reign in or about 332 BCE. And that happens to mark the end of the Nanda dynasty. In trying to go back from that dynasty, especially from the time of Mahapadma Nanda, to the time of the Kurukshetra War, we have to take into account twenty-four Ikshvakus, twenty-seven Panchalas, twenty-four Kasis, twenty-eight Haihayas, thirty-two Kalingas, twenty-five Asmakas, twenty-six Kurus (Pauravas), twenty-eight Maithiles, twenty-three Surasenas, and twenty Veetahotras.

After making allowance for the discrepancies in these dynastic lists as given in different Puranas, we are left with a total of 257 contemporary kings in ten kingdoms, giving an average of twenty-six kings for each dynasty. Now, if eighteen years is taken as the average for the reign of each king, 18×26 will take us back by 468 years. As it is said that the Nanda dynasty ended in 382 BCE, this would land us in (468 + 382) 850 BCE, as the rough starting point of each of the ten dynasties that we are taking into account. But that is not the end of our journey backward. Between the Kurukshetra War and the starting point of each of these ten dynasties, there were a few more kings and dynasties. (I am avoiding their names and numbers to not make our jungle path thornier than it is.) And so, we have to add one hundred years more to 850 BCE, and we conclude with a lusty shout that 950 BCE was the starting point of the Kali Age.[17] But suppose the average is fourteen years per reign, and we land in 846 BCE; and if it is twenty-five, we alight in 1132 BCE!

Are there not too many assumptions, surmises, conjectures, suppositions, guesses, speculations, and so on in the whole process?

As I have already pointed out, there is absolutely no agreement as to the average period of the reign of a king. Furthermore, according to the Puranas, the total duration of the Nanda dynasty, that is, of Mahapadma and his eight descendents, was one hundred years. But the Jain accounts extend it to one hundred fifty-five years while the chronicles of Ceylon reduce it to a mere twenty-two years. That is not the end of the matter, either. How long did Mahapadma rule to extinguish completely the Kshatriya kings and the Kshatriya kingdoms? Some say that he ruled for eighty-eight years, and some others bring down his reign to just a dozen years.[18]

As if this confusion were not enough, some scholars do not accept the synchronism of the Kurukshetra War and the beginning of the Kali

Age. On the authority of Vriddha Garga, Varahamihira of the sixth century CE maintained that the Kurukshetra War took place 653 years after the advent of the Kali Age, that is, in 2449–2448 BCE (both of them were famous astronomers of their times). Kalhana, the Kashmiri historian of the eighth century CE, gave his full support to this view.[19] K. P. Jayaswal, a historian of the present century, held, on the other hand, that the Kali Age, in fact, made its bow in 1388 BCE and that the Kurukshetra War took place thirty-six years earlier, that is, in 1424 BCE.[20]

Is it not presumptuous, I almost said *madness*, to hope that on the basis of such material a definite date for the Kurukshetra War and the singing of the Song Celestial can be assigned? And yet, for about fifteen hundred years, an attempt has been seriously made to decide when exactly that war was fought. As I do not wish to overburden this chapter with too many references, I will set down here the widely different dates assigned to the Kurukshetra War by the more prominent of the disputants during the past fifteen centuries or more. First I will give the date that they opt for and then give within brackets their names. So here we go: 3102 BCE (Aryabhatta and Bhaskaracharya); 3101 BCE (C. V. Vaidya); 2449–2448 BCE (Vriddha Garga, Varahamihira, Kalhana, and D. C. Sen); 1922 BCE (J. S. Karandikar); fifteenth century BCE (Bankim Chandra Chatterjee and Dhirendra Nath Paul); 1468 BCE (M. Rangacharya); 1450 BCE (P. T. Srinivas Iyengar); fourteenth century BCE (H. T. Colebrooke, Lord Elphinstone, H. H. Wilson, Bal Gangadhar Tilak, Seetanath Tattavabhushan, R. C. Majumdar, H. C. Raychaudhuri, A. L. Basham, and Paul Renou); between 1200 and 1042 BCE (A. D. Pusalkar); 1198 BCE (K. G. Sankar); 1197 BCE (K. L. Daftary); 1151 BCE (S. N. Pradhan); about 1000 BCE (E. J. Rapson and Vincent Smith); 950 BCE (F. E. Pargiter); and finally 850 BCE (H. C. Ray Chaudhuri, who opted earlier for the fourteenth century BCE[21]).

More debate on the point will only add more dates to make us more confused, irritated, and bewildered. And yet the Bhimas and the Jarasandhas, Indian and foreign, will wrestle on. Let them fight it out. It will be good for their health. Meanwhile, we cannot overlook one important fact. Of those who took part in this debate, the more sober have formed one firm conviction, and it is that the Kali Age was a fabrication. Who did it? J. F. Fleet pointed his accusing finger at Aryabhatta. K. P Jayaswal was less specific; all he said was that someone did it before the close of the Andhra period, 498 CE. Indologist Winternitz was inclined to agree broadly with Fleet and Jayaswal. The start of the Kali Age, he thought, was based "on the artificial calculation of Indian astronomers, and the association of this date with the conflict of Kauravas and Pandavas is, of course, quite arbitrary."[22] I fully subscribe to this view. The very concept of the Kali Age is based not on reason but on faith. Faith and fabrication always go together, just as reason and truth march together.

FEAR OF DISILLUSIONMENT

Archaeology is mute. And yet it can reveal truth. Literature is articulate, but it has a natural tendency to embroider truth. And when it is that special branch of literature called myth and mythology, truth gets hopelessly enmeshed in its gaudy embroidery. Literary evidence should therefore be treated with extreme caution when one is writing the history of far-off ages. Indeed, it should not be trusted unless it is corroborated by other sources, especially by archaeology.

This is a precaution that is taken by the historians of ancient Sumeria, Babylonia, Assyria, Egypt, Phoenicia, Crete, Media, Phrygia, Lydia, Carthage, Greece, Rome, Persia, China, in short, of every ancient nation. But it is hardly the case with the historians of ancient India. Why? Is it because of fear of disillusionment? Yes, indeed! For two thousand years or more, we as a nation have been living on a diet of myth and mythology. No, I am wrong there. It is more a drug than food. We swallow it in large doses and it makes us euphoric. Ignoring our present, we gloat over our past. We boast about the glory of Ayodhya and the glitter of Hastinapura. We brag about that ancient Disneyland, the Mayasabha of Indraprastha.

If we take up the spade and start to dig, it may, we fear, reveal to us

the truth about our Aryan past in all its stark nakedness. It may scatter
to the winds our illusions about our supposed golden age presided over
by Rama and Krishna. In fact, that happened whenever we excavated
the sites associated with the *Ramayana* and the *Mahabharata*. It blew up
sky-high the myth that the Aryans brought with them a superior civilization when they descended on India as conquerors. As it happened
in several other parts of the world, and as it happened in several other
periods of history, invariably the invaders were the barbarians while
the invaded were the civilized people. The onslaught of the Aryans
meant a violent blow to the higher civilization of the Harappans and
resulted in its gradual decline and death.

And for almost a millennium, say, till the rise of the Magadhan
Empire (and it was the very first empire in Indian history). India had
no more cities like Harappa and Mahenjodaro, no more towns like
Kalibangan and Rangpur, no more ports like Lothal. The Aryans lived
in mud houses, cooked in mud pots, ate out of mud bowls and drank
out of mud cups. Their material culture was poor; they were total aliens
to urban life and its amenities. Together with their cows, they lived in
village settlements, often sharing the same compound with their cows.
This last statement is not meant to be a sneer; it is a statement of fact.
Cow was their unit of exchange; it was their currency; it was their
wealth, their status symbol. The highest luxury for them was to press
the soma juice, a kind of strong liquor, thrice a day, and quaff potfuls
of it. The material culture of the Aryans was thus of the lowest order.
Writing in 1962, Stuart Piggott said: "Like the Amurru in
Mesopotamia, the Aryans were people who had never known a city."[1]
A greater archealogist than Piggott, Sir Mortimer Wheeler, writing in
1966, was far more emphatic, and he stated:

> Let us admit uncompromisingly that no Aryan culture has yet
> been isolated anywhere in India as a material and recognizable
> phenomenon.[2]

The verdict of these two foreigners should have been taken up as a
challenge by the devotees of Rama and Krishna. They should have

stinted neither time nor money nor effort to prove them wrong. Every site that had anything to do with the *Ramayana* and the *Mahabharata* should have been excavated long ago, not perfunctorily, but with utmost diligence to demonstrate how incorrect are the Piggotts and Wheelers. Instead of doing that, they vie with each other in drawing unwarranted conclusions from the shreds of the Painted Grey Ware found over a wide area, a few glass beads and iron arrowheads discovered here and there, and a solitary twelve-room mud house located at the level of the last phase of the Harappan culture. Except to people given to wishful thinking, these prove nothing but the fact of the low level of the material culture of the Aryans during the thousand years from the time they forced their way into India to the rise of the Magadhan Empire with its base in what was predominantly a non-Aryan region.

Of course, it is said that a statement made in the Puranas, namely, that after it was badly eroded by the flood waters of the Ganges in the eighth century BCE, the capital of the Kurus was shifted to Kosambi, has been proved correct by drillings into the bed of the river at Hastinapura. Just because that one statement is corroborated by archaeology, does it follow that the many silly things said about that city in the Puranas should ipso facto be correct? One such silly thing is this: Hastinapura, the Puranas tell us, was founded by Hastin; they also tell us that Dushyanta, and his more famous son, Bharata, had Hastinapura as their capital. In the Puranic genelogical lists, Hastin is the fifth in succession to Dushyanta. How could the city founded by Hastin be the capital of his forefathers?[3] But nothing is too silly or absurd or crazy where Puranas are concerned.

Potsherds, glass beads, arrowheads and a twelve-room mud house— these cannot bear witness to a high material culture; that can be done only by massive monuments. As no such monuments have been found at Hastinapura, A. Vide Ghosh rightly sounded a warning. He said:

A word of caution is necessary, lest the impression is left on the unwary reader that the Hastinapura excavation has yielded archaeological evidence about the truth of the story of the *Mahabharata* and that here at last is the recognition by "official archaeology" of the truth embodied in Indian traditional literature. Such a conclusion would be unwarranted. Beyond the fact that Hastinapura, the reputed capital of the Kauravas, was found to be occupied by a people whose distinctive ceramics were the Painted Grey Ware in a period which might roughly have synchronized with the date of the origin of the nucleus of the *Mahabharata* story, that this occupation came to an end with a heavy flood and that this ware is found at many early sites, some of which are connected, either in literature or by tradition, with the epic heroes, the excavation has no bearing on the authenticity or otherwise of the epic tale. It is indeed tempting to utilize archaeological evidence for substantiating tradition, but the pitfalls in the way should be guarded against, and caution is necessary that fancy does not fly ahead of facts.[4]

But we do allow our fancy to fly ahead of facts where our old myths and mythologies are concerned. We fail to realize that the bulkier the old books are, the greater the interpretations into them and the value of their anthropology, their geography, their history, and the skeleton of that history—I mean, their chronology. The orthodox crowd, and to our deep regret it includes even many of our archaeologists, anthropologists, and historians, are blind to this.

A typical representative of this blind crowd is C. V. Vaidya. "The Mahabharata War or rather battle," he wrote with a grand flourish, "is the first authentic event in the ancient history of India."[5] As if it were not enough, he affirmed that "nobody has doubted the truth of the event." A brasher statement can hardly be imagined. Not only the event, but also the date of the event was questioned very much by very many people, as we have already seen. And people would continue to question these things despite all the shouting, all the wailing, and all the gnashing of teeth by the traditionalists.

In the spirit of a true historian, Vincent Smith said:

From darkness to light. The advent of the Maurya dynasty marks the passage from darkness to light for the historian. Chronology suddenly becomes definite, almost precise; a huge empire springs into existence.[6]

That is too much for the Sanatanists to swallow. "Much earlier," they will tell you at the top of their shrill voice, there were six great emperors who ruled the whole world from their imperial throne in India. And all of them were pure-blooded Aryans and Kshatriyas who descended directly either from Surya (the sun god), or Chandra (the moon god). To hail the Maurya Chandra Gupta, the upstart, as the first emperor, they will declare, is a part of the dirty plot of Europeans like Vincent Smith to deny the honor of hoary antiquity to Indian history. In their bid to counter this plot, they maintain that the Chandragupta who was a contemporary of Alexander the Great was not of the Maurya dynasty, but of the much later one, the Gupta dynasty. This would place the Gupta dynasty in the fourth century BCE. If you dare to protest, they will knock you down by hurling at you all their *pan-changas* and all their Puranas. What counts, they pontificate, is that great divide between the Dwapara and Kali Ages, the Mahabharata War, fought in 3102 BCE. If that takes Asoka back at least by a thou-sand years, as it was pointed out by A. A. Macdonell,[7] and if it does not synchronize with world chronology, let Asoka and the world chronology be consigned to the blazing pits of hell. Being a Rai Bahadur and a little more sophisticated, Vaidya did not say it openly, but the Vijayawada historians and the Vijayawada author to whom I referred earlier, did!

Now we have that new technique called carbon-14 dating. It was a discovery for which Willard F. Libby got the 1960 Nobel Prize for Chemistry. Libby's dating technique enables us to explore the past as never before. With its aid we can establish chronologies for prehistory as well as for the recent geologic and climatic changes. Of course, it has some limitations. It can, as Libby himself explained, take us back in time for a period of forty thousand years only "with an error of mea-surement of about one century in the period zero to twenty thousand years and somewhat larger for older dates."[8] True, since the time of Libby's statement that I quoted, it has been found that a slightly wider margin for error has to be allowed. But that has not taken away the importance of Libby's carbon-dating technique.

And yet, to accept its efficiency is to admit that your panchangas and

Puranas are of no use in fixing a chronology for Indian history. And so the margin of error in radiocarbon dating is exaggerated, indeed, the whole technique is belittled. And we are left wondering whether our Vaidyas are not really mythologists in the garb of historians!

The best thing to do with our Vaidyas is to ignore them; to argue with them is to give needless importance to their chatter, or, their gibberish, if you prefer the stronger expression. Carbon-14 dating has, on the whole, confirmed the correctness of the chronology of Indian history sketched roughly for the first time by Sir William Jones. It was he who identified the "Sandrocottus" of the Greek writers as Chandragupta Maurya and established the synchronism of Chandragupta and Alexander. It was Janes Prinsep who deciphered the Brahmi and Kharoshti scripts and enabled us to read the Asokan inscriptions. It was Alexander Cunningham, the father of Indian archaeology, who pieced together the geography of ancient India. Before these pioneering savants made us realize the place of Chandragupta and Asoka in Indian history, they were either forgotten or derided, denigrated, and denounced. How many of us know that, according to our dictionaries, the word *Vrishala* means "a Sudra, a sinful man" *and* "Chandragupta"? How many of us, again, know that *Devanampriya*, the title that Asoka had taken for himself in his inscriptions, has only one meaning, and that is "an imbecile"? While praising, nay, worshipping the mythical folk heroes of the epics and the Puranas we heaped contempt on the heads of some of our greatest historical personages.[9]

Insofar as this chapter is concerned, what remains to be said is this: the Kurukshetra War was in all probability a myth. In case it was not a myth, it took place about 1000 BCE. Even so, it can hardly be called a war, much less, a great war; it was a local skirmish between some Aryan tribes. Indeed, it was such a trivial thing that it was ignored totally by the entire range of the Vedic literature. Furthermore, the skirmish was perhaps not between the Kurus and Pandavas. These are by no means original ideas that are being advanced by me for the first time; more thorough students of the *Mahabharata* than me postulated them decades ago.

Apart from the authorities whom I cited in my second chapter, there are many others whose verdict is that the Kurukshetra War was a myth. To quote only a few from among them, Vincent Smith was fully convinced that "the entire framework of the story of the *Mahabharata* is essentially incredible and unhistorical."[10] Albrecht Weber was completely persuaded that it was no more than a war "between the Aryan tribes."[11] Romila Thapar, going even further, was reluctant to call it a war: it was, she thought, a "local feud."[12] Basham did, no doubt, give it the status of a "battle," but he held that it was a "battle magnified to titanic proportions."[13] Christian Lassen was perhaps the first to take the stand that "the original struggle at Kurukshetra was between the Kurus and the Panchalas and the career of Pandava brothers and their connection with the Panchalas was included to promote the Brahmanical interests."[14] Pendyala Sastri of Pithapuram may not have even heard the name of Lassen, but on the basis of his independent study of the *Mahabharata*, he also came to the same conclusion as Lassen.

What does all this show? It shows that the historicity of the Kurukshetra War is doubtful; its date is doubtful; the long list of its participant kingdoms is doubtful; its extent and ferocity are doubtful; indeed, everything about it is doubtful, including the singing of the Song Celestial by Krishna. And yet there are owls in the orthodox crowd who tell us blithely the exact date when that war started. Before Galileo turned his telescope to the sky in the first decade of the seventeenth century CE, astronomy was not much of a developed science in any part of the world. In its former crude stages it was more an ally of wily priests and astrologers in fleecing the credulous people, and not an aid to seekers of knowledge to peer a little further into the depths of the vast cosmos. And yet, on the basis of the pre-Galilean astrology, some members of our orthodox crowd venture to fix a chronology for ancient Indian history! None can accuse A. D. Pusalkar of being a heretic, much less a *pashanda*. And yet here is his criticism of our dependence on moth-eaten almanacs to fix a date for the Kurukshetra War:

Astronomical references in the *Mahabharata* itself about the position of the Nakshatras and planets have been utilized for determining the date of the war. But, the same data have yielded various divergent results. As a matter of fact, the statements in the epic are conflicting and self-contradictory, so that in order to arrive at some conclusion it is necessary to reject certain statements or their implications as later interpolations or mere exaggerations. No satisfactory and acceptable result can be arrived at from these data.[15]

The kind of foolish ventures criticized by Pusalkar are by no means confined to India. Over a hundred years ago Bishop Ussher announced to the world on the basis of his study of the Bible that God created Adam on March 23, 4004 BCE.[16] Perhaps inspired by this foolish bishop, some decades ago Velandi Gopal Aiyar came out with the grand announcement that the Kurukshetra War broke out on October 14, 194 BCE.[17] Correcting Aiyar, another luminary has recently stated that the Kali Age began on February 18, 3102 BCE, and that the Kurukshetra War was fought thirty-six years earlier, in 3138 BCE. He gave a generous life span of one hundred twenty-five years to Krishna and assigned 3227 BCE for the Bhagavan's birth and 3102 BCE for his death. In other words, the Kali Age started on the day of the Bhagavan's death. All very neat, very brave, and very stupid!

Another such luminary is S. B. Roy. After retirement from his position as a high-ranking income-tax officer, he is utilizing his genius for figures, tables, schedules, and balance sheets to decide for good the whole range of chronology, not only for India but for the entire world. Indeed, there is no riddle in human history to which this worthy has not a ready answer. As director of the Institute of Chronology, New Delhi, he is throwing a flood of light on every dark corner of history. To enlighten laymen, he has written a small book, and for the study of scholars a large tome.[18]

"Vyasa" says Roy, "represents the grand personality of the intellectual world of the Epic-Upanashadic age." And Roy represents the grander personality of the age of chartered chauvinism in which India, that is, Bharat, is now living. Hats off to our modern Vyasas!

5

"A FRAUD OF MONSTROUS SIZE"

I t was Kipling who in a mood of levity used the phrase, "a fraud of monstrous size" to describe Cheops's pyramid which, five thousand years after its creation, still stands proudly just outside Cairo at the edge of the Sahara. Without the least levity, Kipling's phrase can be applied to the *Mahabharata*. As that tomb is called "the great pyramid," this tome is called "the great epic." That tops the list of the seven wonders of the world on the score of its sheer bulk. On the same score, this should head the list of the seven fantasies of the world, if one were to prepare that list. While that is 451 feet in height and has 3,057,000 cubic yards of masonry,[1] this is eighteen cantos in length and runs to one hundred thousand verses. Whatever sanctity the pyramid enjoyed at one time, it lost it a long time ago; it is now only a tourist attraction. The epic, on the other hand, still enjoys its sanctity, and that is one of the worst calamities of India. The sheer bulk and weight of the *Mahabharata*, and its sheer nonsense, crushes out all common sense, even all common decency, from Indian life and thought.

How over the centuries the *Mahabharata* had grown into its present monstrous size is a tale that is told much too often. So, I need not tell it over again. It is enough to state that the epic itself provides internal evidence that it was the handiwork of three scribes, Vyasa, Vaisampayana, and Souti. Vyasa, it is said, dictated the core theme in eighty-eight hundred verses and called it *Jaya*. Vaisampayana enlarged it to twenty-four thousand verses, and renamed it *Bharata*. Then Souti came along to expand it to a grand total of one hundred thousand verses and called it the *Mahabharata*. But the truth is that, apart from these three, there were many more nameless scribes and scribblers, fabricators and forgers, who put their finger into the prodigious pie.

To tamper with the work of some other author, to interpolate whole passages of your own into it, to twist it out of shape, to alter its very basis and its central message is a heinous crime indeed! And yet in this spiritual country of ours, it has been done since antiquity. There is no religious text, no law code, no treatise on polity, no manual of economics, no epic, no Purana that is not tampered with. And it is done with a clear conscience! Indeed, it is thought that to "improve" the work of others by what you believe to be correct, proper, or true, or what you think will subserve public interest, (in effect this means the interest of your own caste) is a thing that would earn you the right of permanent residence in *Swarga* (heaven). And so the process of "improving" goes on all the time. Even the coming of the printing press has not put a stop to it.

The *Mahabharata* is the worst victim in this respect. Its original form was in all likelihood that of a ballad. When there was no cinema, no radio, no television, perhaps not even the theater, one of the most popular forms of entertainment was undoubtedly the singing of ballads. They were woven around folk heroes or tribal gods. Their authors belonged to a special caste, a mixed one, called "Suta." The Sutas attached themselves to royal courts. They were most in demand during sacrifices. Some of the sacrifices went on and on for a dozen years or more, and to overcome the boredom of the prolonged rituals the Sutas were engaged to recite their ballads. To please their royal patrons, they trimmed the text of the ballads here, expanded it there, and took full liberties with it everywhere. That is how the ballads increased in length from one recital to another and with each fresh recital their tone and tenor also changed. This was true not only of the *Mahabharata* but of the *Ramayana* and Puranas as well.

That, however, is not the end of the story. The original text in Prakrit was changed (as Pargiter suggests) in later time to Sanskrit.[2] At this stage the Brahmans replaced the Sutas. And they went full steam ahead to alter not only the text of the old ballads but also their character, their meaning, and their message. The main thrust of their revision was to make themselves the undisputed gods on earth. Indeed, some of them went much further. The Bhrigus, who were the principal revisers,[3] placed themselves above the gods. One of them, it was claimed, gave a hard kick—perhaps harder than a kick by a judo expert—right on the chest of Vishnu for not showing him proper respect. Prior to this, he was equally incensed with Brahma and Shiva, and laid them under dire courses.[4]

I am no Sanskrit scholar. Nor have I spent a lifetime doing research in Indology. But there are others, Indians and foreigners, who mastered Sanskrit and earned great name as Indologists. They can speak with greater authority than I can. One such was Hermann Oldenberg of Germany. The author of a critical biography of the Buddha, he was known as a prodigy of industry. According to the well-considered verdict of this savant: "The *Mahabharata* began its existence as a simple epic narrative. It became, in course of centuries, the most monstrous chaos."[5] So, I am not the first, nor will I be the last, to apply the adjective "monstrous" to the *Mahabharata*.

Hopkins, the American Indologist was a closer student of the *Mahabharata* than Oldenberg. In his book *The Great Epic of India*, wholly devoted to a systematic analysis of the *Mahabharata* and published for the first time at the beginning of the present century, he described graphically how the epic has come down to us, and I quote:

> In what shape has epic poetry come down to us? A text that is no text, enlarged and altered in every recension, chapter after chapter recognized even by native commentaries as Praksipta in a land without historical sense or care for the preservation of popular monuments, where no check was put on any reciter or copyist who might add what beauties or polish what parts he would, where it was a merit to add a glory to the pet god, where every popular poem was handled freely and is so to this day.[6]

Yes, indeed. As I pointed out right at the beginning of this chapter, we think nothing of tampering with the old texts, be they religious or secular. And in the process of tampering, we throw in everything, relevant or irrelevant, decent or vulgar, true or false. According to Vincent Smith, out of the one hundred thousand verses of the existing text of the *Mahabharata*, only twenty thousand have a bearing on the core theme of the epic, that is, the conflict between the Kurus and Pandus; all the rest is padding, more padding, and yet more padding. Even in the medieval Hindi epic, the *Chand-Raisa*, there is padding, in a big way. Its initial five thousand verses are now lost in a muddy ocean of one hundred twenty-five thousand verses.[7]

What I have said thus far is meant to lead to some pertinent question. When was the core theme of the *Mahabharata* composed? When and how did its expansion begin? When did it stop? What were the motives for tampering with the text?

On every one of these questions, there is wide divergence of opinion among scholars. But it can be said definitely that the *Mahabharata* did not exist as an epic in Sanskrit, as distinct from a heroic laud in Prakrit, at the time of Panini. In his grammar the word "Mahabharata" is used, (as already pointed out) not as a noun, but as an adjective. He, however, mentioned Vasudeva, Arjuna, and Yudhisthira, but the first two as gods.[8] From this we can deduce two things: first, at the time of Panini, the *Mahabharata* did not exist as an epic in Sanskrit; second, the Krishna cult was then in its formative stages, and along with Krishna, Arjuna was also being worshipped as a god.

That Panini was unaware of the *Mahabharata* as an epic is suggested by yet another significant point. His grammar refers to Kunti and Madri. But they are brought in not as the wives of Pandu but as "geographical appellatives; Kunti signifying a woman from the country of the Kuntas, and Madri, Madra woman."[9]

When, then, did the *Mahabharata* assume the form of an epic? The earliest reference to both "Bharata" and "Mahabharata" occurs in Asvalayana Grihya Sutra. But Albrecht Weber thought that it was either an interpolation or that the sutra was of a very late date.[10] However that may be, as the date of the sutra itself is very uncertain, it leaves us hanging in midair.

And so, we are back in the realm of assumptions, conjectures, speculations, guesses, and so on. But of one thing there can be no doubt. Whatever the date when the Mahabharata assumed its present form of an epic in Sanskrit is, it cannot be anterior to Panini. Of course, that grammarian's lifetime cannot be fixed exactly,[11] but the consensus is now in favor of the fifth century BCE. Rapson,[12] Barnett,[13] Hopkins,[14] Macdonell,[15] Winternitz,[16] and some others think that the Mahabharata's initial emergence as an epic should be placed some years after Panini, that is, between the fourth and third century BCE. Weber brings the date down to the third century BCE,[17] and so does Vaidya.[18] Radha Kumud Mookerji brings it down further by a century to the second century BCE.[19]

Whatever might have been the upper limit for the emergence of the Mahabharata as a Sanskrit epic, the lower limit for its present avatar is the fourth or the fifth century CE. And minor additions and alterations and emendations did not stop till as late as the fourth century CE. Vaidya, on the other hand, placed the lower limit only a century below his upper limit, that is, 200 BCE. Nothing else can be expected from a self-proclaimed spokesman of the orthodox crowd, which has a holy horror for anything and everything that comes after Christ. In fact, at the start of the Kali Age itself, it affirms, the fall of man has begun. But to go back to the lower limit for the shaping of the Mahabharata. V. S. Sukthankar, despite his worshipful attitude toward the epic, was honest enough, candid enough, to admit that it might contain "some furtive additions which had been made as late as 1000 CE or even later." And he went on to add:

> The critical edition of the Mahabharata which is being published by the Bhandarkar Oriental Research Institute shows that large blocks of the text of the vulgate must on incontrovertible evidence be excised as comparatively late interpolations. . . . The Southern Recension offers us illustrations of regular long poems being bodily incorporated in the epic, like the detailed description of the avataras of Vishnu put in the mouth of Bhishma in the Sabha, and the full enunciation of the Vaisnava Dharma in the Asvamedhikaparvan,

two passages comprising together about twenty-five hundred stanzas. When we know that these additions have been made [in] comparatively recent times, even so late as the period to which our written tradition reaches back, can we legitimately assume that our text was free from such intrusions during that prolonged period in the history of our text which extends beyond the periphery of our manuscript tradition?[20]

Such is the mulish obstinacy of the orthodox crowd that it clutches at any straw to defend its blind beliefs. One such straw is an inscription of the fifth century CE which states that at that time Vyasa's *Mahabharata* had a total of one hundred thousand verses. The same is the number now; and so it follows, argues the orthodox crowd, that from a time prior to that date there should have been no changes in the text of the epic. But they overlook one point. How easy it is to cut out some old verses here and there so as to make room for new ones and still to maintain the total at one hundred thousand? And this is exactly what had happened.

Now, what remains is the question of motives. The first and foremost motive was to build up the concept of a personal god. Though Gautama, the Buddha, refused to affirm or deny the existence of God, his disciples set him up, soon after his death, as a god. And fantastic were the stories that they wove around him about his miraculous birth, his colorful life until he grew up to be a youth, the renunciation of his young wife and newborn son and his kingdom in his zeal to rid the world of all sorrow and suffering, his all-embracing love and compassion, and his limitless powers to offer succor to his faithful devotees. All this helped to make Buddhism develop rapidly as a major threat to Vedism, or Brahmanism, as some would prefer to call it. To counterattack, it was necessary to create a rival. After trial and error, the folk hero of a tribe of cowherds in and around Madhura proved handy. By about the third or fourth century BCE, he was built up into a god. We see him breaking into the story of the *Mahabharata* rather abruptly at the time of Draupadi's self-choice of a groom (*swayamvara*). She ended up marrying not one but five princes, but that is a different story. From that time onward, Krishna grows and grows, and he dwarfs every other character in the *Mahabharata* and emerges as God.

The next motive, not so obvious, was to change what was a pro-Kuru laud into a pro-Pandu laud. On this point, apart from some Western Indologists, Pendyala Sastri of Pithapuram wrote at length. This sea change, he thought, took place at the sacrifice of Janamejaya. He was a descendent of the Pandus; he was lavish with gifts. Is it not then wise to please him by giving a pro-Pandu slant to the whole theme? So the slant was given and yet truth shows through the cracks that could not be papered over completely.

A third and deeper motive, already mentioned in passing, was to place the priest class right at the top of the social ladder. A reliable historian of ancient India, Rapson was definite in thinking that the *Mahabharata* "has become through the accretions of ages—the work, no doubt, of Brahman editors—a vast encyclopedia of Brahmanical lore."[21]

Yet another writer on ancient India, particularly of the Buddhist period, is T. W. Rhys-Davids, and he says that the *Mahabharata* "has certainly undergone one, if not two or even three, alterations at the hand of later priestly editors." And he adds:

> They must have recast the poem with two main objects in view—in the first place to insist on the supremacy of the Brahmans, which had been so much endangered by the great popularity of the anti-priestly view of the Buddhists and others; and in the second place to show that the Brahmans were in sympathy with, and had formally adopted, certain popular cults and beliefs highly esteemed by the people. In any case, there, in the poem, these cults and beliefs, absent from the Vedic literature, are found in full life and power. And though this line of evidence, if it stood alone, would be too weak to bear much weight, the most likely explanation seems to be that here also we have evidence, to some extent at least, of beliefs not included in the Vedic literature, and yet current among, and powerfully affecting, both the Aryan and the semi-Aryan peoples of India.[22]

Well, whatever are the motives and whichever the agency, it was always sinister, always evil and inhuman. Is this too sweeping a condemnation? No, not in the least! "The *Mahabharata*, completely rewritten just before the Guptas," stated Kosambi, "shows revision in favor of the barbarous sati practice."[23] And if sati is again coming into vogue after more than one hundred fifty years of its abolition by law, thanks to the British, it is due to the pernicious influence of its epics and Puranas, at the top of which stands the *Mahabharata*. Is this a biased charge? No, definitely not! "Perhaps few books," as Sir Percival Griffiths said, "have influenced the pattern of Indian life and thought more than the *Mahabharata*. In a well-known part of this epic occurs the description of a dispute between the wives of King Pandu as to which of them is entitled to die on his funeral pyre."[24]

Well, such is the influence of the *Mahabharata*, persistent, pervasive, pernicious. And with every revision, that influence has become more reactionary, deadlier. A part of that revision, let me add, is the Bhagavad Gita, the Song Celestial, with its exhortation to kill, to kill in cold blood, to kill as a matter of caste duty.

OUTER CITADEL
AND INNER FORT

Unless you breach the outer citadel you cannot storm the inner fort. That is the reason why I have been concentrating my attack on the *Mahabharata*. Once I show how it is a big lie, an outrageous forgery, a pious fraud, I can tackle the Gita easily. The validity of this strategy will be readily conceded when it is remembered that without its dramatic setting the Gita loses much of its appeal.

Right from its start, despite its many groupings and regroupings, its reconnaissances, its ambushes, its sallies, its sorties and skirmishes, its diversionary attacks, its rearguard actions, the *Mahabharata* marches—slowly, tortuously, and yet inexorably—toward the Kurukshetra. It is said to be not merely a battlefield but a "holy field,"a "field of righteousness." On that field two vast armies are arrayed. The horses, numbering hundreds of thousands, are stamping their feet to rush forward, but on being held back, neighing in their impatience. The elephants, somewhat fewer in number, are trumpeting. From the tops of the thickly massed chariots, colorful flags are fluttering in the morning breeze. A drone is rising from the ocean of infantry, spoiling for a fight. And suddenly, drowning everything else, there is the blowing of conches by the legendary warriors of both sides. It is followed by the blare of the kettledrums and tabors, drums and horns.

The tumult is earsplitting. It is resounding through earth and sky. At that dramatic moment, Arjuna asks Krishna to draw up his chariot into no-man's-land so that he could survey the men and their commanders whom he has to encounter. And once he sees standing before him his "fathers and grandfathers, teachers, uncles, and brothers, sons and grandsons, as also companions,"[1] his limbs quail, his mouth goes dry, his body shakes, his hair stands on end, and his bow slips from his limp hands. In a mood of deep despondency, of utter gloom, he says, "I have no desire for victory. Please turn back my chariot." With an indulgent smile, Krishna refuses to oblige, and for exhorting Arjuna to fight the battle of righteousness, he begins to sing his Song Celestial. A hush falls on the Kurukshetra; millions of men thirsting for war stand spellbound; earth and heaven strain their ears not to miss even a single note of that divine song.

Take away this dramatic setting, this thrilling scene, and what remains of the Gita? Only the hotchpotch of faulty cosmology, hackneyed theology, turbid philosophy, primitive sociology, obnoxious ethics, and to create a mood of awe, the oft-repeated claims "I am the God," "I am the Truth," "I am the Life," and "I am the Way." And yet, to a mind that is already captive, it sounds like something great, something profound. Whoever first interpolated the Gita into the already much-interpolated *Mahabharata* at this particular point with scenic tricks and sound effects was a master psychologist. "It is difficult to excel," as P. D. Mehta says, "the Hindu sense of dramatic in religion. . . . The poet author of the Gita could hardly have chosen a more arresting opening scene for his philosophical song."[2] But to deal with the Gita at this stage would be to anticipate, and so, I return to the *Mahabharata* to fire at it a few final salvos.

A Rajagopalachari, a Munshi, or a Sukthankar may appreciate the *Mahabharata* as a great work of literature, but I cannot. They may think that it has a solid kernel of historicity; I do not. They may extol it for its moral grandeur, its eternal verities; I disagree with them. Among the epics of the world, it is the most amorphous, the most tortuous and chaotic. It has neither the unity of theme nor style nor vision that is expected in an epic. To borrow the words of Hopkins, it is "pitched together and patched together" by many hands, including the most detestable of human beings, the priests.[3] If it has one merit, it owes it to its original composers, the Sutas. They were born poets; they were of the earth, earthy; they had the power to sway the hearts of the common people. They could etch character in black and white with practically no intermediate tones, making it typological, and on that score, memorable. For priggishness tinged with self-pity there can only be one Yudhisthira; for the he-man who eats like a wolf and drinks like a whale, gruff in his speech and rough in his manners, there can only be one Bhima; for obstinacy for incapacity either to learn or to unlearn, for standing on dignity unmindful of all consequences, there can only be one Duryodhana; and for—well, even the minor characters in the *Mahabharata*, such as Sanjaya and Sakuni, are typological. The interpolators and redactors could do little or no damage to those characters originally conceived and created by the Sutas. Draupadi is by far the most superb of their creations. And it is these characters who lend to the *Mahabharata* its basic appeal, its unabating interest. But simply on the basis of this one merit, it cannot be rated as a great work of Indian literature, let alone the greatest work of world literature as Sukthankar would have us believe.[4]

Now as for the *Mahabharata* being a work of moral grandeur, it is (to put it mildly) a preposterous claim. To us who are ordinary mortals without any esoteric powers, the morals of the *Mahabharata* are muddy, crude, revolting. But to esoteric geniuses like Sukthankar the *Mahabharata* is "the golden treasury of the ideals of the Indians at their best."[5] But Indians of what age? Of which political setup? Of which economic and social order? At one point of his paean of the *Mahabharata*, Sukthankar says with a thrill in his voice that the epic was "used as a book of education in Bana's time."[6] Bana lived in the seventh century CE, and we are living in the twentieth. Bana lived in a monarchy, and we are living in a republic. Bana lived in a feudal social and economic order, while we are professing to build a society based on socialism, egalitarianism, and secularism. Our world is different from his; our worldview is divergent from his. And yet Sukthankar thinks that the *Mahabharata* should continue to be our textbook; Rajagopalachari publishes a popular translation of the epic at a cheap price so that it could gain the widest circulation;[7] and Munshi spends the terminal years of his life trying to complete his last major literary effort, *Krishnavatara*.[8] And we have in our midst millions of Sukthankaras, Rajagopalacharis, and Munshis! They have a feudal mentality. They have a vested interest in the old order of society. And so they want the *Mahabharata* to be our textbook, the Gita to be our scripture. They refuse to read the history of the world, much less, to learn any lessons from it. This is not the place to recapitulate the story of the fading out of the feudal age in Europe, giving place to the modern era. But I would like to mention one bare fact. Paracelsus, the German alchemist and physician of the fifteenth century CE, "burned the books of Hippocrates and Galen before beginning his lectures on medicine at Prague."[9] It is that defiant spirit, that daring gesture, which led to the birth of modern medicine. If a modern India were to be born, we should cultivate that defiant spirit of Paracelsus and turn our back on a past that shackles on a world that is dead and gone. Undoubtedly, myth has a place in human civilization. As Bronislaw Malinowski wrote:

> Myth fulfills in primitive culture an indispensable function: it expresses, enhances, and codifies belief; it safeguards and enforces morality; it vouches for the guidance of man. Myth is thus a vital ingredient of human civilization; it is not an idle tale, but a hard-worked active force; it is not an intellectual explanation or an artistic imagery, but a pragmatic charter of primitive faith and moral wisdom.[10]

But let it be noted that Malinowski, a great anthropologist, was writing of primitive culture, of primitive society. Is ours still a primitive society? Even Rajagopalacharis, Munshis, and Sukthankars would reject that idea. Why, then, are they zealous in propagating the primitive myths? A reply to this query can be found in Malinowski's essay, "Myth in Primitive Society." In the course of it, he stated that "myth, taken as a whole, cannot be sober, dispassionate history, since it is always made ad hoc to fulfill a certain sociological function, to *glorify a certain group or to justify an anomalous status.*"[11] I have added emphasis to what should be taken special note of. Our Rajagopalacharis, Munshis, and Sukthankars are out to glorify a *certain group* (their own) and to justify *an anomalous position* (again, their own).

A little lower down in the same essay, Malinowski remarked:

> It is clear that myth functions especially where there is a sociological strain, such as in matters of great difference in rank and power, matters of precedence and subordination, and unquestionably where profound historical changes have taken place.[12]

All these conditions mentioned by Malinowski are present in the India of today. There is sociological strain; there is great difference in rank and power; there is social and economic precedence and subordination. Our Rajagopalacharis, Munshis, and Sukthankars are not for wiping out these factors; they are for preserving them; indeed, they would like to strengthen them; therefore, they opt for myth as a buttress to the old order of society. There can be no new society, no new life, unless that buttress is bombarded and blown up.

WHO IS KRISHNA?

Hermann Oldenberg once asked, "Who is Krishna?"[1] It was not an impertinent question. It was asked in all earnestness to know and to understand Krishna, who dominates the Hindu religion and ritual, poetry and drama, song and dance, painting and sculpture —indeed, every aspect of Hindu life and thought. Of course, he has a rival in Rama. But the latter's appeal is by far less widespread. There are few, if any, non-Hindu devotees of Rama. But in the case of Krishna, it is different. As early as the second century BCE, there were some Bactrian Greeks who worshipped him under the name and style of Vasudeva.[2] And today, his influence seems to be spreading like a forest fire in the Christian world. The tongues of that fire have started to spread even to the godless Communist world. To change the metaphor, Krishnaism is now one of the more important export items of India. It is a super-product in the supermarket of America. Krishna consciousness is the escape route from the world of drug culture. It is the panacea for all personal and public ills. To follow Krishna is to attain eternal bliss. A scion of the Ford family of Detroit has given away all his millions to spread the Krishna consciousness.

Along with Oldenberg we, too, should ask in right earnest, who is

Krishna? However, it is a question that is easier asked than answered. Decades ago Bipin Chandra Pal tried to answer it and tied himself up into knots, leaving us and the world not a bit wiser.[3] This need cause no surprise. For there are very many Krishnas, and it is difficult to say who among them is the ersatz Krishna and who the genuine. To start with, there are two Vedic Krishnas. The first is an Aryan *rishi* (seer), and the second a non-Aryan warrior. The rishi Krishna has a son by name Viswaka and grandson called Vishnapu. The grandson, lost for a time, is restored to his family by the Asvins, the twin gods.[4] In this episode, the role of Krishna is only to address a prayer to the Asvins. As it is nothing grand or glorious, the fabricators of the Puranas make their Krishna take up the role of the twin gods. To the delight of his guru, Sandipani, the Puranic Krishna dives into the sea, goes to its very bottom, and rescues Sandipani's son from a demon.[5] What a heroic thing to do! And how precious a gift to offer his guru!

Now, the non-Aryan Krishna is famous warrior (of course, called a demon in the Rig-Veda), and he has an army of ten thousand men under his command. A war is fought between him and Indra, the supreme god of the Vedic Aryans. In that war on the banks of Amshumati, Krishna and his army are badly beaten by Indra with Brihaspati as his ally.[6] Here the one who suffers defeat is, no doubt, a non-Aryan, but does he not bear the name of Krishna? That is surely a blot on that blessed name. And so, the fabricators of the Puranas reverse the roles and make Krishna the victor and Indra the vanquished when they come to write the Vishnu Purana. Krishna opposes the worship of Indra by the gopas of Brindavan; Indra's ire is raised at this affront and he sends down a deluge of rain; the boy Krishna protects all his kinsfolk by lifting up the Govardhana mountain and holding it on the tip of his little finger for seven days as an umbrella; and a humbled Indra asks the clouds to disperse—how greatly the episode enhances the luster of the holy name, "Krishna"![7] The writers of the Puranas were born geniuses in the art and craft of fabrication; the great Viswakarma has not a patch on them!

The next Krishna is the Upanishadic Krishna. He figures in the Chandogya as "Krishna Devakiputra."[8] Is this Krishna the disciple of

Ghora Angirasa? Adi Sankaracharya said *yes* in his commentary on the Upanishads.[9] Anyone can be wrong, but not Sankaracharya, according to our orthodox sections. And so, it is said that Krishna learned his Upanishadic philosophy at the feet of Ghora Angirasa. But then the fact of the discipleship is not quite clear from the Chandogya. Furthermore, according to the Puranas, the teacher of Krishna is Sandipani. But if Krishna is to be credited as a repository of Upanishadic philosophy, he should be linked somehow or other with Ghora Angirasa, and that is done practically by all, right from Sankaracharya down to Hemachandra Raychaudhuri.[10] Apart from Sankaracharya's authority, and he lived about fifteen hundred years after Ghora Angirasa, the only basis for Raychaudhuri's contention is the similarity of certain ideas in the Chandogya and the Gita. By the same token, Krishna should have been the disciple of quite a few other Upanishadic sages, for whole passages from them are found either word for word or with slight changes in the Gita. In this matter, we can hardly withhold our admiration from A. S. P. Ayyar. In his flights of imagination, he beats every fabricator of the Puranas hollow. And he has utter scorn for that Western fetish—historical truth. Neither his sojourn in England for higher studies nor his wide travels in western Europe made the least dent in the iron curtain of his orthodoxy. And so, he writes with a straight face:

> Sri Krishna wanted to teach Ghora Angirasa, the most celebrated teacher of the time and an uncompromising worshipper of the sun, a lesson. He therefore went to him as a disciple. Angirasa taught him all that he knew, and was surprised to see Krishna grasp everything in no time. So, he told him: "You have learned all that I can teach you, O Krishna, son of Devaki. You can leave me now."

As he had gone to Ghora Angirasa not to learn from him but to humble him, Krishna does not leave and give his thanks. Instead, he talks back to him, prefacing his words with "Sir, I presume that you mean. . . ." He delivers a long lecture to poor Angirasa, quoting what Yajnavalkya said to Gargi. Properly impressed and humbled, Angirasa embraces his pupil and says: "Yes, you have understood the inner meaning and mystic significance of my teaching, O Achyuta!"[11] Even a magnifying glass of the highest power will not show even a word of this in the Chandogya Upanishad; what is a wretched magnifying glass compared to the imaginative power of Ayyar! And if Ayyar's imagination was flighty, Bepin Chandra Pal's was perverse. This Brahmo-turned-Vaishnavite made Krishna the son of Ghora Angirasa![12]

The third Krishna is the Krishna of the *Mahabharata*, and its supplement, the Harivamsa. This Krishna is very much a split personality. The man behind the plots and counterplots of the Kuru Pandava conflict is not the same as the theologian-philosopher of the Gita; again, the duo is not same as the divine incarnation we encounter in certain sections of the *Mahabharata* and throughout the Harivamsa. During the long gap between the compilation of the *Mahabharata* and its supplement, the eclipse of the Vedic gods is complete and the trinity, headed by Vishnu, reigns supreme.

When we move next to the Vishnu Purana, written about the fifth century CE, we meet a Krishna who begins his dalliance with the *gopis* (cowherdesses), but in a discreet way.[13] And in that Purana we also encounter a Krishna who in his real form as Vishnu turns the demons on the banks of the Narmada into Buddhists and Jains. For this purpose he sends forth from his being an illusive figure by the name Mahamoha.[14] Such spiteful banalities are as plentiful in the epics and the Puranas as house flies in the rainy session. Rama is supposed to be prior to the Buddha by many centuries. And yet, in the *Ramayana*, its hero Rama calls the Buddha a "thief."[15]

As we go forward in time we reach the Bhagavata Purana. In its pages, Krishna, though eighth in the list of *avataras*, looms large. As a boy, he is prankish; as a youth, he is a Lothario; and as a man, he is prone to a life of ease and luxury. The discretion of the Krishna of the Vishnu Purana in his dalliance with the gopis is slackened in the Bhagavata, but Radha has yet to put in her appearance. This Bhagavata Krishna takes shape between the ninth and the tenth centuries CE; some Puranic authorities extend its lower limit to the thirteenth century CE.[16]

Next in line is the Krishna of the Brahma Vaivarta Purana. In this late Purana of the fourteenth or fifteenth century CE,[17] Radha appears for the first time to initiate unbridled eroticism. Next only to Krishna, she dominates Vaishnavism. To justify the amorous goings-on between Radha and Krishna, there is, of course, much tall talk of the human and divine souls, of the surrender of the individual self to the supreme self (paramatma), of the merger of the finite in the infinite. But it can neither cover up nor condone the stark reality. Only an imbecile or a hypocrite can see the merger of the infinite in the following passage from the Brahma Vaivarta, as translated by Nirad C. Chaudhuri:

Narayana *uvacha* [Thus spake Narayana]:

Krishna pulled her [Radha] with both of his arms to his breast and stripped her of her clothes. Then he kissed her in four different ways. In the combat of coitus the bells in Radha's girdle were torn off, the color on her lips was wiped off by the kisses, the leaves drawn with sandal paste on her breasts were rubbed off, her hair came loose, and the vermilion marks on her forehead disappeared.

Then Radha mounted Krishna and had reversed coitus. The red lack on her feet was rubbed off, she had gooseflesh on her body, and in her swoon could not perceive whether it was night or day. Afterward, Krishna had coitus with her in eight positions, and tore her body to shreds by biting and scratching. The bells in Radha's girdle and her anklets made sweet sounds, and unable to bear any more, Radha ceased from the combat of coitus.[18]

As Chaudhuri proceeds to show, there is an even more vulgar, lewd and revolting passage in the same Purana. To make the meaning of the passage clear, he makes the following introductory remarks:

Krishna now felt that in his preoccupation with Radha he was doing injustice to the other gopis, who were equally devoted to him, and so he went out to satisfy them in the park. There were, however, nine hundred thousand of them, and in order to satisfy them Krishna became nine hundred thousand different men. These exact figures are given in the text, and it adds that the park resounded with the coitus of one million eight hundred thousand persons. Then it proceeds to describe the collective sexual orgy.[19]

And here is the description of that orgy as translated by Chaudhuri from the Brahma Vaivarta as only he could do with his equal mastery of both Sanskrit and English.

Narayana *uvacha* [Thus spake Narayana]:

Then the supreme guru of all the yogis assumed many forms and had intercourse with them in such a manner as would satisfy them. O Narada! From all this coitus arose the charming sound of bells, bangles, and anklets of the women. All of them swooned from pleasure. . . . Recovering consciousness, Krishna began to bite and scratch them, and they him. Krishna scratched their breasts with his nails, and made marks on their firm buttocks. They were beautiful in their nakedness.[20]

It is this particular Krishna about whom Vallabhacharya, Chaitanya, and other leaders of Vaishnavism go into ecstasies; it is this Krishna around whom Andal, Chandidas, Jaydev, Mirabai, Suradas, Vidyapati, Potana, Narsi Mehta, and a host of other poets and poetesses weave their songs; and it is also this Krishna in whom his modern biographers see the divine combined with the human, completely, perfectly. Writing toward the end of the last century, Dhirendra Nath Pal says:

The little kingdom of love and devotion, beauty and sublimity, that Krishna founded in the beautiful forests of "Vrindavana" had now extended far and wide—from the snowcapped Himalayas in the north to the dense forests in the south, from the Vrisni city of Dwaraka in the west to Bhismaka's great kingdom in the east.[21]

At the end of the first part of his voluminous biography in two parts, this worthy says that Krishna is a "towering personality—wonderful man among men—yet he was a great mystery, none could understand him—nor his teachings, nor what and who he was."[22] And yet it did not deter Pal from writing a big book to make us understand "what and who" Krishna is!

Mohan Lal Sen goes on better than Pal. His biography of Krishna is in three volumes, and a major part of the first volume is devoted to Krishna's sport with the gopis in Brindavan. Indeed, the subtitle of the volume is *Brindavana Leela*. In his unbounded admiration for Krishna and his *leelas* in Brindavan, he rhapsodizes thus:

> In no other man in history we find such humanity and divinty so harmoniously blended together! As a man, Sreekrishna shows the highest human perfection in every higher sphere, in culture, in valor, in intelligence, in the breadth of vision and in the catholicity of views. All the noble qualities of man, and all the potential energies of the human race find their fullest expression in him![23]

Apart from being the perfect man, Krishna is also the perfect god. To know why, Sen tells us, "Turn to his Brindavana Leela, it is all love, it is all divine! Hence Sreekrishna is God incarnate on the earth, at least, the greatest and the wisest not only of the Hindus but of men at large."[24] Men at large, I am sure, are not given to voyeurism like the devotees of Krishna to glue their eyes to Brindavana or any other *vana* (park) to satiate in (to drink in) scenes of sexual orgies.

A more recent biographer of Krishna is Pratap R. Parekh. Though he entitles his book, *Krishna: Myth or Reality*, at no point has he the faintest doubt in his mind that Krishna is very much a reality. He gives in his appendices not only Krishna's geneology but also his horoscope. Like the rest of his tribe, he lingers in and around Brindavan! He is enthralled by the sight of the garden, "fresh and green with recent rains" and glistening in the full moonlight in the month of Shravan; he is bewitched by "Krishna's dalliance with the gopis and his grand affair with Radha," and he pours scorn on the prudish fellows who question the propriety of Krishna's conduct. "Don't you know," he asks them, "that powerful men of extraordinary abilities [I am quoting here his very words] have somehow overstepped the norms of dharma and established laws . . . just as fire is not considered blameworthy when it devours, destroys, and wreaks havoc, so also men of strength and powerful abilities are not afflicted for such breaches. *Tejiyashan nadoshaya.* Law applies to the weak, not to the strong."[25]

The same point is stressed by Hanurman Poddar in his monograph of one hundred pages dealing exclusively with Krishna's sport with the gopies. "Carnality and illicit love," he says, "cannot be conceived to exist in one who possesses . . . the divine qualities," and if one thinks that they exist, one must be having a sinful mind. Indeed, according to Poddar, an unfaithful wife should be given higher honor than the faithful wife for three reasons. To quote his exact words: "These are (1) constant thought of the beloved, (2) an insatiable longing to meet the beloved, and (3) complete blindness to the faults of the beloved. Since the wedded wife remains under the same roof with her husband all the twenty-four hours, none of these things is present in her. No doubt the gopis used to see the Lord every day: yet, since the sentiment of a paramour was predominant in their love, a moment's separation would appear unbearable to them."[26] Can perversity go futher? Yes, it can. For here is A. S. P. Ayyar who declares strindently: "Sri Krishna is the father of all men, the husband of all women."[27] The second proposition, he says, is "a normal corollary of the first." How? It is a thing that only his twisted brain can understand!

However, all this is not merely specious pleading on the part of the devotees of Krishna to justify the goings-on between their god and the gopis but a special feature of Hinduism. It has two sets of laws, one for the weak and another for the strong; two sets of norms, one for the high and another for the low; two codes of ethics, one for the gods and another for the mortals.[28] Small wonder, there is such a lot of doublethink and doublespeak in Indian life.

The same type of doublethink and doublespeak are very much in evidence in many other modern biographies of Krishna, including *Sree Krishna: The Lord of Love*, by Baba Premanand Bharati, and

Lord Krishna: Love Incarnate, by Monika Varma. Baba's style tends to become fervid the moment he thinks of Radha, and here is a sample:

> Radha was she, youthful, lovely, she, his playmate of the forest, she, with love-look in her face, she, the queen of love among them, giving all and asking naught.[29]

We cannot accuse Donald R. Kinsley of doublethink and double-speak. He may be misguided, but he is honest. He is typical of the present younger generation of Americans who, in a bid to still the restlessness of their spirit, are resorting to hashish, opium, mescaline, or mysticism. The last in the list may take the form of yoga or sex. Indian Babas and Bhagavans are making big money in America because they are meeting a real need. And one of the Bhagavans who migrated there recently is an exponent of the doctrine of "salvation through sex." His influence can be detected in the fulsome praise that Kinsley bestows on Krishna. Here is the case he makes out for free sex with special reference to Krishna:

> The intimate and playful themes that run through Krishna's love for Radha and the festival nature of his dalliance with the gopis portray a vision of the divine that is approachable, warm, irresistible, blissful, and intoxicating. Krsna moves in a realm of love and love making that invites (indeed, demands) a total, impassioned response. All those who enter this realm are freed from bondage to the ordinary and customary, freed to behave imaginatively and spontaneously. The erotic aspect of this other world is not degrading but life affirming. Erotic dalliance shuns the world of taboos and lives for the moment. It is an ovation to all that is vigorous and full of joy. The young god Krsna is an unrepentant reveler stirring all those who join with him to uncontrollable frenzy. In the world of the great lover Krsna, the gopis, as representatives of the human, expand themselves; they plumb depths and reach heights of emotion that are impossible within the humdrum world of habitual action. They leave behind the ordinary and participate in the extraordinary. Under the influence of the intoxicating and intoxicated god they lose their inhibitions and revel in playful freedom.[30]

This passage, I am sure, would make the heart of every devotee of Krishna jump with joy. Turning around to the critic of their lord of love, they will tell him: "You are dead to all finer sensibilites, all higher values. You will do well to sit at the feet of this American saint to learn a lesson or two on Indian spiritualism, on the meaning and message of Brindavan."

Be that as it may, it is time to ask ourselves who among these many Krishnas is the real one. The soberer of the traditionalists will point to the Krishna of the *Mahabharata*, and particularly of the Gita. So let us take a closer look at that Krishna in our next chapter.

KRISHNA AS MAN

We may or may not like Krishna, the Lothario of the Puranas. It is a matter of taste and temperament. When we turn from that Krishna to the Krishna of the *Mahabharata*, we can not help disliking him, for he is hypocritical. Of course, I am speaking not of the devotees of Krishna but of men with a rational mind, with an impartial outlook and a judicious approach. To devotees, whoever may be their god, the subject of their devotion is the embodiment of ultimate truth, of ethereal beauty, of supreme divinity. Devotion has a lethal effect on man the thinker. How else can one explain the equal devotion shown by many to Rama and Krishna? They are believed to be two incarnations of the self-same Vishnu. And yet how widely they differ! With rare exceptions, Rama is a stickler for truth; Krishna is not. Rama is monogamous; Krishna is not. Except on two or three occasions, Rama is fair in war; Krishna is not. And yet their devotees see nothing conflicting in their character! Such is the lethal effect of devotion on the thinking process.

Turning our back on the devotees, let us return to the Krishna of the *Mahabharata*, and see him through the eyes of foreign scholars. From among them, I am selecting three who were not of British nationality. For the Britishers, having been the imperial rulers of this country, may be open to the charge of anti-Indian bias, and more so, of anti-Hindu bias.

Now, let us first take up E. W. Hopkins (1857–1932), the doyen of American Indologists. He mastered, apart from Greek and Latin, two of the ancient languages of Asia, Sanskrit and Pahlavi. He specialized in philology. He wrote on the Hindu caste system and Hindu ethics. Of the Hindu epics and Puranas, he made a thorough study of the *Mahabharata* and wrote an authoritative analysis of it from the linguistic, poetical, ethical, and other angles. He taught as professor at Yale University and many were the academic honors he received in his long and distinguished career. And this is what Hopkins says of Krishna, taking the words from the mouth of Sanjaya: "Krishna is a pious hypocrite."[1] For a moment, let us leave out Hopkins and ponder over the words of Sanjaya. At the end of the Gita, it is on record that Sanjaya said to Dhritarashtra: "O King, as I recall again and again this dialogue, wondrous and holy, of Krishna and Arjuna, I thrill with joy again and again, and often as I recall that most wondrous form [*Viswarupam*] of Hari [Krishna] great is my astonishment, O king, and I thrill with joy again and again." It is this very Sanjaya who says toward the closing stages of the Kurukshetra War that "Krishna is a pious hypocrite." Surely there must have been compelling reasons for Sanjaya to change his opinion of Krishna so radically during the course of the eighteen days of that war. Now, to return to Hopkins. Fully endorsing Sanjaya, this is what he says:

> Krishna served as the charioteer of Arjuna, the chief Pandu and epic hero; and though he promised not to fight in person he did all he could to keep up and intensify the enmity between the Pandus and their related foes, the Kurus, not avoiding even tricks opposed to knightly honor. It is not likely that such shameful acts as those recorded of him by his own followers would have been invented of a god, but rather that the tricks belonged to him as a hero, and that no amount of excuse, of which there is enough offered, could do away with the crude facts of tradition, which represented the man-god Krishna as a clever but unscrupulous fighter.[2]

Next let us turn to Maurice Winternitz (1863–1937), an Austrian by birth. He studied classical philology and philosophy and even got his doctorate by the age of twenty-five. Then, coming under the influence of Max Muller and Gorge Buhler, he specialized in Indology. Staying and teaching at Oxford for some years, he helped Max Muller in getting ready the press copy of the Rig-Veda and also in preparing the bulky index to the forty-nine volumes of *Sacred Books of the East*. Later he shifted to Prague to teach Indology at the University of Prague, and he rose in a dozen years from the post of a lecturer to full professorship. Working intensely for fifteen years, he wrote *A History of Indian Literature* in about sixteen hundred pages. When he died in 1937 at the age of seventy-four, Rabindranath Tagore paid a glowing tribute to "his amazingly wide scholarship, his devotion to truth, and the courage with which he held to his idealism."[3] And this is what Winternitz has to say in his book, *A History of Indian Literature*, on Krishna the man: "It is striking that all the treachery emanates from Krsna, that he is always the instigator of all the deceit and defends the conduct of the Pandavas. And this is the same Krsna who in many parts of the *Mahabharata* and more especially in the Harivamsa, is praised and glorified as an incarnation of Vishnu the highest god, and as the ideal and prototype of every virtue."[4] At another place in the same book, Winternitz calls Krishna "the cunning friend of the Pandavas."[5]

The German sociologist Max Weber (1864–1920) was even more caustic. His special distinction was to apply the perspectives of sociology to the study of the major religions of the world. Of his books on religion, the most important is *The Protestant Ethic and the Spirit of Capitation*. Of no less merit is his book *The Religion of India* with its subtitle *The Sociology of Hinduism and Buddhism*. In that book he anticipated by several decades that religion would greatly hamper the growth of the scientific spirit in India. How correct he proved in his forecast! Well, here is the estimate of the character of Krishna made by Weber: "What strikes the Occidental about the redeemer Krishna, and what separates him from later redeemers who are presented as free of sin in the theology of the sects is Krishna's indubitable nonvirtuousness. In the *Mahabharata* he suggests to his protégés the grossest and most unchivalrous offenses against the mores."[6]

Apart from the three non-British scholars—one an American, the second an Austrian, and the third a German—whom I have quoted, there are many others who expressed a poor opinion of Krishna the man. Among Indian pandits, Sukthankar had the fullest knowledge of the case against Krishna, and to the best of my knowledge his is the ablest summary of that case. It reads:

> That paradox of paradoxes! A philosopher on the battlefield! An ally who gives away his powerful army to swell the ranks of his opponents; and himself, though the omnipotent lord of all weapons, takes a vow, before the commencement of the war; not to hold a weapon in his hands! A god who avows impartiality toward all living beings, and yet like a wily and unscrupulous politician secretly plots for the victory of the Pandavas and the annihilation of the Kauravas! Standing on the field of battle, this self-styled avatara preaches the lower morality and the mere man (Arjuna) the higher! A grotesque character who claims to be the highest god and behaves uncommonly like a "tricky mortal."[7]

Sukthankar, being very astute, introduced his refutation of the case against Krishna at the beginning of his summing up. It is in the four words, "The paradox of paradoxes." Once you start talking of paradoxes, enigmas, puzzles, riddles, and mysteries, you step out of the realm of the mind and enter the domain of mindlessness. In that domain reason has no place, argument is of no avail, and sanity can hardly breathe. In that domain ambiguity, equivocation, conundrum and sophistry reign supreme. And so Sukthankar tells us that "Sri Krishna is a mortal and yet not a mortal." Lest we should miss his point, he reiterates, Krishna is "a paradox, a riddle, to say the least." Without allowing us to get a word in edgewise, he affirms, "And what is so very strange in that? Is not life a paradox, a riddle?" Proceeding further, he avers, "the double character of Sri Krsna gives rise to apparent contradictions in his words and actions which have been the despair of the modern interpreters of the *Mahabharata*." Unlike the stupid modern interpreters, Sukthankar and his like are "furnished by nature with a bifocal stereoscope apparatus [perhaps made in Dwaraka] which instantly combines the twin views of the god who has become man and the man who has become [a] god—views taken at slightly different angles—into a single, perfectly focused image of god-man or man-god, with complete effect of solidity, reality, and perspective." To hit the nail right on our stupid head, the self-appointed spokesman of the god-man or man-god adds pontifically:

> It is only the modern critic who, starting from entirely different modes of thought, standards of conduct, and norms of expression, approaches this stupendous product of Indian genius suspiciously, hesitatingly, superciliously—when he comes across anomalies, in the character and behavior of Sri Krsna—which are more apparent than real—finds his progress impeded by a blank wall of total incomprehension and comes sooner or later to a dead stop.[8]

Not being lucky as Sukthankar and the like, the modern critic lacks "a biofocal stereoscopic apparatus," and the poor creature sees a glaring credibility gap in the words of Krishna. He also finds outrageous trickery in Krishna's actions. According to Krishna's dictum, "an enemy's abode should be entered through a wrong gate and a friend's abode through the right one" (Sabha, XXI, 53). And this is exactly the way he enters the palace of his dreaded enemy Jarasandha; he enters it at midnight accompanied by Bhima and Arjuna, all the three disguised as Brahmans. When informed about the arrival of some Brahmans, Jarasandha comes out to do them honors and Krishna loses no time in getting him killed by Bhima. The account of the wrestling match that goes on for fourteen days between Bhima and Jarasandha is convincingly shown to be untrue by Pendyala Sastri of Pithapuram.[9] And he is equally convincing when he writes that Krishna plays trickery in killing Kamsa and Sisupala.[10]

In these three cases, the accusation of trickery may be questioned, but surely not in the case of Bhishma, Drona, Karna, and Duryodhana. Even Sukthankar cannot deny that "these were killed by subterfuges or tricks." But he conveniently foists the guilt on the Pandavas alone and finds excuses for them. Here are his actual words:

> It is indeed true the Pandavas make themselves guilty of some slight breaches of pugilistic conventions in the course of the long, drawn-out, and bitter war of annihilation fought out on the plains of Kurukshetra. Bhishma, Drona, Karna, and Duryodhana were all killed in the war by subterfuges or tricks which violate the strict code of chivalrous and knightly combats. But the Kauravas are just as unscrupulous, if not indeed more so; only they are discreet and diplomatic in the extreme.[11]

"It is indeed true that the Pandavas make themselves guilty of *some slight breaches* of pugilistic conventions in the course of the long, drawn-out, and bitter war of annihilation fought out on the plains of Kurukshetra" (emphasis mine). In one sentence how did, one wonders, Sukthankar manage to compress so many sophistries! Going against the covenants for the conduct of war in every crucial situation cannot be "some slight breaches of pugilistic conventions." And what does pugilism mean? According to *Webster's New World Dictionary*, it means "the art or practice of fighting with the fists; boxing; prize fighting." Which of these three was the Kurukshetra War? And was it a long, drawn-out war? There is in European history a Hundred Years' War and a Thirty Years' War. The First World War lasted for four years and the Second went on for about six years. In the case of the Kurukshetra War, it was all over in eighteen days.

How can it be called a long, drawn-out war? Furthermore, did not the Kurukshetra consist of a single plain? Of the prose translations of the Gita into English, the one by John Davies is still rated one of the best in being the nearest to the original. It opens thus: "Dhritarashtra spoke: when my forces and the Pandavas met together on the sacred plain, the Kurukshetra [plain of the Kurus], eager for a fight, what did they do, Sanjaya?"[12] It may be noted that the singular for "plain" is used here not once, but twice! Why, then, the use of the plural by Sukthankar? Is it not to suggest that it was a mighty war spread over a wide area? Strictly speaking, the armed clash on the Kurukshetra was more a battle than a war. More important, it was Krishna and not the Pandavas who should be held really guilty of the breach of the rules of war agreed to by both the parties before the commencement of hostilities.

After his gem of a sentence, Sukthankar proceeds to say that if the Pandavas sinned, the Kauravas sinned even more. Obviously, he thinks that two wrongs make one right. To further extenuate the Pandavas, he argues that while the Pandavas are "truly ingenuous and guileless," the Kauravas are "sanctimonious hypocrites." Surely it is the Pandavas, and not the Kauravas, who always prattle about dharma. But in the whole of this passage, Sukthankar evades the real issue. The individual primarily guilty of trickery and deceit is Krishna, but Sukthankar keeps him out of the dock by the simple device of omitting his name from the list of the accused.

As we have had enough and more of Sukthankar, we may now leave him behind together with his sophistries and go ahead. Of all the trickeries of Krishna, easily the worst is the way he brought about the defeat and death of Duryodhana. In her book, *Politics and Ethics in Ancient India*, Manorama Jauhari has a whole chapter entitled "Unfair Deaths in the *Mahabharata*." At the close of the chapter she says: "The Pandavas *violated the code of fighting mostly* under the advice of Krishna himself" (emphasis mine).[13] She would have been more right had she written "*solely* under the advice of Krishna." Being very clever and shrewd, Krishna often takes care to proffer his crooked advice indirectly. His advice to kill Duryodhana by hitting him below the belt, that is, by breaking his thighs, is conveyed to Bhima not directly but through Arjuna. Balarama, Krishna's half-brother, is so outraged by the foul play that he makes a move to punish Bhima with his special weapon, the plough. The right thing for him should have been to raise his weapon against Krishna. Being aware that Balarama has little trust in his word, and less in his morals, Krishna has obviously taken the precaution of passing on his unfair advice through Arjuna without being noticed by Balarama. And when Balarama is about to punish Bhima for his dastardly deed, Krishna intervenes to pacify him. After Balarama's departure in sheer disgust, the words addressed by Krishna to Yudhisthira in justification of the unjust means adopted in the war are these: "This man [Duryodhana] could not be killed by righteous means, nor could your other enemies been slain, if I had not thus acted sinfully."[14]

Being as much "a pious hypocrite" as Krishna, Yudhisthira sheds a few crocodile tears over the foul play against Duryodhana and chides Bhima for kicking the head of the fallen foe. But almost the next moment he rejoices saying, "The earth has been conquered [by us], ourselves having acted according to the counsels of Krishna." Though Yudhisthira, also called Dhramaja, the King of Righteousness, is mightily pleased with himself, the gods are not. To indicate their low opinion of the Pandavas and "the god-man or man-god," who is their adviser, the gods shower flowers on the dying Duryodhana. Here is a vivid description of the scene in the *Mahabharata*:

> A thick shower of fragrant flowers fell from the sky. The Gandharvas played upon many charming musical instruments. The Apsaras in a chorus sang the glory of king Duryodhana. The Siddhas uttered loud sound to the effect—Praise be to King Duryodhana! Fragrant and delicious breezes mildly blew on every side. All the quarters became clear and the firmament looked blue as the lapis lazuli. Beholding these exceedingly wonderful things and this worhip offered to Duryodhana, the Pandavas headed by Vasudeva became ashamed. (Salya Parva)

In preparing the critical edition of the *Mahabharata*, did Sukhthankar omit this incident as an interpolation?[15] I do not know. As he is too shrewd to do such a rash thing, he should have retained it. After all, is not everything only apparent? So the flowers are apparent; their showering is apparent; the shame felt by the Pandavas and the god-man or man-god is apparent. Unless you have "a bifocal stereoscopic apparatus" made in Dwaraka, such things are beyond the reach of your poor vision, outside the range of your puny intellect!

KRISHNA AS STATESMAN

Highly complex was the personality of Bankim Chandra Chatterji. An official of the British government in India, he was a patriot at heart. A nationalist in general, he had pro-Hindu proclivities. A rationalist and humanist in his early life, he turned to religion as he grew older and developed a strong streak of obscurantism. An innovator in literature and the first in India to master the art and craft of the novel, he ended by looking up for inspiration to the *Mahabharata* and its Krishna. Did he seek personal salvation through Krishna? To be sure, he stated unreservedly that personally he was a believer in the divinity of Krishna. And yet, his *Krishnacharita* in Bengali was conceived and written, not as the biography of a god but of a statesman.

Though Bankim Chandra's warm admiration for Comte cooled off during his later life,[1] the influence of that French thinker was never totally obliterated. Hence Bankim Chandra was more concerned with the future of India than with his personal salvation. It was that concern which urged him to set up Krishna as a symbol of a resurgent India—united, free, powerful.

That was a basic mistake made by the pioneer of modern Indian literature. For one thing, it was almost impossible to free Krishna from the myth, the mythology, and the rest of the sticky mess of the Puranas. For another, even the Krishna of the *Mahabharata* has too many frailties to serve as an inspiring model for a statesman. More important, a nation cannot march forward toward its future by fixing its gaze backward on its past. Krishna, be he of the Puranas or of the *Mahabharata*, can be a symbol only of the past, and certainly not of the future. His times were different, the historical forces in operation during his times were different. And this is the case with Rama, too. While Bankim Chandra's symbol for a new India was Krishna, Gandhi's was Rama. Often Gandhi talked of "Ramarajya." Such was his obsession with Rama that his day opened with Ramdhun and closed with Ramdhun. When he was once asked to state categorically what he meant by "Rama" and "Ramarajya" he said that his Rama was not the son of Dasaratha, the Prince of Ayodhya, but only another name for God. But he was not consistent in this matter. Further, he wrote that "Ramnama" can cure all ills, physical, mental, and spiritual. Be that as it may, both Gandhi and Bankim Chandra were mistaken in the symbols that they had chosen for the new India and we are now paying a very heavy price for the wrong choices they made.

It should be said to the credit of Bankim Chandra that, despite his personal belief in the divinity of Krishna, he scrupulously kept out all supernaturalism from his *Krishnacharitra*. He dismissed the exploits of Krishna, amorous and the rest, retailed in the Harivamsa, Vishnu, Bhagavata, Brahma Vaivarta, and the other Puranas as either fanciful or fantastic. He refused to accept the Krishna of Jayadev and Vidyapati as genuine. Indeed, he thought that their Krishna was vulgar. He did not accept as true quite a few things said even in the *Mahabharata* about Krishna. In his zeal to be rational, he often went too far. An example may be given. By saying that the war with Naraka of Pragjyotisha, and the wholesale appropriation of the large harem of that king was a myth, Bankim Chandra reduces the number of Krishna's wives from 16,002 to a mere twenty-two, ten are mentioned only in the Harivamsa, and so they, too, go. Now out of the remaining twelve, two are referred to only at one place in the *Mahabharata*, and so out they go. Next, Satya is only the shortened form of the name of Satyabhama, and Rohini is another name for Jambavati. Thus only eight are left. Of these eight, we know nothing about five except their names; hence they should also be dropped. As it is nonsensical to say that Krishna married Jambavati, the daughter of a bear, one more has to be eliminated, and thus Krishna is left with only two wives. Finding it impossible to dismiss Satyabhama in a like manner, Bankim Chandra has to admit that Krishna is bigamous but likes to forget that fact. So, ignoring the existence of Satyabhama, he finally affirms that Krishna has only Rukmini as his wife and thus is monogamous! It is rather an ingenious exercise in ratiocination!

By following more or less similar lines, Bankim Chandra tried his level best to present Krishna "as a far-sighted statesman, bent upon achieving the unity of India." Despite all his literary genius, he failed in his objective. After a fair and critical study of *Krishnacharitra*, this is the summing up by Bimanbehari Majumdar:

> Bankim Chandra concludes his brilliant work with the observation that Krsna was an ideal person in whom the synthetic development of all the mental and physical faculties took place simultaneously. He was not merely a great hero, but according to the testimony of Bhisma, a scholar well versed in all the Vedas and Vedangas. Bankim proved that Krsna was the "wisest and greatest of the Hindus." But Rabindranath offers a perfectly valid criticism against the *Krsnacharitra* when he says that the hero of the work is not really Krsna but the rationalism of Bankim Chandra.[2]

In recent years, K. M. Munshi attempted to outbid Bankim Chandra in establishing Krishna as the greatest statesman ever born in India. Although he did not live to complete his highly ambitious work, *Krishnavatara*, he was very near the end of the mighty task he set for himself. In the introduction to his saga, Munshi says with his usual flamboyance:

> Wise and valorous, he was loving and loved, farseeing and yet living for the moment, gifted with sagelike detachment and yet intensely

human; the diplomat, the sage, and the man of action with a personality as luminous as that of a divinity. The urge, therefore, came
upon me, time and again, to embark upon a reconstruction of his
life and adventures by weaving a romance around him.[3]

Yes, what Munshi has woven is a romance, giving free rein to his
riotous imagination. According to him, Krishna's life mission was no
less than to unify India and to forge it into a mighty nation under the
hegemony of Yudhisthira with himself as the real power behind the
throne. At a time when Bihar and the rest of India east of it were outside the Aryan pale, when all the land south of the Vindhyas was considered unholy, if not the very purgatory, an attempt to unify India
into a single nation is something wholly incredible. Luminaries like
Munshi conveniently forget that during Buddha's lifetime, there were
as many as sixteen *Mahajanapadas*, fourteen to the north of the Vindhyas and two to their south. As Niharranjan Ray pointed out:

> . . . these sixteen Mahajanapadas were, by about 400 BCE, reduced
> to four, and by about 324 BCE, to only one, which was the great
> and sprawling Maurya Empire. Here was thus a political process at
> work, a process of formation of larger and larger states obliging the
> smaller ones to merge themselves into the larger and more powerful
> ones on the one hand and transforming the tribal oligarchical ones
> to monarchical ones on the other.[4]

There is only one inference that can be drawn from this, but Ray
failed to draw it, clearly, firmly. That is done by D. C. Sirkar without
hemming and hawing, as most of our historians do where the so-called
hoary tradition, and hence hoary history, is concerned. In no uncertain terms he affirmed that "all stories of earlier *digvijayas* [earlier than
the Maurya] and empire building described in the Puranas have to be
regarded as belonging to the domain of mythology and folklore and
not of history."[5] Indeed, as Hopkins suggested, the very idea of a vast
empire was beyond the "pre-Asokan imagination as it is reflected in
the literatures."[6] Not to speak of unifying India, Krishna could not
unify his own people, the Yadavas. Incidentally, what was the number

of Yadavas in Dwaraka alone? To draw attention to the fantasies which the Puranas purvey, I may quote here a passage from Bimanbihari Majumdar. It reads:

> The Matsya and the Agni Puranas state that the total number of the Yadavas at Dvaraka was three crores. The Skanda Purana increases the number to fifty-six crores. It also relates that Krsna had as many as nine lakhs of golden palaces. The Bhagavata says that the number of the Yadavas could not be counted even in ten thousand years. It gives an idea of the total population by stating that the strength of the teaching staff for the Kumaras of the Yadava family was three crores eight thousand and eight hundred. The Yadavas probably solved their food problem by importing foodstuff from the heavens.[7]

Apart from these countless crores (!) of Yadavas at Dwaraka, there were more of them at Madhura, Vidarbha, Avanti, Mahismathi and some other places. They lived under different regimes refusing to accept Krishna's leadership. And at the time of the Kurukshetra War, a majority of the Yadavas, as pointed out by Pusalkar, were with the Kauravas and not with the Pandavas. Here is the relevant passage:

> The Yadavas were divided in their allegiance. Krishna was the non-combatant adviser of the Pandavas and Balarama remained neutral. Yuyudhana and Satyaki, among the Vrishnis and Yadavas, came to the Pandavas, while Nila of Mahishmati, Vinda and Anuvinda of Avanti.
>
> Kritavarman of the Bhoja-Andhaka-Vrishnis, Vidarbha, Nishada, and Salva supported the Kaurava forces.[8]

It may be necessary to mention here that the Bhojas, Andhakas, Vrishnis, et al., were different clans of the Yadavas.[9] Even from the Yadava clan of Dwaraka, it was only Krishna who supported the Pandavas; the Yadava army as a whole fought on the side of the Kauravas. Of course, it is said in the *Mahabharata* that it was Krishna who gave the choice to Arjuna to choose either him as a noncombatant counselor or his large army, and that Arjuna gladly chose Krishna. This should be treated as a deliberate misstatement. For Dwaraka was an oligarchic republic and not a monarchy. And Krishna's office was that of *sangha mukhya*. Indeed, he referred to himself as such in the Santi Parva of the *Mahabharata*. He had obviously to share that office as well as the power which it confers with another, for he also called himself in the same parva *ardha-bhokta*, that is, "enjoyer of the half." In all likelihood, the second sangha mukhya was Balarama. And he preferred to stay neutral, joining neither the Kauravas nor the Pandavas. Two of Krishna's own sons, Pradyumna and Samba were, likewise, neutral. Apart from all this, the point I am trying to make is this: When Krishna was unable at any time in his long life to unify his own Yadava people, is it not preposterous to claim on his behalf that he was a great statesman who unified the whole of India?

Indeed, his failure as a leader of men in general, and of his own tribe in particular, was total. Who can question this verdict if he bears in mind the total annihilation of the Yadavas in fratricide? To trace its cause to a curse laid by some sages is a silly excuse; it all started with a drunken brawl. Krishna himself joined in the massacre in its final stages. To call such a man a far-sighted statesman, a great unifier of the nation, is to take leave of one's senses.

10

KRISHNA AS GOD

In every respect, Krishna the god is even less credible than Krishna the man and Krishna the statesman. He enters the *Mahabharata* as a man and exits as a god. In the Puranas both his entry and exit are as a god. So in looking at his godhood we have to take into account the epic as well as the Puranas.

Krishna's childhood exploits, each more miraculous than the next, are not taken seriously by Bankim Chandra Chatterji, though he affirmed profound faith in Krishna's divinity. He dismissed those exploits as allegories. Pendyala Sastri of Pithapuram is more perspicacious in explaining those supposed miracles. Putana is no she-demon; it is the name of a children's disease, and there is a clear reference to it in the old textbooks of Indian medicine. Out of superstitious fears, certain ceremonies are performed even now in backward villages to ward off perils to children from malevolent spirits. Of these spirits, one is called Kesin, a second Sanderatha, and a third Ulukhala. The first two from among these three, says Sastri, are blown up as the two demons Kesin and Sakatasura* sent by Kamsa in his vain bid to kill Krishna. With regard to the uprooting of a pair of trees by Krishna by dragging

---

*A synonym of Sanderatha.

between their adjoining trunks a wooden pestle to which his mother tied him with a rope, explains Sastri, it's nothing but the supposed evil spirit named after a pestle (Ulukhala).[1] The rest of the miracles in Krishna's childhood are like figments of superstitious imagination.

Even in the matter of another miracle supposed to have been performed by Krishna when he grew up to be a man, Sastri has shown a mind that is both acute and critical. When Draupadi is being stripped of her robes in the court of the Kauravas, it is said, she prays to Krishna and he saves her from dishonor with his supernatural powers. According to Sastri, Draupadi mentions in the *Mahabharata* thirteen times in all how she is dishonored at the Kauravas' court; but only in three out of these thirteen references she brings up the attempt to disrobe her, and in the other ten cases she speaks only of her being dragged by her hair into the royal court. On the only two occasions when she complains directly to Krishna about the humiliations she suffered, she does not refer at all to the attempt to disrobe her nor does she thank Krishna for coming to her rescue. Indeed, at the time of the alleged attempt to strip Draupadi, Krishna is away from Dwaraka fighting a war with Salva. Only after his return from the war does he hear for the first time of Yudhisthira's gamble and its bitter consequences. So his going to Draupadi's rescue in response to her prayers is baseless. Furthermore, neither Bhasa nor Bharavi nor Kshemendra, three of the famous poets and playwrights of ancient India, refer to the alleged attempt to disrobe Draupadi, even though they write on the *Mahabharata* themes. By these and other cogent arguments, Sastri makes a powerful case against the alleged attempt to disrobe Draupadi and Krishna's timely intervention.[2]

On another point Sastri is no less incisive in his argument. He shows that after the initial dispute as to who should be honored first at the Rajasuya sacrifice of Yudhisthira, Sisupala, who has a rightful grudge against Krishna, leaves the assembly hall to prepare for a fight. He is pacified by Yudhisthira and brought back. Even after his return, Sisupala continues to voice his protest against giving the first place of honor to Krishna when the latter suddenly hurls his quoit (*chakra*) at his detractor and kills him. In a like manner, says Sastri, Jarasandha is killed by Bhima in a wholly unguarded moment at the instigation of Krishna.[3]

A more serious charge against Krishna is made by Sitanath Tattavab-hushan. With reference to the early life of divine Krishna, he says: "His first act in this part of his life was the assassination of his maternal uncle Kamsa. 'Assassination' is not too strong a term for it, for though Kamsa had given him provocation, he was not killed in the course of a battle or even in a single combat."[4] How did Krishna, then, kill his uncle? Getting up the platform on which Kamsa was sitting, watching wrestling matches, Krishna held him by the hair and hurled him down to death when he least suspected such a peril. After referring to Krishna's killings of Sisupala, Satadhanva, Salva, and others, Tattavabhushan remarks thus:

> Killing seems to be the most divine act in the eye of our Purana writers—one which proves divinity more than any other act. And this killing of Paundra was a specially divine act, since the fellow not only denied Krishna's divinity, but assumed Vishnu's fourfold insignia—the conch, the quoit, the club, and the lotus—and declared himself to be the real Vasudeva. He is also said by one authority to have invaded Dvaraka. In the fight that ensued, he showed great bravery but was at length overpowered and killed by Krishna. Another account makes Krishna himself proceed to Paundra's capital in response to his challenge to return to him the insignia and kill him by throwing them upon him. This was perhaps a more godlike procedure than the former.[5]

Krishna is no less famous for his abductions. He carries away Ruk-mini a day before the time fixed for her wedding with Sisupala. He kid-naps Mitravinda from her swayamvara grounds. His marriage with Lakshmana, daughter of the king of Madra, is also forcible seizure. And by right of forcible seizure conquest, he adds sixteen thousand women from the harem of Naraka to the list of his wives. As befitting a divine being, he has 16,008 wives in all (according to Bankim Chandra's version, the Puranas put the number at 16,022). And his children, says the Harivamsa, number one hundred eighty thousand, all sons—no daughters, not even one.

Krishna's life span, according to the Bhagvata, is one hundred twenty-five years. On its basis, Bankim Chandra makes a little calculation and it shows that Krishna gives birth to fourteen hundred and forty sons per year or four sons per day. That it is an underestimate is shown by Bimanbehari Majumdar. "Krishna, in his human form," says Majumdar, "could not have produced a son during the first fourteen years of his life, nor after his eightieth year. This leaves only sixty-six years for procreative work, during which period on an average 7.5 sons had to be born a day if the Puranic total regarding the number of sons is to be believed at all."[6]

Yet another great thing that the Puranas tell us about Krishna is the thorough way in which he plans Dwaraka. A city without its redlight district is no city. London has its Soho, Paris its Montmartre, Tokyo its Ginza; should not Dwaraka have its own center for night life? And so, according to no less an authority than the Harivamsa, "the Lord settled thousands of public women at Dwaraka." Where the Lord is concerned, the figures always run into thousands and hundreds of thousands; anything less is unthinkable. Furthermore, would not there be fights among men, as the Harivamsa asks, unless enough women are there to go around? Along with thousands of public women, the Lord also sees to it that thousands of pubs are opened. The champion boozer of the city is the Lord's own half-brother, Balarama. Rarely is the toddy pot absent from his hand; hence, toddy has come to be known as *halipriya*, that is, "the favorite drink of Balarama, the bearer of *halam*, the plough." And, of course, all kinds of meats are on sale. They include, as the Harivamsa again tells us, the meat of birds, deer, and buffalo. The Lord himself is neither a vegetarian nor a teetotaler. The gay life of Dwaraka is summed up thus by Bimanbehari Majumdar:

> The Yadavas, according to the Harivamsa, used to take these women to the seaside along with their wives, brothers, sons, and grandsons, and amuse themselves with water sports, drinking, and eating. In one passage, the sons of Krsna and the chiefs of the family are described to have discarded all their clothes and ornaments while engaged in the water sports in the sea. Men as well as women amongst the Yadavas were addicted to drinking.[7]

Whether or not it was a holy city, Dwaraka was certainly a gay city when Lord Krishna was presiding over its destinies. Resenting such an observation, though it is based on the Harivamsa, the orthodox legions will certainly be livid with rage. Indeed, the great Sukthankar denounced the "sheer stupidity" of the "modern critic" who misses "the obvious." In his view, "the illiterate Indian is right to a large extent" in understanding the inner significance of *leela* [play] of the Lord than his 'educated' brother."[8] The "educated" fool fails to take note of the fact that Krishna not only claimed to be God but also gave a glimpse of his cosmic being more than once. How grand, how graphic, how awe inspiring is that glimpse that he gave to Arjuna on the Kurukshetra battlefield! Only the fool of a modern critic would say that Arjuna, being in a state of nervous shock, could be easily made to believe anything.

The best judges in such matters can only be Krishna's own folk, the Yadavas. And they never thought of him as a god nor worshipped him. On this point Bimanbehari Majumdar is very clear. He writes:

> From a careful perusal of all the source materials it is evident that he was regarded by his kinsmen as a leader endowed with exceptional mental and physical powers but not as an incarnation of God. The attitude of Akrura and Krtavarman toward him in the long-drawn struggle over the Syarnantaka gem and the conduct of his cousin brothers Sisupala and Dantavakra and of his sons and grandsons, especially at Raivataka and Prabhasa, show that they seldom manifested the awe and reverence or the spirit of complete self-surrender which are usually evoked when one comes into contact with God. The Bhagavata regrets that the Yadavas were the most unfortunate beings, because they failed to recognize him as God, though they lived with him.[9]

Let alone others, his own children, especially Pradyumna and Samba, showed him scant respect and landed him in many troubles. Unmindful of the ill repute that such an outrageous act would bring to his family, Pradyumna made love to his foster mother, Mayadevi, and ultimately married her. As a notorious Don Juan, he resorted to any trick to get the woman who caught his fancy. In the guise of the head of a theatrical party, he entered the capital of Vajranabha in the company of his brothers and uncles, and after staging a few plays, says the Harivamsa, succeeded in seducing Vajranabha's daughter Prabhavati. And Samba, according to the Varaha Purana, seduced Krishna's sixteen thousand wives acquired from Naraka's seraglio. Unable to control his jealously, anger, and shame, Krishna laid the curse of leprosy on Samba.

Indeed, something worse followed. After the near total extinction of the male population of Dwaraka in fratricide, and just before his own death, Krishna sent word to Arjuna to come over and rescue the womenfolk and the few surviving men. An old, sad, weak, and dejected Arjuna carried out the mission but not with much success. As he was proceeding to Hastinapura with the survivors, barbarians called the Abhiras, armed only with sticks, attacked the party and carried off many women. Without the use of any force, but voluntarily, indeed, with alacrity and glee, the whole lot of Krishna's wives, except three, went away with the Abhiras. Perhaps they were tired and bored by too much nearness to divinity!

Apart from the members of his own family and the Yadavas in general, even others did not obviously take seriously Krishna's oft-repeated claim that he was God, for he castigated the nonbelievers in his divinity as "fools." Quoting verse 11 from chapter 9 of the Gita, Hopkins says, "The Gita itself admits that those who worship Krishna as the all-god or recognize him are few in number."[10] Even Patanjali's Mahabhshya, adds Hopkins, "does not recognize Krishna as all-god, but as hero and demigod." Winternitz, too, comes to more or less a similar conclusion. He writes:

> As regards Krsna, the race of the Yadavas, to which he belongs, is described in several places in the *Mahabharata* as a cowherd tribe of rough manners, and he himself is repeatedly scorned by hostile heroes as "cowherd" and "slave." In the ancient heroic poem, he was certainly nothing more than a prominent leader of that cowherd tribe and had nothing divine about him. Even behind the Krsna legends of the Harivamsa there seems to be a foundation of older legends, in which Krsna was not yet a god, but the hero of a rough tribe of cowherds. It is difficult to believe that Krsna, the friend and

counselor of the Pandavas; Krsna, the herald of the doctrines of the Bhagavad Gita; Krsna, the youthful hero and demon-slayer; Krsna, the favorite and lover of the cowherdesses; and finally Krsna, the incarnation of the exalted god Vishnu, can be one and the same person. It is far more likely that there were two or several traditional Krsnas who were merged into one deity at a later time.[11]

Sitanath Tattavabhushan is far more explicit than Hopkins and Winternitz. He thinks that "the story of Krishna is more or less mythical and legendary." Without stopping at that, he adds, "if all that the *Mahabharata* and the Puranas say about him [Krishna] is true, he cannot have been the incarnation of God."[12] The best summing up is, however, by D. D. Kosambi. Mincing no words, he boldly and frankly writes thus:

The many-faceted god [Krishna] . . . is inconsistent, though all things to all men and everything to most women; divine and lovable infant, mischievous shepherd boy; love of all the milkmaids in the herders' camp, husband of innumerable goddesses, most promiscuously virile of bedmates; yet devoted to Radha alone in mystic union, and an exponent of ascetic renunciation withal; the ultimate manifestation of eternal peace, but the roughest of bullies in killing his own uncle Kamsa, in beheading a guest of honor like Sisupala at someone else's fire sacrifice; the very fountainhead of all morality, whose advice at crucial moments of the great battle (in which he played simultaneously the parts of deus ex machina and a menial charioteer) nevertheless ran counter to every rule of decency, fair play, or chivalry. The whole Krishna saga is a magnificent example of what a true believer can manage to swallow, a perfect setting of opportunism for the specious arguments of the Gita. It reflects the relationship between a highly composite society with [a] relatively primitive level of production and its religion.

That is hitting the nail right on the head, and it is a thing that only Kosambi could do.

11

WHO WROTE THE GITA?

As we have dateless history, we have nameless authors. One such author or a group of authors wrote the Gita. Yes, it was written, and not spoken, much less was it sung. What is the authority for such an explicit statement? The Gita itself. Turn to one of its closing verses (18.70). In that verse Krishna says, "And whoever studies this sacred dialogue of ours . . ." and so forth.[1] Mark the word "studies." Surely at the time he was engaged in his philosophical dialogue with Arjuna, Krishna was not aware that they were being overheard by Sanjaya. Nor was he aware that Vyasa was using his supernatural powers to tape-record the dialogue. Or am I wrong?

Did he, being a god, know these things? In the alternative, did he foresee that Arjuna would have a nervous breakdown on the Kuruk-shetra, that he would have to tell Arjuna not to be a sissy but to stand up and fight, and then meet the situation prepared with the text of his discourse in advance? This, I submit, is not being facetious or indulging in an exercise in word splitting. Only a written text can be studied, not an extempore talk given to tackle an unexpected development. And yet Krishna says, "And, whoever studies this sacred dialogue of ours . . ." and so on. I am not, I submit again, being profane, but surely even gods are expected not to be boastful and vulgar. Is it proper for Krishna to refer to his dialogue with Arjuna as "sacred," especially when he did practically all the talking? Perhaps we should not, as Sukthankar would hasten to point out, apply our norms of good taste to gods!

However that may be, my contention is this: the text as well as the tenor of the Gita clearly indicate that it is a work put together by different authors at different times. It is equally clear that given Krishna's life and work and times, as they are described in the *Mahabharata* and the Puranas, he could not have been the author of even the hotchpotch that passes muster for the philosophy of the Gita. Can one see a philosopher in the prankish boy of the Bhagavata? Can one see a philosopher in the promoter of the pubs and brothels of the Harivamsa? Can one see a philosopher in the philanderer of the Brahma Vaivarta? Can one see a philosopher in the "trickster" of the *Mahabharata*? Of course, I am speaking of a man with an open mind, one who is not dead to all reason, and not of a devotee of Krishna. A devotee has a closed mind or a muddled mind, prone to be frenzied. Indeed, the greater the frenzy into which he works himself, the nearer he feels to his beloved god. Brushing aside the devotee, we can say that when Krishna is not being prankish or philandering, he can surely be a Machiavelli, but never a Socrates. He is wholly out of character as a philosopher.

There are quite a few other reasons to take the view that Krishna was not—indeed, he could not be—the author of the Gita. His education was perfunctory. His discipleship of Ghora Angirasa was, as we have already seen, a myth propagated by Adi Sankaracharya. And his stay with Sandipani of Avantipur, near Varanasi, as a student was (according to a Puranic account) only for a short period. Moreover, he was too much of a dilettante to have studied much in later life. He was more interested in a belle than in a book. Bhishma's tribute to him as a master of the Vedas and the Vedangas, that is, of all the branches of knowledge, sacred and secular, need not be taken seriously. At his Rajasuya sacrifice, Yudhisthira should have given the first place of honor to Bhishma, the oldest, the cleanest, the wisest, and the most valorous man present in that assembly of kings, priests, and warriors. Instead, he asked Bhishma himself to suggest to whom that honor should go. In that delicate situation, Bhishma must have thought it best to suggest the name of some nonking like himself, lest the one king being given the first place should be resented by the rest of the kings. And so he suggested Krishna's name. This should have enraged practically all the kings in the assembly, though it was left to Sisupala to question the propriety of Bhishma's suggestion. In his blunt protest, Sisupala called Krishna, among other names, an ignoramus. So Bhishma had to take the stand that Krishna was indeed the master of the Vedas and the Vedangas. Ignoring the circumstances under which this particular praise was given to Krishna, to argue (as some of Krishna's admirers do) that his mastery of all branches of knowledge was acknowledged by no less a person than Bhishma, and hence Krishna should undoubtedly have been the author of the Gita is totally wrong.

Now let us assume for a moment that Krishna was not mythical, and that the Kurukshetra War did take place. If so, what was Krishna's age at the time of the war? The *Mahabharata* is vague and confusing in its answer to this important question. According to one calculation, Krishna should have been sixty-four at the time of Draupadi's swayamvara, which he attended in the company of two of his sons; over eighty when Arjuna married Subhadra; and over ninety-four when he and Arjuna took part in the Kurukshetra War. If this is considered absurd, the figure cannot be reduced to an appreciable extent. It is said at many places in the *Mahabharata* that Krishna died thirty-six years after the Kurukshetra War, and it is generally believed that Krishna's life span was one hundred twenty-five years. It means that at the time of the war Krishna's age was eighty-nine years. C. V. Vaidya, the field marshal of the orthodox armies, made his own calculation. "If we take 3185 BCE as the date of Srikrishna's birth," he wrote, "he was at the time of the Rajasuya about seventy-one years of age, being at the time of the Mahabharata War eighty-four." Thus he reduced our earlier estimates of ninety-four and eighty-nine to eighty-four. Even if the figure is eighty-four, is it not an advanced age to participate in a war? "No," said the field marshal. "Considering that Lord Roberts actively worked as the commander-in-chief of the British forces in South Africa at the age of eighty-two, we need not wonder at Srikrishna taking the reins of Arjuna's chariot at the age of eighty-four." The field marshal wants us to believe that conducting a modern war from the army headquarters, located far behind the firing lines, is the same thing as taking charge of a chariot in the actual battlefield of ancient times. He also wants us to forget that according to the *Mahabharata* itself all the charioteers, except Krishna, were dead by the end of the war. Better homework would have enabled the field marshal to know that in ancient wars a warrior fighting from a chariot always showed eagerness to kill his foe's charioteer. This is what Hopkins wrote on the subject with reference to the Kurukshetra War itself:

> The ensign and charioteer are often aimed at first, and these with the horses being laid low, the knight-to-knight combat first begins. . . . It was a very mean and cowardly practice and engaged in without compunction. The driver was absolutely helpless. The opposing knight looked on him as he did on the horses and shot him to stop the car. No qualms of honor seem to have been felt; yet the driver was the most protected man in the field. The "code" had not touched him.[2]

That being the case, Krishna functioning as a charioteer in his eighties or nineties to Arjuna, who was nearly of his own age, is highly incongruous. What is still more incongruous, almost bizarre, is Krishna singing his Song Celestial, standing between two great armies poised for battle. As Sitanath Tattavabhushan rightly remarked: "[That] the teachings filling eighteen chapters could not be imparted in a battlefield is plain to everyone not blinded by bigotry. That this Bhagavad Gita is an interpolation awkwardly introduced into the original poem will be evident to everyone who certainly examines the place and the way it is sewed up, as it were, with the main current of the narrative." In continuation, he also says that the Gita "cannot be the utterance of a man who lived, if he actually took part in the war, in or about the twelfth century BCE."[3]

It was perhaps Weber who suggested for the first time in 1863 that the Gita was a much interpolated work. "The Bhagavad Gita," he wrote, "can, of course, only be regarded as in part a combination of the most highly diverse pieces."[4] In plainer words, he thought that it was potpourri. Monier-Williams, writing in 1877, did, no doubt, praise the Gita as "a pearl" that "lies inlaid" in the *Mahabharata*, and yet he agreed with Weber that it was an interpolation. "Its author," he said, "was probably an earnest Brahman and nominally a Vaishnava, but really a philosopher with a mind cast in a broad mold." Whoever that "philosopher" was, he was not Krishna. According to Monier-Williams, the achievement of that nameless philosopher was this:

> Finding no rest for his spirit in the extreme dogmatism of any one system of philosophy, as commonly taught in his own time, much less in the narrow-minded exclusiveness, and corrupt forms of Brahmanism which surrounded him, he was driven to construct an eclectic school of his own. This he had done with great perspicacity and beauty of language in the Bhagavad Gita, combining various theories into one system, by interweaving, so to speak, threads from the Sankhya, Yoga, and Vedanta, so as to form a many-colored woof of thought, which is shot across a stiff warp of the doctrine of love (*bhakti*) for Krishna, and of stern devotion to caste duties (*dharma*). Of these cross threads the most conspicuous are those of the Sankhya, for which the author of the Gita has an evident predilection. As a necessary result of its composite character, the work is, of course, full of inconsistencies.[5]

This one-time Boden Professor of Sanskrit in the Oxford University had almost a genius for letting his blows fall softly. So, he first praises the Gita as "a pearl," and later on says in dulcet tones that "the work is, of course, full of inconsistencies." It means that the pearl is not in one piece but splintered. And as he hints, it is not even of one color! Being frank and blunt, Hopkins did not mince his words. And this is what he wrote on the Gita in 1885:

> Despite its occasional power and mystic exaltation, the Divine Song in its present state as a poetical production is unsatisfactory. The same thing is said over and over again, and the contradictions in phraseology and in meaning are as numerous as the repetitions, so that one is not surprised to find it described as "the wonderful song,

which causes the hair to stand on end." The different meanings given to the same words are indicative of its patchwork origin, which again would help to explain its philosophical inconsistencies.[6]

Like Weber, Richard Garbe was convinced that the Gita was a work much tampered with and hence highly inconsistent. As I have no access to Garbe's writings on the subject in German, I will quote here as they were summarized by an Indian scholar. "According to Garbe," says K. N. Upadhyaya, "the text is a composite work." He believed that the original kernel was a Sankhya treatise, which was later worked over and expanded by an adherent of the later Vedanta philosophy. He thought he could detect and eliminate these later Vedantic accretions, and he printed them in a type of smaller size in his translation of the Bhagavad Gita.[7] According to Garbe, the original Gita consisted of only 528 verses. Jacobi thought likewise, though he was not specific about numbers.[8]

While largely agreeing with Garbe, his pupil Rudolf Otto differed from his teacher on some minor points. Taking up Garbe's work at the point he left it off, Otto published in 1933, 1934, and 1935 his own theses on the Gita. The English version of his theses appeared in a single volume in 1939 with the title *The Original Gita*. Its main stand is that, out of the seven hundred verses of the present text, only 128 constituted the original Gita "while the insertion of the rest of the individual treatises may have been effected very much later, and was presumably a rather prolonged process."[9]

Of course, Otto knew no more than we do who exactly the various writers were. He was, however, sure that the original Gita was "no construction by some theologian nor is it doctrinal literature, but is essentially the masterpiece of an indisputably great epic poet, of the genius, in fact, who could imagine so splendid a figure as that of Karna. More especially is the magnificent theophany of chapter 11 the creation of an epic poet."[10]

S. C. Roy had an altogether different theory of his own. In his book, *The Bhagavadgita and Modern Scholarship*, he held that the Gita was much earlier in its composition than the *Mahabharata*, and that by adding about eighty verses that have a reference to the Mahabharata War and the persons connected with that war, it was interpolated into the epic. And he was positive that the original Gita was pre-Buddhistic.[11]

Like Roy, Surendranath Dasgupta also believed that the Gita was an independent work of the pre-Buddhistic period that was interpolated into the *Mahabharata* at a later date because of "the sacredness that it had attained at the time."

> The Gita may have been a work of the Bhagavata school written long before the composition of the *Mahabharata,* and may have been written on the basis of the Bharata legend, on which the *Mahabharata* was based. It is not improbable that the Gita, which summarized the older teachings of the Bhagavata school, was incorporated into the *Mahabharata,* during one of its revisions, by reason of the sacredness that it had attained at the time.[12]

Franklin Edgerton is a more recent researcher on the Gita. Unlike the authorities whom I have quoted in this chapter, he says, "My own interpretation tacitly assumes the unity of the Gita."[13] And yet, he, too, is fully aware of the absurdity of a long philosophical discourse being delivered while standing between two armies, and that, too, after the war drums were sounded for the start of the hostilities. "It is likely," he wrote, "that the Bhagavad Gita was not a part of the original epic narrative. Possibly it was composed or inserted in its present position, by a later interpolation."[14]

Unlike me, Gajanan Shripati Khair has veneration for the Gita. He uses it as his "prayer book."[15] Indeed, his veneration for it is so high that he declares that "the echo of the Gita composed twenty-six centuries ago still resounds in the hearts of the Indian people."[16] To his mind, it is more than an echo; it is a jet engine that carries forward the Indian people into the rarefied realms of spiritualism and away from the mud and slush and stench of materialism. "The value of the Gita is not diminished," he affirms, "but all the more enhanced in the modern age."[17] Despite such high veneration for the Gita, he is definite that Bhagavan Krishna had not much to do with its authorship.

After years of laborious research, or "investigation," as he prefers to call it, he published his conclusions in a book entitled *The Quest for the Original Gita.* According to it, the dialogue between Krishna and Arjuna on the battlefield conducted in prose was later versified by the original author of the Gita; still later, two others interpolated their own religious, ethical, and philosophical views into it. Here is Khair's own able summing up of his conclusions:

> The first author composed some portions of the existing first six chapters of the poem. The second author added six more chapters of his own. . . . The third author recast the whole poem by adding his own verses to the chapters of the first and second poets, composed six entirely new chapters, inserted them in the middle of the poem, and shifted the chapters of the second author to the third sextet.
>
> . . . The first author propounded the theory of Yoga and Karma, and refuted the *sannyasa* and nonaction principle of the contemporary Sankhya philosophy. The second author added the practical details of Karma-Yoga and supplemented the poem by the contemporary Sankhya metaphysics and cosmology. The third author brought Karma-Yoga within the understanding of the common people by associating it with devotional theism based on the worship of Vasudeva Krsna. This is the germ of the later Bhagavata Dharma. He also tried to integrate the diverse forms of worship and religious practices.[18]

To demarcate the portions written by the three different authors, Khair printed the full text of the Gita toward the end of his book in three different colors, assigning red to the first author, blue to the second, and black to the third. The dominating color is black. For the third author has a domineering temperament. Of him, Khair writes:

> The third author is entirely different from the first two. He is not concerned with logical exposition but straightaway proclaims his doctrines and commands his audience to accept them on faith. Whatever topic he touches is clothed in sentiment, eloquence, and forcible diction. Logic, coherence, and consistency are subordinated to the indoc-

trination of the main principles underlying his philosophy. The audience is carried away smoothly along the current of his rhythmic, forcible, sublime, and emotional discourse. The logical rational argument of the first author and the scholarly practical treatment of the second are entirely overshadowed by the quantitative mass and qualitative merits of the composition of the third author.[19]

The authorship of the Gita is thus a matter of serious doubt, of endless debate. Where Khair has recognized three authors, others can discover a dozen or more. Had it not been the work of many authors spread over many generations, it would not have been the medley, the melange, and the mess that it is. Only men with blurred vision can see any basic unity in its thought; only men with a bigoted mind can find in it a systematic philosophy. What Winternitz has said about the *Mahabharata* as a whole applies much more aptly and truly to the Gita. Here is the relevant passage:

> Anyone who has really read the whole of the *Mahabharata* and not only the most magnificent portions of it is bound to admit that our present-day text of the epic contains not only much that is diverse in content but also much that is diverse in value. In truth, he who would believe with the orthodox Hindus and the [like-minded] Western scholars that our *Mahabharata*, in its present form, is the work of one single man, would be forced to the conclusion that this man was, at one and the same time, a great poet and a wretched scribbler, a sage and an idiot, a talented artist and a ridiculous pedant—apart from the fact that this marvelous person must have known and confessed the most antagonistic religious views, and the most contradictory philosophical doctrines.[20]

AND WHEN?

I f we know little about the author or authors who wrote the Gita, we
know even less about the time of its writing. This is a matter not to
be wondered at. For we lack a sense of history. That is due directly to
another thing which we lack, namely, a sense of time. We live in a
milieu in which one year really has no meaning; it is after all a day to
the gods. We abide in an ethos in which a lifetime has not much importance; it is just one out of our countless births in the past, and one in
the countless births in the future. What really matters is the ultimate
merging of the individual soul in the unborn, undying, undifferenti-
ated, uncircumscribed, unmoving, unhungering, unfeeling, unseeing,
unhearing, unsmelling, unmating supreme soul (*Brahman*).

And when that happens, time has a stop. So why bother when a
Kapila lived, when a Kannada taught, when a Kanishka ruled, or when
a Kalidas wrote. Such philosophers, kings, poets, and the rest, however
eminent, are mere shadows that flicker for a while and fade out on the
screen of time. Unmindful of them, we should look to the reality that
lies behind time and space. When such are our basic assumptions, how
can we emerge out of the make-believe world of Brahma, Vishnu, and
Siva or of Rama and Krishna or of the Fish, the Tortoise, and the

Boar? How can we have a sense of time or a sense of history? How can we sketch a reliable account of ancient India? How can we decide who wrote the Gita and when?

All that can be attempted is to make some reasonable guesses on the basis of this religious text or that mythological theme or something else equally undependable as a source of history. One such guess is that the Gita was pre-Buddhistic. As we have already seen, S. B. Roy and Surendranath Dasgupta were of the opinion that the Gita existed as an independent philosophical work prior to the Buddha and Buddhism and that in a later age it was interpolated into the *Mahabharata* with some modifications here and there. What is the basis for this opinion? The fact that there is no reference at all to the Buddha or Buddhism at any place in the Gita certainly proves that the interpolators into the *Mahabharata* were more clever than the interpolators into the *Ramayana*. The latter, being idiotic, made Rama denounce the Buddha as a thief, forgetting the fact that Rama is supposed to have lived centuries earlier to the Buddha. Though there is no direct reference to the Buddha or Buddhism in the Gita, his unseen presence is felt in most of the verses of the Gita. In fact, it was written to repulse the serious threat posed to the continued existence of Vedism, or "Brahmanism" as some would like to call it, by the rapid spread of Buddhism and other non-Brahmanical religions like Jainism and Lokayata.

Futhermore, though there are no references to the Buddha and Buddhism in the Gita, the *Mahabharata* as a whole is not free from them. The words "Buddha" and "Prati-Buddha" occur here and there in the text of the epic. Another significant word, which appears with greater frequency is *eduka*, which stands for "dagoba" in Pali and for "stupa" in Sanskrit. As it is clearly stated at one place that the nation was littered with the edukas, it is justifiable to presume that the epic as a literary work in Sanskrit came into being after Buddhism emerged as a major religion.

To embarrass those who plump for the antiquity of the Gita, there is a clear reference to the Brahma Sutra in the Gita (13.4). If the reference here, stated Bimanbehari Majumdar, is "to the famous Brahma Sutra of Badarayana, the Bhagavad Gita must be post-Buddhistic, because the sutras 18–32 of the second section of the second chapter of the Brahma Sutra refute the Buddhistic theory of momentarism and nihilism. But Sankaracharya does not interpret the Brahma Sutra here as the book of aphorisms; he takes it as referring generally to passages treating of Brahman."[1]

Opinion is much divided on this point. But apart from a reference to the Brahma Sutra there is also in the Gita a definite reference to "Vedanta" (15.15). Though there is an attempt to explain away this word, too, taken together with the earlier reference, this can be considered reasonable proof for the presumption that the Gita was a post-Buddhistic and post–Brahma Sutra composition.[2]

A fairly comprehensive review of these different views is put in a nutshell by K. N. Upadhyaya, and I quote him here with thanks:

The chronology of the Bhagavad Gita has been widely discussed by scholars both of the East as well as of the West, and widely have they differed in their opinions, so much so that the range of difference covers a period of at least one thousand years.

To mention a few of them, Dr. Lorinser thinks that the Gita might have been composed after about 500 CE, for he sees in it influences of the Christian religion. Talboys Wheeler regards it "evidently a product of a Brahmanical age and presumably also a later age." According to Garbe, the original Gita belongs to 200 BCE, and its present form to 200 CE. K. T. Telang thinks that "the latest date at which the Gita can have been composed must be earlier than the third century BCE, though it is altogether impossible to say at present how much earlier." Rudolf Otto feels that "the third century BCE is perhaps too low a limit for "the original Gita while the insertion of the individual treatises may have been effected very much later, and was presumably a rather prolonged process." John Davies in his work on the Bhagavad Gita concludes that "the Bhagavad Gita cannot probably be referred to an earlier period than the third century [CE]" and with regard to the question of the author's acquaintance with Christian doctrines, he agrees with A. Weber that it "is still subjudice." W. Douglas P. Hill thinks that "this theory (of a Christian influence on the Gita) is now almost universally dis-

credited" and that "the internal evidence points to the second century BCE as the period when the Gita in its present form appeared."
R. G. Bhandarkar thinks that the Gita is at least as old as the fourth
century BCE. B. G. Tilak tries to establish through his long-drawn
arguments that the Gita must have been in existence in its present
form at least in 500 BCE. According to Radhakrishnan, "its date
may be assigned to the fifth century BCE though the text may have
received many alterations in subsequent times." Swami Vireswarananda thinks that "the date of the Gita and the original *Mahabharata*, of which the Gita is a part, can be fixed before the time of
Buddha. Both of them are pre-Buddhistic, for they contain no reference to Buddha and Buddhism."

These diverse and mutually conflicting views, it is clear, will prove
more a hindrance than a help in deciding the issue, and one is bound
to feel bewildered amidst this welter of conflicting opinions.[3]

Though reluctant to add to the welter, I should, I think, mention
two more opinions. G. S. Khair with his thesis of three different
authors of the Gita thinks that the first author wrote in the sixth century BCE; the second, about a century later; and the third, by about
the third century BCE.[4] In glaring contrast to this, D. D. Kosambi is
positive that "the Sanskrit used is of about the third century CE,"[5]
hence, "its composition can hardly have been possible before the end
of the third century."[6] I am very much inclined to agree with this date.
But my extensive study of the subject makes me believe that the Gita,
in view of its glaring inconsistencies, could not have been the work of
a single author, and that it took its present shape sometime after
Patanjali and the date indicated by Kosambi.

All this would surely make Vaidya, the field marshal of the
orthodox armies, furious, and he would order a counterattack all along
the front, deploying every brigade, opening up every gun, throwing in
every tank, and ordering every plane to give cover to the ground forces.
It is an outrage, nay, a sacrilege, to doubt the truth recorded in the
Mahabharata, the earliest of itihasas (histories) in the world, that on
the day the Kuru-Pandava War started in 3002 BCE, it was Lord
Krishna who delivered the great discourse that has come down to us

with all its pristine purity and its inviolable sanctity, and since that day serving as a beacon light not only to India but to the whole world. "What is so strange," he would thunder at you, "in Krishna delivering a long philosophical discourse right on the battlefield at the age of eighty-four? Did not Hindenburg write at the age of seventy-one long war dispatches to his sovereign as supreme commander of the German armies during the First World War?"

But we can protect ourselves from the field marshal's attack by taking cover behind S. K. Belvalkar, who is only a little less orthodox than Vaidya. According to him, evidence can be found in the *Mahabharata* itself to show that there was a time when the Gita in its present form was not a part of the epic. Despite its length, the relevant passage deserves to be quoted in full:

The Krisna-pratijana-bhanga episode occurs twice in the Bhisma-parvan: once on the third day of the battle and once again on the ninth day. The two accounts are more or less similar. Now, on a detailed comparison of the two passages, from the point of view of vocabulary, grammar, meter, and contents, it has been found that the earlier portion of the third day account is more primitive and original than the corresponding portion of the ninth day's account, while the later portion of the third day's account is exaggerated and secondary when compared with the corresponding portion of the ninth day's account. This naturally suggests the possibility of the earlier portion of the third day's account having been once followed by the concluding portion of the ninth day's account. What concerns us to note here is that the secondary (i.e., initial) portion of the ninth day's account contains an unmistakable reference to the Bhagavad Gita teaching, which is absent in the corresponding earlier and "original" version of the third day—a circumstance which supports the inference that there was a stage in the development of the epic story in which Bhishma fell at the end of the third day's fight, and in which there was no Gita taught, on the opening day; or if there was some Gita taught, it must, at any rate, not have been our present poem of seven hundred stanzas.[7]

It means that the Gita got into the *Mahabharata* with the help of a very clever and highly daring smuggler or gang of smugglers. It also means that the Mastans and Bhakias have been with us from ages!

GITA AS SCRIPTURE

The Gita is no Veda or Vedanga. The scriptural authority that it now possesses is a late acquisition. As I suggested earlier, none took it seriously prior to Adi Sankaracharya. And his interest in it was not because of its intrinsic merit but because of its utility to promote his own special brand of thought, his own sectarian and caste interests. He was a master of polemics. He could cleverly twist inconvenient words to suit his purposes. He could dexterously turn the arguments of his opponents to discomfit them. He could easily round the most awkward corners with the aplomb of an acrobat. He was undoubtedly a genius but a sterile genius. He was a master builder, not of mansions to live in, but of graves to lie in. After his emergence as a leader of thought, India withered as it never did earlier. Who can deny that the nation's decay and decline started roughly after the eighth century CE, that is, after Sankaracharya's time? Who can gainsay that after his time all creativity in literature, science, and thought dried up? My assessment of the acharya's life and teaching and influence may be dismissed as arrant nonsense. But even the orthodox folk have to admit that it was Sankaracharya who rescued the Gita from its well-deserved obscurity. With his alchemy, he made the old, cheap, and dull brass shine like burnished gold. Even S. A. Belwalkar had to own it, though tacitly, when he said that the Gita attained its "dominant position" during "the last twelve hundred years,"[1] that is, after Sankaracharya's lifetime.

Once the acharya of Kaladi showed the way, the other acharyas—Ramanuja, Madhva, and Vallabha—used the Gita to subserve their own sectarian ends. A curious fact about the four acharyas of the second revival of Hinduism—the first occurred during the time of Patanjali—is that all the four were from South India. No less a curious fact is that each of the four hailed from each of the four major linguistic areas of the south: Sankara from Kerala, Ramanuja from Tamilnadu, Madhva from Karnataka, and Vallabha from Andhra.* Each was a proponent of a particular school of Vedanta, and together they were, so to say, the four pillars of the dark age in India, which lasted from the eighth to eighteenth century and beyond. In post-Independence India their influence, never totally absent, seems to be growing apace.

However that may be, the four acharyas utilized the Gita to their utmost advantage. Sankara made it the scripture of Advaita; Ramanuja shaped it into the gospel of Visista-advaita; Madhva forged it into the vulgate of Dvaita; and Vallabha turned it into an oracle of Suddhaadvaita. Taking a cue from these acharyas, literally hundreds of others either wrote commentaries on the Gita or wrote commentaries on commentaries. This latter practice of rechewing the cud already chewed is very much prevalent among Hindu theological writers. It is an index of the aridity of their mind, the sterility of their thought. Those who are interested to know which were all the commentaries on the Gita, and all the commentaries on those commentaries, can refer to the second volume of Surendranath Dasgupta's *History of Indian Philosophy*.[2] What he has given is a long list; and yet, it is by no means exhaustive. Furthermore, his list does not contain the commentaries in the different regional languages; it omits the most famous one in Marathi, *Jnanesvari*.

---

*True, Vallabha was born near Raipur in the present Madhya Pradesh while his parents were on a pilgrimage to Varanasi, and his lifework was mostly in the north, but all the same he was of Andhra origin. His surname is Kambhampati. His ancestral village, Kakaravada, is in the Krishna District. Even today his descendants prefer marrying Andhra girls.

Unlike Jnanesvara, Tikkana, the foremost Telugu poet, had obviously
no high opinion of the Gita. For in translating the Bhishma Parva of
the *Mahabharata* into Telugu, he wisely condensed the seven hundred
verses of the Gita into a mere thirty-five with seventeen prose links,
most of them being not more than a line or half a line.

But all are not Tikkanas. And so translations of the Gita with or
without commentaries roll out of the presses unendingly. This happens
not only in India and in the Indian languages, but all over the world and
in all the major, and even in some of the minor languages of the world.
The very first of its translations into English appeared in 1785. Translated by Charles Wilkins under the title *Bhagavt-Geeta; or, Dialogues of
Kreeshna and Arjoon*, its publication was actively promoted by the then
governor-general of India, Warren Hastings.[3] The court of directors of
the company ordered it to be published "under the patronage of this
court, on condition however that an expense not exceeding £200 shall
be incurred by the company in the publication."[4]

It was "the first published translation into a European language of
any major Sanskrit work."[5] Its French rendering by M. Parraud (*Le
Bhaguat-Geeta*) appeared in 1787. After going through the Gita in its
English translation, William Blake did a drawing entitled "The Brahmans." And yet, the Gita seems "to have had comparatively little
immediate public impact."[6] That came much later. Of all English
translations, it was Edwin Arnold's free and poetical rendering *The
Song Celestial*, first published about a century ago, which gained for the
Gita wide and uncritical acclaim.

I do not know which was the translation read by Henry David
Thoreau, but he said, "In the morning I bathe my intellect in the
stupendous and cosmogonal philosophy of the Bhagavad Gita, in
comparison with which our modern world and its literature seem
puny and trivial." His friend, Ralph Waldo Emerson, was no less
effusive: "I owed," he wrote, "a magnificent day to the Bhagavad Gita:
It was the first of books: it was as if an empire spoke to us, nothing
small or unworthy but large, serene, consistent, the voice of an old
intelligence which in another age and climate had pondered, and thus
disposed of the same questions which exercise us." No wonder, these

two men were counted in their day as the leading lights among the
Boston Brahmans cutting across continents and cultures; the Gita,
thus, continues to appeal, and every year produces its bumber crop of
reprints, translations, glosses, interpretations, expositions, theses,
and—overshadowing all—plaudits and panegyrics.

Two things, both of a dubious nature, enable the Gita to enjoy its
high prestige; first, the equivocation of its teaching and the elasticity
of its medium. It speaks not with two but with a multitude of tongues.
Reserving discussion of the first point to another chapter, I will only
mention here that the Gita was the much-venerated scripture of
Gandhi as well as his assassin, Godse! Now, as for the second point,
Sanskrit has few, if any, equals for its elasticity and its consequent
inexactness. A single word in Sanskrit can mean a score or more
things, widely different, utterly divergent. Take the simple word *sri*.
The revised edition of Apte's Sanskrit-English Dictionary gives
twenty different meanings for that word, ranging from wealth to
poison. The same dictionary lists twenty-three separate meanings for
dharma, and they include religion at one end and bow (stringed
weapon) at the other. And the compounds of that word are more than
one hundred fifty! Further, each of these meanings of the words and
their compounds has very many shades, tones, undertones, nuances,
and connotations. Such words as *dharma*, *karma*, and *yoga*, which occur
very frequently in the Gita, cannot only be highly equivocal, but something worse, positively deceitful. This, I think, is largely true of all
priestly languages, and Sanskrit is preeminent among such languages.
You need not take me seriously on this matter, as I am no Sanskrit
scholar, but D. D. Kosambi ranked among the masters of that language, and this is what he said about it:

> At its best, Sanskrit literature is exquisite, with an intricate pattern
> of beauty. Even at its best, it does not give the depth, [the] simplicity
> of expression, the grandeur of spirit, the real greatness of humanity
> that one finds in the *Pali Dommapada*, the *Divina Commedia*, or *Pil-
> grim's Progress*. It is the literature of and for a class, not a people.
> The language suffered from its long, monopolistic association

with a class that had no direct interest in technique, manual operations, trade agreements, contracts, or surveys. The class did have
leisure enough to write their tenuous ideas in a tortuous manner
above the reach of the common herd, and to unravel them from such
writings. Prose virtually disappeared from high literary Sanskrit.
Words that survived in literary usage took on so many different sup-
plementary meanings that a good Sanskrit text cannot be inter-
preted without a commentary. The glosses are often demonstrably
wrong and succeed only in confusing the text.[7]

Very correctly this describes my own experience in studying the
different translations of the Gita in English and Telugu with the aid
of the commentaries that often go with them. I have in my personal
collection nearly forty of its English translations and more than half
a dozen Telugu renderings. The English ones range from Sankara,
Ramanuja, Madhva, and Sridhara through Wilkins, Davies, and
Arnold to Telang, Besant, and Radhakrishnan, and further down to
such popular peddlers of the Gita like Prabhupada, Mehesh Yogi, and
Chinmayananda. I have also thirty to forty expositions written by different authors from Aurobindo to Zaehner. Read together, they make
confusion worse confounded. For the Gita is as "trickish" as its putative parent Krishna.

And it is as thievish as its real author or authors. Upadhyaya wrote
a large chapter on the sources of the Gita in his book *Early Buddhism
and the Bhagavadgita*.[8] It shows the blatant plagiarism the Gita is guilty
of. Not only does it borrow its main ideas, concepts, and postulates
from the Upanishads, but it also lifts whole passages from them. Of
course, in bringing out these points Upadhyaya was very polite, almost
apologetic. To be fair to him, it is best, I think, to quote him directly,
though, it means quoting at some length. Here is what he stated:

The influence of the Upanishads on the Bhagavad Gita is only too
patent. The entire description of the eternity and immortality of
atman, the absoluteness and transcendence of Brahman, its nega-
tive and paradoxical characterization, the reference to lordly powers
and the supreme nature of God (paramatman), the symbolic medi-

tation of "Om" (*Sabda Brahman*), the description of the two pathways of pitryana and devayana, the ultimate unity behind the multiplicity of the world, an abiding and imperishable element behind the impermanent and perishing features of it, the nature and the state of nirvana and the ideal conduct of Sthithaprajna—in short, most of the metaphysical elements of the Bhagavad Gita are drawn from the Upanishads. Not only are the ideas taken but very many verses as well, literally or with some variations, are the same as those of the Upanishads. Besides, there are numerous other short passages, words, and expressions which clearly seem to be borrowed from the Upanishads. Some images also of the Bhagavad Gita are similar to those of the Upanishads.[9]

Upadhyaya proceeded next to print in parallel columns all the passages lifted verbatim from the Upanishads, and they total up to twenty-two.[10] Apart from these, he also had drawn attention to "other passages conveying the same ideas and having somewhat similar expressions," and they, in their turn, total up to thirteen.[11] But that is, by no means, the end of the Gita's plagiarism. Quite a few of its images, about whose aptness and beauty and power the admirers of the Gita crow a lot, are also copied from the Upanishads. Upadhyaya noted seven of them.[12] Maybe others can find some more. This is perhaps what is meant by saying that the Gita is the quintessence of the Upanishads!

All religious scriptures are, no doubt, guilty in this respect. But the first prize in plagiarism should go to the Gita. Is it a shining honor?

14

HAS THE GITA A PHILOSOPHY?

The word *philosophy* was first used by Pythagoras. And it was Plato who sought to develop it into a special discipline. This does not mean that there was no philosophy before Pythagoras and Plato; it was very much there. Indeed, when man started to ask, now in wonder, now in fear, and always out of his insatiable curiosity, why the sun rose and set, wherefore the moon waxed and waned, how the clouds formed and rained, whether flood and storm and lightning and thunderbolt were indicative of the wrath of gods, what is life and why death, in a word, when he started to ask questions about himself and the nature around him, philosophy was born.

In its initial stages, philosophy comprised every branch of knowledge—logic, aesthetics, polity, economics, science, and ethics. In fact, this continued in a broad way right down to the eighteenth century. The writers and editors of the French encyclopedia consisted of poets, playwrights, novelists, artists, statesmen, economists, scientists, and others, but all of them were collectively known as *philosophers*. The emergence of philosophy as a special discipline is, thus, comparatively late. Its speciality consists in taking into account the totality of knowledge as well as experience and to provide a meaning, a direction, and a purpose to life. Neither knowledge nor experience is static; they grow, they expand; hence, philosophy also should grow and expand. It should move with times, change with the age. Marx, for one, held that philosophy should not content itself with explaining the world but proceed to change it.

As far as India is concerned, the synonym for philosophy is *darshana*. It means direct perception. Of what? Of that airy nothing, the soul in its two forms, the individual and the universal (the *atma* and the *paramatma*). And so the very term *darshana* has put Indian philosophy on the wrong track. Since the basic philosophical questions are the relationships of man to nature, of thinking to being, of consciousness to matter, and of man to man, there can be no philosophy without observing the external world, without thinking rationally and without taking cognizance of the discoveries of science and every single addition to the sum total of knowledge and experience. As Will Durant stated, "the world is her [philosophy's] subject matter, and the universe is her speciality."[1] If either is taken as an illusion, there can be no philosophy. Indeed, "without science," to quote Durant again, "philosophy is impotent; for how can wisdom grow except on knowledge fairly won, with honest observation and research and recorded and chartered by impartial minds? Without science, philosophy becomes decadent and dishonest, isolated from the flow of human growth, and falling more and more into the dreamy futility of scholasticism."[2] But Indian philosophy scoffs at science. It tells you that the only reality is the soul and all else including your world and the very universe around you is an illusion, *maya*. It tells you to close your eyes, to shut your ears, to control your breath, to dull your senses and to still your mind, so that you could have the direct perception of the ultimate reality, the atma and the paramatma. Of course, my reference here is to the idealistic school of philosophy, that is, the Vedanta, with its divisions and subdivisions, and its derivatives, deviations, and deceptions. This particular school has either smothered the materialist schools or perverted them beyond recognition. It has a high potential for mental disease and moral death.

And the Gita is not even a treatise on what passes for Indian philosophy. In the very first sentence of the introductory note to his translation of the Gita, Radhakrishna said, "The Bhagavad Gita is more a religious classic than a philosophical treatise."[3] Here he spoke in comparative terms, wrongly suggesting thereby that the Gita was also a philosophical treatise, though in a secondary way. In fact, it is nothing of the sort.

Doubt can be philosophy but not dogma; incredulity can be philosophy but not equivocation. Viewed from either of these standpoints, the Gita is not a philosophical treatise. It is full of dogmas. Indeed, it can be called the dictionary of dogmas. From *adhyatamavidya* through *maya* and *mantra* to *yogadharma*, it is a proponent of every conceivable dogma. This cannot be done without being equivocal and so it has made dogma almost a fine art of equivocation. As Hopkins correctly pointed out, the Gita is "a medley of beliefs," and *Webster's New World Dictionary* says that the term *dogmas*, taken collectively, means "doctrines, tenets, or beliefs." The Gita, to quote Hopkins again, is "uncertain in its tone"; in other words, it is evasive and equivocal. And as he proceeded to add, it is "an ill-assorted cabinet of primitive philosophical opinions."[4]

Arun Shourie agrees fully with Hopkins, though he avoids such blunt expressions as "medley" and "primitive." He writes:

The Gita is an ambivalent, almost an equivocal work. This ambivalence is testified to by the ease with which so many commentators— Shankara on one side and Tilak on the other, Gandhi on one side and should one say Godse on the other—have been able to use it as the scaffolding for such divergent points of view. If he had an unequivocal message Krishna should have spoken a little less obscurely.[5]

Steeped as he was in the tradition of the Gita, Radhakrishnan could see a method and a meaning in its very obscurity. And so he stated that the Gita embraced "within its synthesis the whole gamut of the human spirit, from the crude fetishism of the savage to the creative affirmation of the sage."[6] Only another Radhakrishnan could, I suppose, tell us where exactly the philosopher fits in between the savage and the sage. Be that as it may, Radhakrishnan was convinced that the teacher of the Gita "refines and reconciles the different currents of thought, the Vedic cult of sacrifice, the Upanishads, that is, teaching of the transcendent Brahman, the Bhagavata theism and tender piety, the Samkhya dualism, and the Yoga meditation. He draws all these living elements of Hindu life and thought into an organic unit. He adopts the method not of denial but of penetration and shows how these different lines of thought converge toward the same end."[7]

Not to speak of others, even Radhakrishnan's close friend, D. S. Sarma, failed to see any "organic unity" in the Gita. He was definite that "the Gita as a whole is rather irregular." But he was an even greater admirer of the Gita than Radhakrishnan. And so, while Radhakrishnan saw unified thought in chaos, Sarma saw sublime poetry in irregularity. The Gita, he said, "is irregular as the mountains are irregular, as the forests are irregular, as the ocean is irregular. The fact of the matter is, it is a poem, a collection of songs—not a work of theology or philosophy."[8]

Between these two, whom should we take seriously? Should we agree with Radhakrishnan's opinion that the Gita is "more a religious classic than a philosophical treatise" or agree with Sarma that it is neither?

Such indeed is the dogmatic and equivocal nature of the Gita that it gives rise to endless questions. Some of them are posed thus by Arvind Sharma:

> Is the Gita the word of God incarnate as the pious Bhagavata believes? Is it an Advaita, a Visistadvaita, a Dvaita, or a Suddhadvaita work? Does it propound Karma Yoga, Jnana Yoga, or Bhakti Yoga, or all of them, or all of the various other yogas enumerated? Is it a Vedantic revision of a theistic poem? Is it a Vishnuite remodeling of a pantheistic poem? Is it a Krsnaite version of a Vishnuite poem? Is it an Upanishad of the "Svetasvatara" type adopted by the Krsna cult? Is it a late product of the degeneration of Upanishadic monistic thought in the transitional period from theism to realistic atheism? Is it an old-verse Upanishad, later than "Svetasvatara," worked into the Gita by Krsnaism? Does it merely reflect different streams of tra-

dition flowing through a confused mind? Is it the application of the Upanishadic ideal to the *Mahabharata* reality?

Will the real Gita please stand up?⁹

No, the Gita will not stand up. For it is too evasive and equivocal on almost all vital questions. Is God personal or impersonal? According to the Gita, he is now this and now that (11.17, 18). He is even the neuter Brahman (14.27). Is God mutable or immutable? He is both (13.14). Is he interested in man or is he indifferent? Yes (9.22) and no (11.32, 33, 34). Does he love man or is he vengeful? Again, yes and no. One moment he is all love (18.64), all compassion (10.22 and 16.19, 20), all forgiveness (9.32), and in the very next, highly vengeful (16.19, 20). Is the world real? Yes, very much so (7.4). No, no! It is all an illusion (7.14). Should you be guided by the Veda? Yes indeed! "Let the scripture be thy authority for determining what should and what should not be done" (16.24). No, never! "You should free yourself from the authority of the Veda; What is the use of a pond in a place flooded with water everywhere?" (2.45, 46). Which is preferable—bloody Vedic *yajna* or simple worship, *pooja*, with flowers? Yajna, of course (3.9–15). No, no! Only simple worship, only pooja (9.26). There is no end to this ambiguity and ambivalence, this inconsistency and incongruity, this evasion and equivocation.

And yet the admirers of the Gita—or should we call them "the apologists?"—dismiss these as not real but only "apparent" contradictions. It shows that they are either willfully blind or dogmatically perverse. "The high god," as Kosambi rightly pointed out, "repeatedly emphasizes the great virtue of nonkilling (*ahimsa*), yet the entire discourse is an incentive to war."¹⁰ Is this an apparent contradiction? The supreme deity preaches that one should do his duty disinterestedly, and yet at two places (3.37 and 11.33), he tells Arjuna: "If slain in war, you go to heaven; if victorious, you enjoy the earth." Is this also an apparent contradiction? The Lord says, "I am the same to all beings. None is hateful or dear to me" (9.29). The same lord tells Arjuna later, "you are dear to me" (18.65). Is this, too, an apparent contradiction? Of these very many contradictions, or "inconsistencies," as he prefers to call them, this is what K. T. Telang had to say:

It seems to me that all these are real inconsistencies in the Gita, not such, perhaps as might not be explained away, but such, I think, as indicate a mind making guesses at truth, as Professor Max Muller puts it, rather than a mind elaborating a complete and organized system of philosophy. There is not even a trace of consciousness on the part of the author that these inconsistencies exist. And the context of the various passages indicates, in my judgement, that a half-truth is struck out here, and another half-truth there, with special reference to the special subject then under discussion; but no attempt is made to organize the various half-truths, which are apparently incompatible, into a symmetrical whole, where the apparent inconsistencies might possibly vanish altogether in the higher synthesis. And having regard to these various points, and to the further point, that the sequence of ideas throughout the verses of the Gita is not always easily followed, we are, I think, safe in adhering to the opinion expressed above, that the Gita is a non-systematic work, and in that respect belongs to the same class as the older Upanishads.[11]

Now, simply because of occasional flings of the Gita at the Vedas and the Vedic rituals, some of the commentators of the Gita affirm that it raises the standard of revolt against the established religion. Nothing can be farther from the truth. What it does is to be all things to all men, that is, dupe as many people as possible in as many ways as possible. Franklin Edgerton, never half as critical of the Gita as Hopkins, was forced to admit:

> The curious many-sidedness, tolerance, or inconsistency—whichever one may choose to call it—of the Bhagavad Gita ... is shown nowhere strikingly than in its attitude toward what we may call orthodox established religion.[12]

Another name for "the curious many-sidedness, tolerance, or inconsistency" of the Gita is, of course, eclecticism. Among others, Radhakrishnan took the same stand when he claimed that the Gita "refines and reconciles different currents of thought." This sort of eclecticism can run amok. It happened in the India of the past and is happening in an even worse fashion in the India of the present. Eclecticism is not integration. Different ideas and concepts, borrowed from different sources by an eclectic, do not generally merge into an integrated whole, but abide side by side as separate entities and lead to a split personality, to a double life, and ultimately to downright hypocrisy. As Radhakrishnan himself admitted there can be, what he had chosen to call "cheap eclecticism," and this can, as he rightly warned, lead "the Indian thinkers into misty vagueness."[13] And this is exactly the demerit of the Gita. None can definitely say what it stands for. None can definitely say what it stands for either as theology, philosophy, ethics, or sociology.

But of one thing it leaves no scope for any doubt. Its only philosophy—if it could be called a philosophy—is the philosophy of surrender. You should surrender your mind, your will, your freedom, and surrender everything else absolutely, abjectly. In the Gita Arjuna starts with the affirmation *nayotse* ("I will not fight") and ends up with *karishye vachanam tawa* ("I will do thy bidding"). That is executing a full circle—from defiance to obedience, from rebellion to surrender, from freedom to servility. And therein lies the core of the Gita, its central message, its final triumph.

"Why is man prone to obey and why is it so difficult to disobey?" asked Erich Fromm, the German-born American psychoanalyst, and he proceeded to answer his own question in his usual brilliant way:

> As long as I am obedient to the power of the state, the church, public opinion, I feel safe and protected. In fact, it makes little difference what power it is that I am obedient to. It is always an institution, or men, who use force in one form or another—and who fraudulently claim omniscience and omnipotence. My obedience makes me part of the power I worship, and hence I feel strong. I can make no error, since it decides for me; I cannot be alone because it does not let me do so, and even if I do sin, the punishment is only the way of returning to the almighty power.[14]

Krishna did claim again and again that he was omniscient and omnipotent; it is for you to decide whether or not he should be taken seriously. And as an omniscient and omnipotent god, he demanded utter surrender, not merely from Arjuna, but also from you and me, from everyone, born and unborn. Here is an inkling of his claims as well as demands:

By Me all this universe is pervaded through My unmanifested form. All beings abide in Me but I do not abide in them. (9.4)

Under My guidance, nature [*prakriti*] gives birth to all things, moving and unmoving and by this means, O Son of Kunti [Arjuna], the world revolves. (9.10)

Always glorifying Me, strenuous and steadfast in vows, bowing down to Me with devotion, they worship Me, ever disciplined. (9.14)

I am the father of this world, the mother, the supporter and the grandsire, I am the object of knowledge, the purifier. I am the syllable Aum and I am the rk, the sama and the yajus as well. (9.17)

[I am] the goal, the upholder, the Lord, the witness, the abode, the refuge, and the friend. [I am] the origin and the dissolution, the ground, the resting place and the imperishable seed. (9.18)

But those who worship Me, meditating on Me alone, to them whoever perseveres, I bring attainment of what they have not and security in what they have. (9.22)

On Me fix thy mind; to Me be devoted; worship Me, revere Me; thus having disciplined thyself, with Me as thy goal, to Me shall thou come. (9.34)

Is there, I wonder, a parallel to such big claims and boastful demands in the whole range of theological literature of the world? Perhaps not. And Krishna does not stop even at that. Going futher, he condemns and despises and damns those who doubt his omnipotence and omniscience. To illustrate this, it is, I think, more than enough to quote a couple of verses from the Gita:

The deluded despise Me clad in human body, not knowing My higher nature as Lord of all existence. (9.11)

Partaking of the deceptive nature of fiends and demons, their aspirations are vain, their actions vain and their knowledge vain and they are devoid of judgement. (9.12)

When such is the philosophy that is claimed as the highest in the world by many of the leaders of Indian thought, and even by some foreign worthies like Thoreau and Emerson, need we be surprised that our nation as a whole or large segments of it surrendered over the centuries to the Iranians, Greeks, Bactrians, Kushanas, Hunas, Sakas, Arabs, Turks, Moghuls, Afghans, Portuguese, French, and British? And as late as 1962, was it not given a rude kick by the Chinese? It is only one small step from obedience and surrender to sacerdotal authority to obedience and surrender to secular tyranny. As a people we have taken this step again and again.[15]

No devotee, I am sure, will be able to appreciate the following penetrating observations of Erich Fromm regarding modern Europe:

From Luther to the nineteenth century one was concerned with overt and explicit authorities. Luther, the Pope, the princes, wanted to uphold it; the middle class, the workers, the philosophers tried to uproot it. The fight against authority in the state as well as in the family was often the very basis for the development of an independent and daring person. The fight against authority was inseparable from the intellectual mood which characterized the philosophers of the enlightenment, and the scientists. This "critical mood" was one of faith in reason, and at the same time of doubt in everything which is said or thought, in as much as it is based on tradition, superstition, custom, power. The principles *sapere aude* and *de omnibus es dubitandum*, "dare to be wise" and "of all one must doubt" were characteristic of the attitude which permitted and furthered the capacity to say *no*.[16]

Will we in India ever enter the critical mood? Will we ever develop faith in reason? Will we ever learn to doubt whichever is based "on tradition, superstition, custom, power"? No, as long as we glory in the Gita and grovel before Krishna.

15

ETHICS OF THE GITA

"The study of ethics," as Bertrand Russell said, "traditionally, consists of two parts, one concerned with moral rules, the other with what is good on its own account. Rules of conduct, many of which have a ritual origin, play a great part in the lives of savages and primitive peoples. It is forbidden to eat out of the chief's dish, or to see the kid in its mother's milk; it is commanded to offer sacrifices to the gods, which, at a certain stage of development, are thought most acceptable if they are human beings. Other moral rules, such as the prohibition of murder and theft, have a more obvious social utility and survive the decay of the primitive theological systems with which they were originally associated. But as men grow more reflective there is a tendency to lay less stress on rules and more on states of mind. . . . What they value is a state of mind, out of which, as they hold, right conduct must ensue; rules seem to them external, and insufficiently adaptable to circumstances."[1]

In other words, ethics is something wider, deeper, and more universal than morals. In ancient India ethics never developed, as it did in Greece, into a special branch of study. True, Gautama, the Buddha, gave an ethical base to his religion. But the rise of Mahayana and other sects, differing from the Mahayana only in minor doctrinal details, undermined that ethical base. As further reference to the subject will be out of place here, all that need be said is this: as Russell put it truly and pithily: "Ethics is mainly social."[2]

An ethical system with a social bearing can develop only in a society that has some social coherence. Because of our castes and subcastes, we lack it. Along with social coherence, we also lack social conscience. If ever we had it, our karma and *punarjanma* (rebirth) theories weakened it, our Vedanta crippled it, and finally, our supreme goal of *mukti, moksha,* or *nirvana* killed it. How can an individual goal foster a social conscience, a collective spirit? If you want release from the cycle of birth and death, you should, Krishna tells you, even cultivate "absence of affection for son, wife, home, and the like."[3] In the commentary on the verse, Sankaracharya leaves no scope for any doubt. He says:

> Affection is an intense form of attachment and consists in complete identification with another, as in the case of a man who feels happy or miserable when another is happy or miserable and who feels himself alive or dead when another is alive or dead. They like others who are very dear, other dependents. Unattachment and absence of affection are termed knowledge because they lead to knowledge.[4]

If you are really serious about "nonseparation" with the supreme god you should go further and—do what?—develop "DISTASTE FOR THE SOCIETY OF MEN."[5] What a horrid thing to preach! And yet . . . and yet . . . Ranganathananda tells us:

> In these days of conflict, struggle, and confusion, we can have no better guide to show us the path to freedom and peace than the message of the rational, universal, and comprehensive spirituality which Krishna taught in his Gita over two thousand years ago. It is God's message to man—eternal, ancient, and ageless. Momentous problems are there before us which stagger the wisdom of the earth's bravest and best. Let us hope and pray that the new interest that is evident in many quarters in the Song Celestial, as Edwin Arnold called the Gita, may be productive of real and lasting benefit to humanity at large.[6]

How can a scripture that makes a reluctant Arjuna take up his arms again and kill his kinsmen to gain a petty kingdom promote world peace? How can a scripture that tells Arjuna that he has no freedom of action, that he should kill his guru and his grandsire and the rest because they were already killed by Krishna himself—well—how can such a scripture promote freedom? These are perhaps great esoteric truths that only Swami Ranganathananda can comprehend. I find that among the books I collected on the Gita there is one entitled *The Esoteric Gospel of Gita* by Susruva. Being a very unesoteric person, I could not understand, try however much, what the author meant by the following two sentences: "In this path there is just no way to codify the fruits of the individual's experience for easy imitation by the masses. There is always an element of risk, a gap of uncertainty, as the sole portals to self-knowledge lie within oneself."[7]

Among the other books that I have—books that have a direct bearing on the ethics of the Gita—one is the *Ethics of the Gita* by G. W. Kaveeshwar, a professor of philosophy. On page 198, he speaks of "the final goal for the tendency to action" that the Gita placed before humanity. I presume that he means Karma Yoga when he speaks of "the final goal for the tendency to action." With this plausible explanation, I proceed to quote him:

> The final goal for the tendency to action, placed by the Gita before humanity, is naturally in line with the general current of Indian philosophical thought. The Gita has all along been regarded as the quintessence of such ancient Indian philosophical literature as the Upanishads. The final . . . is beyond the reach of mind and of language too.[8]

And yet this learned professor has written a whole book of more than three hundred pages mostly on what is "beyond the reach of mind and of language too."

Kaveeshwar seems to have read Plato, Kant, Mill, Russell, and other leading lights of European thought. It did not, however, occur to the professor of philosophy that it is foolish to write on subjects that are beyond the reach of both mind and language. Most of our academic philosophers indulge in such foolishness; it is their forte, their fortune, their future!

As real yogis, that is, without caring whether the end product of their labors is good, bad, or indifferent, some of our philosophy professors link up Sankara, Ramanuja, Madhva, or even a lesser Vedantists with some European or American theologian or philosopher. It helps them to pass off as equal masters of both the Eastern and Western thought. The provocation for these remarks is the little return by way of intellectual stimulation that I get from a majority of the books belonging to this genre. One is *Ethics of Butler and the Philosophy of Action in the Bhagavadgita according to Madhusudana Sarasvati: A Critical and Comparative Study*, by S. S. Sarma. What a mouthful of title! Joseph Butler was not much of a philosopher. The other Butler (Samuel) finds a place in Russell's *History of Western Philosophy* but not this Butler (Joseph). Nor was Madhusudana much of an original thinker; at best, he was a scholarly commentator. Why drag down the first from his Christian heaven and the second from his Hindu svarga? To be sure, they may have both stressed the virtue of duty for duty's sake. But is it such a profound truth as to deserve from our professor "a critical and comparative study"? This question is all the more pertinent as he admits that "ethics was not treated separately and independently in Indian thought."9

A more pretentious work of this genre is *The Concept of Perfection in the Teachings of Kant and the Gita*, by B. S. Gauchhwal, a philosophy lecturer. One of the great discoveries made by this luminary is that "the similarities between the two [Kant and Gita] are so numerous and close that no serious student can ignore them as mere [sic] accidental. Indeed, they were so impressive that they easily invite speculation as to whether the German philosopher could possibly have been acquainted with the main spirit of Gita teaching."10

Disturbing him for a moment from his profound speculation, we may be permitted to ask the philosophy lecturer some searching questions. Kant died in 1804; the first English translation of the Gita appeared in 1785, the French in 1789, and it was only in 1808 that

Friedrich Schlegel published in German some extracts from the Gita in his anthology of Sanskrit classics.[11] Is it not silly to say that Kant was influenced by a book of whose existence he was in all probability unaware? Then, again, while Kant was a thorough-going monist, is not the Gita ambivalent on the point? Has not S. S. Raghavacharya written a treatise to expound that, according to Ramanuja, the Gita is a scripture of "Vishista-Advaita"?[12] Furthermore, one of the cardinal principles of Kant's philosophy is to treat every human being as an end in himself? Can this be said of the Gita? Does it not tell you that if you are really an enlightened man you should treat a savant and a dog as equals (5.13)?

The late P. N. Srinivasachari was also a professor of philosophy. His treatise *The Ethical Philosophy of the Gita*[13] is a rehash of the atma and paramatma, the Kamya Karma and Niskama Karma, and the rest of the vaporousness that has been smothering all original thought in this country for more than two thousand years now.

But some of the other writers on the Gita are worse; I refer to the late Sir H. V. Divatia. Starting off with the general statement, "Like its philosophy, the ethics of the Gita is inseparably connected with its metaphysics,"[14] the noble knight plunged straight into the muddy waters of the karmic laws, the atma and paramatma, and the rest of Hindu theology with all its dogmas. And he ended up by stating, "The metaphysical concept of the Gita underlying its social ethics may be regarded as too high and unapproachable."[15] Obviously the "past karma" of Divatia was of a high order. For he had the best of the two Indias, the British India and Independent India. Likewise, we can be sure that after having the best of this world, he is going to have a good time in the other world. How hateful is the cant and hypocrisy of our upper castes and classes! Attributing their own social prestige, economic privilege, political power, and the rest of the good things of life to those two big and black lies, the past birth and the good karma accumulated in that birth, they lecture to the victims of an unjust and cruel social order on such virtues as meekness, poverty, suffering, and above all, on respect to the prince in his castle and the priest in his chapel.

What Kaveeshwar, Srinivasachari, Divatia, and others present to us is not, it cannot be, ethics; it is the old dope of Vedanta in new capsules. Kaveeshwar talks of Utilitarianism and Divatia of Socialism in the context of the ethics of the Gita. Only a glib tongue can do that!

Whatever these and other commentators on the Gita might say, the concern of ethics should be not with God and his angels but with man and his fellow men. Its aim should be "the greatest happiness of the greatest number." It should set its sights on a free, just, egalitarian, and happy society. It should promote amity, not strife; it should work for peace, not for war. Is not the Gita a total alien to all these objectives of a sound ethical system?

There are many systems of ethics. They range from the one formulated by Hammurabi through the one proclaimed by Asoka to the one sketched by Marx and Engels. According to Will Durant, they can ultimately be divided into three broad systems. As he is not only a popular but a precise writer, it is, I think, best to quote his own words:

> Ultimately, there are but three systems of ethics, three conceptions of the ideal character and the moral life. One is that of Buddha and Jesus, which stresses the feminine virtues, considers all men to be equally precious, resists evil only by returning good, identifies virtue with love, and inclines in politics to unlimited democracy. Another is the ethic of Machiavelli and Nietzsche, which stresses the masculine virtues, accepts the inequality of men, relishes the risks of combat and conquest and rule, identifies virtue with power, and exalts an hereditary aristocracy. A third, the ethic of Socrates, Plato, and Aristotle, denies the universal applicability of either the feminine or the masculine virtues; considers that only the informed and mature mind can judge, according to diverse circumstance, when love should rule, and when power; identifies virtue, therefore, with intelligence; and advocates a varying mixture of aristocracy and democracy in government.[16]

The ethics of the Gita belongs to the second system. Krishna, the putative author of the Gita, was both a Machiavelli and a Nietzsche in a superlative degree. The Italian statesman and the German philosopher stood equally for naked autocracy. The former pleaded for a strong prince, and the latter, for a superman. Neither cared whether the means were fair or foul as long as the end was achieved. Falsehood, trickery, deceit, treachery, murder—anything is permissiable as long as it furthers your objective. Love, pity, and compassion weaken your will; you should not allow any of them to sway you. Might is right; war is the ultimate instrument of policy. Roughly such was the ethics of Machiavelli and Nietzsche. Is not Krishna's ethics very much the same? This may be true, it can be argued, of the Krishna of the *Mahabharata* and of the Puranas, but not of the Gita. My contention is that it applies to both the Krishnas in an equal measure, and I will proceed to present my case, avoiding the points made in the earlier chapters.

Was not Krishna a leader of the Yadu clan, which lived, not under kingship, but under an oligarchic democracy? Why, then, did he not lend all his support to democratic forces? Why did he encourage monarchy as a first step toward imperialism? Why did he claim, "Of men, I am the monarch" (10.27)? Had he not enough influence with the Pandavas to ensure a peaceful settlement of their dispute with the Kauravas? Why did he not use it to that effect? True, he went as an envoy of peace to Hastinapura. But why, then, did he present unacceptable demands in the guise of opting for the barest minimum? The popular impression is that the Pandavas were prepared to give up their claim to their half-share of the kingdom, provided they were offered five towns together with their hinterland. But what is forgotten is that two of them were snatched by Drona from his boyhood friend and later enemy, Drupada. Being honorable men, how could the Kauravas ask their teacher Drona to give up his possession so that they could make peace with the Pandavas? Krishna was well aware of this and yet he did his best to paint the Kauravas as so proud and power-drunk as not to agree to the lowest minimum terms in the interests of peace.

And once the war started, why did Krishna pretend to be a non-combatant? In reality, did he not play a more crucial role in the war than any combatant? Had he allowed Arjuna to retire from the fray, would the war have continued? Most decidedly not. And for making Arjuna change his mind, did not Krishna use every means, such as persuasion, as not temptation, intimidation, blackmail, and browbeating?

Was it not blackmail to tell him that if victorious he would enjoy a kingdom and if he fell on the battlefield he would enjoy heaven? That this is no baseless indictment is amply proven by the following verses taken from the Gita:

> Besides, men will ever recount thy ill fame and for one who has been honored, ill fame is worse than death. (2.34)

> The great warriors will think that thou hast abstained from battle through fear and they by whom thou wast highly esteemed will make light of thee. (2.35)

> Many unseemly words will be uttered by thy enemies, slandering thy strength. Could anything be sadder than that? (2.36)

Asking Arjuna to act against his conscience, holding out the threat that otherwise he would be ridiculed and reviled, is not worthy of an ethical teacher; in fact, it is a form of intimidation or blackmail to which only an unethical person would resort.

From blackmailing, Krishna proceeded to browbeating. He told Arjuna, "Being a fool, you think you will be killing Bhishma, Drona, Karna, and others. In fact, they are already killed by me." To an Arjuna much bewildered and broken down by then, Krishna gave a stunning glimpse of his cosmic form. It was something ghoulish and blood-curdling. It should have been a case of hallucination on the part of Arjuna or Krishna should have been an adept in hypnotism.

However that may be, the core teaching of the Gita, as Prem Nath Bazaz has put it boldly, succinctly, and truly is this: "Murder with impunity."[17] Elaborating this point, D. D. Kosambi wrote that the ostensible moral of the Gita is, "Kill your brother if duty calls, without passion; as long as you have faith in Me, all sins are forgiven," and he went on to add:

> But the history of India always shows not only brothers but even father and son fighting to the death over the throne, without the slightest hesitation or need for divine guidance. Indra took his own father by

the foot and smashed him, a feat which the Brahman, Vamadeva, applauds. Ajatasatru, king of Magadha, imprisoned his father Bimbisara to usurp the throne and then had the old man killed in prison. Yet, even the Buddhists and [the] Jains as well as [the] Brahadaranyaka Upanishad praise the son (who was the founder of India's first great empire) as a wise and able king. The Arthasastra devotes a chapter to precautions against such ambitious heirs-apparent; he could circumvent them if he were in a hurry to wear the crown. Krsna himself at Kurukshetra had simply to point to the Yadava contingent, his own people, who were fighting in the opposite ranks. The legend tells us that all the Yadavas ultimately perished fighting among themselves.[18]

In another context, Kosambi reverted to the subject, and wrote:

... Krsna as he appears in the *Mahabharata* is singularly ill suited to propound any really moral doctrine. ... At every single crisis of the war, his advice wins the day by the crookedest of means which could never have occurred to the others. To kill Bhisma, Sikhandin was used as a living shield against whom that perfect knight would not raise a weapon, because of doubtful sex. Drona was polished off while stunned by the deliberate false report of his son's death. Karna was shot down against all rules of chivalry when dismounted and unarmed; Duryodhana was bludgeoned to death after a foul mace blow that shattered his thigh. This is by no means the complete list of iniquities. When taxed with these transgressions, Krsna replies bluntly at the end of the Salya-parvan that the man could not have been killed in any other way, that victory could never have been won otherwise. The calculated treachery of the Arthasastra saturates the actions of this divine exponent of the Bhagavad Gita. It is perhaps in the same spirit that leading modern exponents of the Gita and of ahimsa like Rajaji have declared openly that nonviolence is all very well as a method of gaining power, but to be scrapped when power has been captured: "When in the driver's seat, one must use the whip."[19]

To those who admire and adore the Gita, these are minor points. They will tell you that the Gita is not merely the quintessence of the Upanishads but something more; it brings them down to earth. Unlike

the Upanishads, the Gita, you are told, asks you firmly to come down
to the world and to fight its battles. But even on this problem, as Arun
Shourie points out, the Gita is not consistent. It tells you to act not to
make the world a better place to live in or to make your fellow men
better citizens to live with, but to seek the merger of your individual
soul with the supreme soul. To quote the actual words of Shourie:

> The similarity of the Gita to the basic Upanishadic doctrine as well
> as its characteristic ambiguity can be seen by recalling its view about
> the goal itself and about the knowledge that will lead us to the goal.
> In the Gita, as in the Upanishads and, of course, in the Brahma
> Sutras, the highest goal is the same—freedom from the cycle of
> birth and death, the submergence in Brahman. And in the Gita, as
> in the other works we are considering, internalizing the same
> knowledge of one's nondifference from the Brahman remains the
> way to merging with Him.[20]

With his wonted thoroughness Shourie proceeds to quote verse
after verse from the Gita in support of his contention. This merger
business is, to my mind, the most narrow, the most selfish and the
meanest goal to aspire for. The ideal man should seek merger not with
a mythical paramatma but with life in general and with humanity in
particular. Countless generations lived and died to make us what we
are today. We owe all our humanity and everything that goes with it—
our arts and crafts, our science and philosophy, our culture and civilization, and all the graces of life that make it meaningful—to the
heritage handed down to us by those past generations. What is more
desirable, more noble, more self-fulfilling than safeguarding that heritage unimpaired and handing it over to the next generations, and if we
could, to enrich it in howsoever small a measure?

But to get back to the Gita, while action without seeking some personal gain can be noble, action without any care for its evil consequences to other men and the world at large is something reprehen-
sible, even diabolical. You should refuse to act when you are sure that
only something ill, something evil, would come out of it. To justify
your unjustifiable action as your caste duty or as an inevitable expres-

sion of your nature, prakriti, is to make yourself a robot, an unfree man, a member of a herd of wolves and jackals. I can think of nothing more shocking, more despicable than the doctrine "kill, kill one and all, kill without the least constraint, because it is your caste duty, because it is in consonance with your nature."

To sum up, the ethics of the Gita is wholly Machiavellian and Nietzschean. It is not entirely without significance that Machiavelli spent his last years in comparative obscurity after divestment of his public office and a term in prison, that Nietzsche died in a madhouse, and that Krishna met his end after being shot by an aboriginal hunter who mistook him for a quarry?

16

SOCIOLOGY OF THE GITA

S ociology is the science of society, and not the science of the soul. And yet, M. K. Sharan has written a book entitled *Bhagavad-Gita and Hindu Sociology* without even a passing reference to the science of society. Indeed, I could not spot the word "sociology" anywhere except in the title of the book. In spite of being a double MA, and PhD, he does not seem to have even heard the names of such recent sociologists as Durkheim, Weber, Mannheim, Hertz, Maciver, not to speak of the earlier masters like Hobbes, Locke, Bentham, Comte, Mill, Spencer, Marx, and Engles. His knowledge of society and sociology is so abysmally poor that it can be called nil. But for a few inanities on caste, he ignores society and sociology and retains all the old and stale stuff on atma, brahma, dharma, karma, maya, yoga, and the rest of the fantasies of Vedanta. As if he had made a profound discovery, he states with a solemn face that the Gita is "essentially a book of devotion."[1] Why, then, did he pretend that his subject is the sociology of the Gita?

To madden you further, Sharan often forgets what he said a page or two earlier. Now he tells you, "In those times, Bhishma, Krishna, and others who were Kshatriyas were as much honored as teachers by the Brahmans as men of their own class."[2] Next, in praising Krishna, he tells you, "At the Rajasuya sacrifice of king Yudhisthira he took for himself the humble office of washing the feet of Brahmanas."[3] Almost in the next breath he tells you, "During the great war he [Krishna] was always as cool as in peaceful times . . . ," but the truth is otherwise.[4] Breaking his vow not to be a combatant, Krishna, according to the *Mahabharata*, jumped down twice from his charioteer's seat to attack Bhishma, but was prevailed on by Arjuna to desist.

Sharan may be unaware of it, but the Gita has its own brand of sociology. To my mind, its kernel is in four of its key verses. The first of them is:

> The fourfold order was created by Me according to the divisions of quality and work. Though I am its creator, know Me to be incapable of action change. (4.13)

To soften the blatancy of the claim, to mitigate its absurdity and enormity, Radhakrishnan uses the expression "the fourfold order."[5] Sankaracharya's prose translation of this verse (as rendered into English by Alladi Mahadeva Sastri) is practically the same, the nominal difference being that in the place of "the fourfold order" it prefers "the fourfold caste."[6] But the acharya's commentary on the verse is typical of the man and is too clever by half. Though it is a bit lengthy, it deserves to be quoted in full:

> The four castes (varnas, lit., colors) have been created by Me, Isvara, according to the distribution of energies (*gunas*) and of actions. The energies are *Sattva* (goodness), *Rajas* (fairness, activity) and *Tamas* (darkness). The actions of a Brahmana (priest), in whom Sattva predominates, are serenity, self-restraint, austerity, &c. (XVIII–42). The actions of a Kshatriya (warrior), in whom Rajas predominates and Sattva is subordinate to Rajas, are prowess, daring, &c. (XVIII–43). The actions of a Vysya (merchant), in whom Rajas predominates and Tamas is subordinate to Rajas, are agriculture, etc. (XVIII–44). The action of a Sudra (servant) in whom Tamas predominates and Rajas is subordinate to Tamas, is only servitude. Thus have been created the four castes according to the distribution of energies and actions. This fourfold caste does not exist in other worlds. Hence the limitation "in this world of man" (IV–12).

(Objection):—Oh! then Thou art the author of the act of creating the four castes, and as such Thou art bound by its effect; wherefore Thou art not the eternal Lord nor the eternally unbound.

Answer:—Though I am the author of this act when viewed from the standpoint of maya, still know thou that I am in reality no agent and therefore not subject to *samsara*.[7]

And here is the translation of the same verse by John Davies, who is faithful to the original:

The four castes were created by Me, according to the apportionment of qualities (or modes) and works. Know that I, the uncreating and unchanging, am the creator of them.

In a footnote Davies adds the comment:

This apparent contradiction is usually explained by the dogma that he who works without "attachment" does not really work. We may, however, interpret the passage thus: "As Vishnu (or Brahma) I am the author of the castes, but not in my supreme form as Brahma."[8]

It should now be clear that what Krishna meant was not "the four-fold order" (a single unit) but the four castes (four different and rigid entities). A Hindu is born into a caste; he lives and dies as a member of that caste, and even his life after death depends on the zeal and devotion with which he had discharged the duties of his caste during his lifetime. There is no scope whatsoever for social mobility, and in particular, for vertical mobility. In a class society a man may be the son of a laborer, but that would not preclude him from rising to the status of a lord, spiritual or temporal; nothing of the kind is possible in the caste system.

Krishna does not deny his responsibility for the iniquitious system; on the contrary, he owns it as his own creation. But here, too, he shows his genius for equivocation. On the one hand, Krishna claims that he fixes the caste status of each man in strict accordance with that man's good or evil deeds in previous birth or births, and the temperament that those deeds invested him with, and on the other hand, Krishna declares, "I am nonagent; I am immutable." He may or may not have been the lord of the *jagat* (universe) but he was certainly the lord of jugglery.

Taking their cue from the lord of jugglery, the commentators on the Gita maintain that the caste system is not man-made but god-made; it is "therefore" sacrosanct. To attack it is to show defiance of God, to undermine it is to sabotage what is a god-ordained social order. To be sure, it is an order based on the high and the low, the underprivileged millions at the bottom. But then, God is only nominally the creator of the system; it is, in fact, the past karma of men that creates the system. The role of the god is confined to deciding the caste of each man according to his natural aptitudes, his pronounced proclivities, his *swabhava*. How can the swabhava of a man be known before his birth? But is not God all-seeing, all-knowing? And so he can decide the swabhava of a man even before he enters the womb of his mother. Indeed, all the previous births of that man yet to be conceived, and yet to take birth, are fully known to God. Did not Krishna tell Arjuna, "I know all your past births, you don't" (9.5)?

Well, whatever may be the abominations of the caste system, God can be so forgiving, so loving and gracious that he can come to the succor even of those born in sin. Here is the relevant verse as translated by Sankaracharya.

> For, finding, refuge in Me, they also who, O son of Pritha, may be of a sinful birth—women, Vysyas, as well as Sudras—even they attain to the Supreme Goal.[9]

Being extremely shrewd, the acharya avoided all comment on this vicious verse. It is a verse that cannot—should not—be passed over silently. For it is a slur on more than 90 percent of the members of the Hindu society. About 50 percent of that society, like any other, consists of women. Out of the rest, 40 percent or a little more comprise the Vysyas, the Sudras, and the untouchables left unmentioned in the

Gita, perhaps because they are also unmentionable in its view in certain contexts. Are they all of sinful birth? In fact, Sankaracharya is willfully faulty in his translation. The correct version should be "born out of the womb of sin." What a scandalous thing to say! No, it is much worse than that. It is insolent, contumelious, outrageous, filthy. Its filthiness becomes all the more offensive when we look at the very next verse. As translated, again by Sankaracharya, it runs thus:

How much more then the holy Brahmans and devoted royal saints! Having reached his transient joyless world do they worship Me! (9.33)

So while a little over 90 percent of the populace are born out of the "womb of sin," a part of the remaining are "holy" and the balance are both royal and saintly. This reminds one of that insufferable imperialist Kipling who referred to all nonwhite people as "the lesser breeds without the law."

There is another wrong statement or lying suggestion in the verse. The kings and the priests, being at the very top of the social ladder, being the wielders of all power and the controllers of all wealth, command every comfort and spend a joyful life. And yet we are asked to believe that they somehow drag on their days in "this transient joyless world," pining for the union of their atma with the paramatma. This is obviously intended to ward off the wrath of the oppressed and suppressed masses from the two privileged castes.

The verse that castigates more than 90 percent of the people as those who are "born of a sinful womb" is so repulsive, obnoxious, and horrific that I want to discuss it at some length. For it shows, as perhaps nothing else can, the true nature of the Gita.

Chinmayananda is properly shocked by this verse. So he says:

Born out of the womb of sin: (*papayonayah*)—This term qualifying women, trades and workers would be a blasphemous calumny against a majority of mankind—an unpardonable crime, even if the statement comes from the divine mouth of a prophet.[10]

Yet the traveling salesman of the Gita had no difficulty whatsoever to find any number of silly excuses for what he himself stigmatized as "a blasphemous calumny" and "an unpardonable crime."[11] How mealy-mouthed the traditional commentators of the Gita can be! They have a nimble mind, a glib tongue, an easy conscience. In this matter even Radhakrishnan is not above blame. After translating "those who are born out the womb of sin," as "lowly born" he comments on the verse thus!

> The message of the Gita is open to all without distinction of race, sex or caste. This verse is not to be regarded as supporting the social customs debarring women and Sudras from Vedic study. It refers to the view prevalent at the time of the composition of the Gita. The Gita does not sanction these social rules. The Gita gets beyond racial distinctions in its emphasis on spiritual values. Its gospel of love is open to all men and women, persons of all castes as well as those outside caste.[12]

Surprisingly, even John Davies is no better. He translates the verse thus:

> For they who find refuge in Me, O son of Pritha! though they have been conceived in sin, women, too, Vysyas, and even Sudras, these go to the highest way.[13]

And his comment is partly ambivalent and partly apologetic. It reads:

> Those who are born of unlawful connection. The Vysyas are the mercantile and agricultural caste. The Sudras are the lowest caste, placed by Manu (XII–43) in the same rank with lions, tigers and boars. Even these, and women also, might attain to the state of Brahma, i.e., might be absorbed into his being. This goes beyond the prevalent Hindu doctrine. Women alone cannot perform any religious rite (Manu V–155), nor may they repeat the mantras, hymns of the Vedas (IX–18). They may, however, rise to heaven. I have not

noticed in any other passage that they might attain to nirvana. It is singular, as Thomson has pointed out, that the Vysyas should rank so low, and this must be regarded as a sign of the comparatively late date of the poem.[14]

F. T. Brooks, the disillusioned Theosophist who was the private tutor of Jawaharlal Nehru when Nehru was a boy, is tricky in his translation. Deviating from the original, he renders the verse thus in metrical form in four lines.

Verily, they who seek shelter in Me,
Though they be born, on account of past sins,
As women, or traders, or lowliest serfs,
They too win their way to the Goal beyond All.[15]

Without comment of their own, Kees Bolle,[16] A. J. Bahn,[17] Shakuntala Rao Sastri,[18] Annie Besant and Bhagavan Das (in their word-for-word translation),[19] Besant (in her individual translation),[20] Paramananda,[21] Vireswarananda,[22] Sivananda,[23] Arthur Osborne and G. V. Kulkarni,[24] Nehal Chand Vaish,[25] and P. Lal,[26] more or less follow Sankaracharya's translation. Thirteen other translators of the Gita into English, whose work I examined, are Sitanath Tattavabhushan and Srischandra Vedantabhushan Bhagavataratna,[27] Chidbhavananda,[28] Swarupananda,[29] Keshavadas,[30] Prabhavananda in collaboration with Christopher Isherwood,[31] William Q. Judge,[32] Dilip Kumar Roy,[33] Kumar Kishore Mohanty,[34] Swami Purohit,[35] Edwin Arnold,[36] Juan Mascaro,[37] and Prabhupada.[38] They are either evasive or misleading or casuistic or downright dishonest. To me, it was a matter both of pain and surprise that Sitanath Tattavabhushan made a deliberate attempt to mislead by putting "those of sinful birth" and "women, Vysyas, and Sudras" in two different categories (as Davies did). Like Homer, he was perhaps nodding when he reached the particular verse. Dilip Kumar Roy, I presume, was so much shocked by the verse that he omitted it altogether from his translation. The remaining, including Edwin Arnold, fall back on subterfuges, some clever, others stupid. Among the loudmouthed apologists for this abominable verse, the first place should be assigned to A. S. P. Ayyar whom we met earlier. He translates the verse thus:

> For those who take refuge in Me, O Partha, though they are of the womb of sinner women, Vysyas and Sudras—even they attain to the highest state. (9.32)

The irrepressible Ayyar was ebullient in his talk and effusive in his writings. He was excellent as an after-dinner speaker, and it is a pity that he strayed into literature and religion. However, he had an agile mind and he showed it in converting the "sinful womb" into "the womb of the sinner women." This enabled the showy and shallow Ayyar to start off grandiloquently:

> The Gita is gospel for all humanity, indeed for all living things. It knows no preference, caste or creed. The words Manava, Jantava, Manushya, Nara, Bhoota and Jana are used by it. It does not know of any chosen race. We may well say of Krishna, "In Him there is neither Brahman, nor Kshatriya, nor Vysya, nor Sudra, native, nor foreigner, high nor low, man nor woman, human being nor lower animal, but all are one in Krishna Vasudeva."[39]

And then Ayyar tells us, tongue in cheek:

> Though they are born of the womb of sin: This clause must, in my opinion, refer to illegitimate sons, including those among Brahmans and Kshtriyas, and not to women, Vysyas and Sudras, as interpreted by many commentators.[40]

The man who invaribly designated himself on the title pages of his numerous books as "M. A. (Oxon), I. C. S. Bar-at-Law, Fellow of the Royal Society of Literature of the United Kingdom" was obviously taking his readers to be a set of fools who could be made to swallow any nonsense! Indeed, he once told them, as though he was the all-India commissioner of census operations at the close of the Dwapara Age,

that Krishna had ninety million children![41] (He did not enumerate
how many of them were male, how many female.)

Now the fourth key—and vicious—verse in the Gita is verse 35
in chapter 3. First I give its translation by Sankaracharya and follow
it with his commentary:

> Better one's own duty, though devoid of merit, than the duty of
> another well discharged. Better is death in one's own duty; the duty
> of another is productive of danger.

> [Commentary:] For a man to die doing his own duty though devoid
> of merit is better than for him to live doing the duty of another,
> though perfectly performed. For, the duty of another leads to
> danger, such as hell (*naraka*).[42]

What can be more unambiguous and unconditional? You should
never, never, deviate from the duty that your caste enjoins you. You
may have no aptitude for it, but still you have to stick to it. Are you a
better judge of your swabhava (aptitude or nature) than Krishna? It was
he who made you take birth in a particular caste in accordance with
your swabhava. If you are deficient in merit in your *swadharma* (caste
duty), it is due to your own sins in your past birth or births. In case your
demerits in your swadharma keep you at the starvation level, it is just
punishment for your very many lapses in your former births. You may
be able to serve yourself and society better by changing over to what is
not your caste duty, but it is bound to end in peril. You are too ignorant, too powerless, too much subject to maya, to know what that peril
could be. Only God knows that peril, and he warned you of that
unnamed peril, and that should be enough to deter you from being
foolish or rash. Being himself a mini-Bhagavan, Sankaracharya has
given you a hint of that dire peril.[43] It can be a spell in hell.

But Aurobindo, the pontiff of Pondicherry, patronized by princes
and their diwans, by bankers and their agents, thought otherwise. He
said that the Gita did not lay down that "it is a law of a man's nature
that he shall follow without regard to his personal bent and capacities

the profession of his parents or his immediate or distant ancestors, the son of a milkman be a milkman, the son of a doctor a doctor, the descendants of shoemakers remain shoemakers to the end of measurable time, still less that by doing so, by this unintelligent and mechanical repetition of the law of another's nature without regard to his own individual call and qualities a man automatically furthers his own perfection and arrives at spiritual freedom."[44] If this is not bluff, it can only be bunkum! Of the score of top men who greatly hampered the march of India toward freedom of thought, freedom of spirit, and freedom of action, the pontiff of Pondicherry was decidedly one.

Apart from the four verses to which I have drawn pointed attention, there are many others in the Gita that make it the credo of casteism. Look at some of its opening verses. The wail of Arjuna is not merely because of the death of his kinsmen at his hands if he were to give them battle, but also because of casteist reasons. As a result of war and the destruction it causes, there will be lawlessness, women will then become corrupt, and that in its turn will create confusion in the caste system. And with the confusion of the caste system, "the immemorial laws of caste and the family are destroyed" (1.41 and 43). It is this that grieves Arjuna more than the slaying of his grandsire Bhishma, his guru Drona, and others dear to his heart.

And so the only sociology of the Gita is the sociology of caste with all its banalities and brutalities.

THE GITA AND SCIENCE

A long with a host of other sciences, the Gita also teaches modern science. Indeed, it anticipated by many millennia the latest discoveries in nuclear physics. If you are dumbfounded by such a statement, knight of the British Empire, Harsidhbhai Vijubhai Divatia, will call you names, the least offensive of which may be, "You are a silly ass." To open the eyes of all the silly asses in India and elsewhere he has devoted a whole chapter entitled "The Gita and Modern Science" in his book *The Art of Life in the Bhagavad-Gita*. Of course, he owns that his chapter "is not an attempt to read all the discoveries of modern science into the *Gita*." "That would," he admits, "be a tall claim to make."[1] But still the inescapable fact is there for all to see that Darwin, Huxley, Spencer, and their followers, who professed "agnosticism, if not complete atheism" have been proven wrong by the findings of modern science.

According to the noble knight, the materialists of the nineteenth century, headed by Darwin and Huxley, postulated that the higher forms of life evolved from the lower. Their two main concepts were the struggle for existence, and the survival of the fittest. Their stand was that "life was determined by organic changes which nature brought about in the bodies and this material form determined the evolution of mind which was regarded as a condition of the brain. It was the brain that determined the condition of the mind and not *vice versa*. . . . Material law thus prevailed in nature and human development was determined by biological changes, as man evolved from monkeys."[2]

All this is piffle. To support his contention, Sir Harsidhbhai quotes, among others, Sir Oliver Lodge, Sir Richard Gregory, Sir J. A. V. Butler. As all the three were knights like Sir Harsidhbhai, we have to take for granted that theirs is the last word on modern science. And according to that last word: "It is consciousness that bursts forth through physical nature and conditions its organic forms. . . . The whole universe is a vast biological organism and each small organism in the universe is its component part. It is one principle, call [it] energy or call it soul, that permeates and vibrates through this universe. . . . These observations support the Vedantic view of maya and the existence of one spirit or energy in the universe which we know through our senses as matter. The whole cosmos is Brahma; its different manifestations are due to the limitations of our senses."[3]

And so you see that modern science brings us back to maya and Brahma. Forgetting his earlier promise not to make too tall a claim on behalf of the Gita, the noble knight states:

> The Indian sages did not and could not express their ideas in the precise scientific terminology of the modern age. Their ideas are clothed in a poetic and figurative language, but behind that outer garb, they have expressed some eternal truths of life which modern science has expressed in scientific terminology. Any student of natural science who reads the Gita with an open mind . . . can discover for himself the underlying thoughts common to the Gita and modern scientific research.[4]

Without stopping at that Sir Harsidhbhai expresses deep regret that neither Gregory nor Hegel read the Gita. Had they done it, he is sure, the former would have been a greater scientist and the latter a greater philosopher. We can only wonder why Sir Harsidhbhai, despite his mastery of every aspect of the Gita from its ethics to its epistemology stopped short with the judgeship of the Bombay High Court and did not go up to the International Court at the Hague!

The Savonarola of Salem—I mean C. Rajagopalachari[5]—was not merely a sedulous propagandist of the Gita; he tried to implement one of its teachings through the use of state power. During his second spell as the chief minister of the Madras State, he made a determined effort to enforce what the Gita chooses to call swadharma. On the pretext that it could be the only solution for solving the growing unemployment problem, he proposed that each boy should spend half a day in learning his father's craft, trade, or profession, and give only the other half to his general education. This was nothing short of bringing Varnashrama Dharma through the backdoor. The people of Tamil Nadu could easily see through the game and they resisted his move so stoutly that he had to beat a hasty retreat! In some respects our Sankaracharyas are even worse than our Savonarolas. According to S. G. Sardesai, one of them "declared in Poona, a few years ago, that women and Sudras must be despised because, according to the Gita, they were 'born of sin' (*Paapa yoni*)."[6] Why did the acharya omit the Vysyas? Is it because they are some of the biggest donors to their monasteries?

Now to return to the Savonarola of Salem. Assuming the role of a scientist he tells us:

> It is well known that physical characteristics and mental traits are passed on from parents to children. This heredity does not explain what is sought to be explained by the law of Karma. Bodies are shaped by heredity, but not souls. The soul has no father or mother but is self-existent. Any soul may be lodged in any body in which it has earned the fitness to function. Bodies are only the tenements provided for souls even as engineers may build in similar or varying types for citizens to choose and live in, according to their needs.[7]

The tenement provided by the divine engineer for the soul of Rajagopalachari should have been of excellent quality, for it served him—rather, his soul—very well indeed! But the more pertinent questions are these: Hadn't he ever heard of DNA and RNA? Didn't anyone tell him that it is DNA and RNA, "the molecular cousins," and not karma, that determine the hereditary qualities of a living being? Was he ignorant that after the discovery of the content and structure and function of DNA, there has been an explosion in the science of genetics?

However that may be, what amazes me is the self-assurance with which the propagandists of the Gita bring up science and scientists in their talks, discourses, commentaries, and expositions. Do they not know that all scientists, too, have their blind spots? Have they never heard that no less a master scientist than Newton was very much a superstitious person?[8] Are they not aware that Sir Oliver Lodge, Sir William Crookes, Alfred Russel Wallance, and some others, though scientists of front rank, practiced what is called "spiritualism" and deluded themselves that they were actually talking to Alexander the Great, Shakespeare, Napoleon, and other such illustrious dead?[9] Did they never hear that James D. Watson, who shared the Nobel Prize for Medicine and Physiology with Francis Crick and Maurice Wilkins in 1962 for his contribution to the discovery of the structure of DNA, has gone on record that "one could not be a successful scientist without realizing that, in contrast to the popular conception supported by newspapers and mothers of scientists, a goodly number of scientists are not only narrow-minded and dull, but also just stupid."[10] Do not these words remind us of our Bhagavantams and Swaminathans?

Without pressing this point further, I wish to know why the peddlers of the Gita fail to mention those scientists who scoffed at presuppositions like atma and paramatma, karma, and punarjanma of the Vedanta. To make good the lapse, may I have your permission to quote just three scientists? Albert Einstein, who revolutionized such basic concepts as time, space, and matter stated firmly and frankly:

> I cannot imagine a god who rewards and punishes the objects of his creation, whose purposes are modeled after our own—a god, in short, who is but a reflection of human frailty. Neither can I believe that the individual survives the death of his body, although feeble souls harbor such thoughts through fear or ridiculous egotism.[11]

A far more emphatic denial comes from Francis Crick, a member of the team that discovered the structures of DNA in 1953. "The problem of the origin of life," he says, "is, at bottom a problem of organic chemistry."[12] Carl Sagan fully agrees with Crick. For the sake of those who have not heard of him, I may add that Sagan is a distinguished space scientist and one of the most brilliant writers on the latest developments in cosmology. This is what he says with all the authority of a leading scientist:

> In a very real sense human beings are machines constructed by the nucleic acids to arrange for the efficient replication of more nucleic acids. In a sense our strongest urges, noblest enterprises, most compelling necessities, and apparent free wills are all an expression of the information coded in the genetic material: we are, in a way, temporary ambulatory repositories for our nucleic acids. This does not deny our humanity; it does not prevent us from pursuing the good, the true, and the beautiful. But it would be a great mistake to ignore where we have come from in our attempt to determine where we are going.[13]

Yet we have charlatans in our midst who prattle all the time that there is nothing new in modern science that was not already envisaged by Vedanta. It is, I hold, the uttermost limit to which stupidity could go. To prove that this is no irresponsible or irreverent opinion, I proceed to give a few patent, all too patent, nonsensical things that are set down in the Gita as scientific truths! Whatever your wretched Darwin and Huxley might say to the contrary, Brahma created men through yajnas (sacrifices) and after creating them told them that the only way by which they could propagate themselves was by performing yajnas (3.10). Clouds are formed by yajnas, and for getting good and timely rains they should carry on yajnas (3.15). They should feed the gods regularly through yajnas, and the gods will feed them in return, also regularly (3.12). Now what is the moon? If you think that it is a satellite of the earth, you are wholly wrong; it is the greatest of stars (10.21). What is a crocodile? It is not a large lizardlike reptile living in water but a fish (10.31). What has the highest speed, the ultimate speed? It is not light but wind (10.31). What are the most unmoving things in the world? The Himalayas, though your foolish geologists tell

you that they are the youngest mountains in the world, that they consist not of hard granite but of dry mud, and that they are still growing
in height (10.25). What is the biggest lake? If you think that a lake is
a big pond of fresh water, you are wrong. A lake is an ocean (10.24).
Which is the first among the sensory organs? It is *manas*, the mind
(10.22). What are basic to the nutritive value of foods? Not your pro-
teins, carbohydrates, fats and vitamins; it is all idiotic. The nutritive
and other values of foods depend on their tastes (sweet, sour, or other
tastes), their hardness or softness, their hotness or coldness, and
finally their freshness or staleness. Foods are of three kinds, like the
men who eat them—high, middling, and low (17.8, 9, and 10). Such
are some of the great scientific truths that the Gita teaches us! By the
way, do you know that in Krishna's time there was electricity? In his
English translation of verse 6 from chapter 15, Prabhupada tells us
that Krishna had no use for it, though the Lord could have, had he
cared, lighted up his abode with electricity. So self-effulgent was the
Lord that he had no need for the sun, the moon, or electricity.[14]

Such is the science of the Gita, the quintessence of the Vedas and
the Upanishads, the book of all knowledge, sacred and secular. And as
long as the Gita is venerated as the repository of the highest knowledge, advance of science in India will be tardy, lame, and marginal. To
a scientist, his world should be real, not an illusion; to him, his senses
should be the sources of knowledge, not snares; to him, life should not
be splintered, it should be of a piece. All this is well brought out by one
of our modern and seminal thinkers, the late Jacob Bronowski, and I
quote from his book *Science and Human Values.*

> Is it true that the concepts of science and those of ethics and values
> belong to different worlds? Is the world of what is subject to test,
> and is the world of what ought to be subject to no test? I do not
> believe so. Such concepts as justice, humanity, and the full life have
> not remained fixed in the last four hundred years, whatever
> churchmen and philosophers may pretend. In their modern sense
> they did not exist when Aquinas wrote; they do not exist now in civ-
> ilizations which disregard the physical fact. And here I do not mean
> only the scientific fact. The tradition of the Renaissance is of a

piece, in art and in science, in believing that the physical world is a source of knowledge. The poet as much as the biologist now believes that life speaks to him through the senses. But this was not always so: Paolo Veronese was reproved by the Inquisition in 1573 for putting the everyday world into a sacred painting. And it is not so everywhere now: the ancient civilizations of the East still reject the senses as a source of knowledge, and this is as patent in their formal poetry and their passionless painting as in their science.[15]

I wish you would ponder over this passage and then tell me whether it is fortuitous that out of the three Indian-born scientists who have thus far won the Nobel Prize for Science, two won it for their work done in the United States after they decided to not return to the holy land of the Vedas and to renounce their Indian citizenship. A true scientist cannot think, he cannot work, he can hardly breathe in the midst of the vacuity and vapidity of Vedanta.

WHY THE GITA?

Gautama, the Buddha, was no revolutionary and Buddhism no revolution. "Complete change, turning upside down, great reversal of conditions, fundamental reconstruction, especially forcible action by nation etc., to substitute new ruler or system of government"—that is the definition of a revolution by the seventeenth edition of *The Concise Oxford Dictionary*. Buddhism comes nowhere near this definition. The changes it attempted cannot be called complete, much less were they fundamental. Nor did it bring about a total reversal of the status quo by turning everything upside down. Furthermore, it removed no king or government by forcible action, nor did it introduce any new order of society. At best, it was a radical reformation. However radical, a reformation cannot by its very nature be a revolution. Reform is tinkering; revolution is recasting after smashing the old mold.

Even before the time of the Buddha there was a revulsion againt the Vedic sacrifices and the large-scale waste of cattle and other wealth that they entailed. And during his time, apart from himself, Mahavira, Gosala, Ajita, and others were questioning the divine authority of the Vedas. In general, there was a strong resentment against the pretensions of the priests who were claiming to be *bhudevas* (gods on earth).

What the Buddha did, along with the other teachers of his time, was to strengthen these social and religious tendencies. In this matter, he was more successful than the rest because of the massive royal support he and his religion received during his lifetime from Bindusara and others, and after his time, from Asoka and Asoka's successors. In the teaching of the Buddha what hurt the priest caste most was not so much the questioning of the authority of the Vedas or the efficacy of the Vedic sacrifices. To an extent, it was done by the Upanishads even before the advent of the Buddha. It was not even the Buddha's opposition to the caste system that was hurtful. True, he recognized no caste inside the Sangha (Buddhist order), but outside the Sangha he did not mind the prevalence of the caste system. All that he did was to affirm that by birth alone one would not become a Brahman, and that a Kshatriya was really superior to a Brahman. Indeed, Hermann Oldenberg, a greater authority on Buddhistic studies, was reluctant to call the Buddha even a social reformer. Any assumption, he wrote, to make out that the Buddha had "broken the chains of caste and won for the poor and the humble their place in the spiritual kingdom which he founded would be unhistorical." And he proceeded to add:

> Anyone who attempts to describe Buddha's labors must, out of love for truth, resolutely combat the notion that the fame of such an exploit, in whatever way he may depict it to himself, belongs to Buddha. If anyone speaks of a democratic element in Buddhism, he must bear in mind that the conception of any reformation of national life, every notion in any way based on the foundation of an ideal earthly kingdom, of a religious Utopia, was quite foreign to this fraternity. There was nothing resembling a social upheaval in India. Buddha's spirit was a stranger to that enthusiasm, without which no one can pose as the champion of the oppressed against the oppressor. Let the state and society remain what they are; the religious man, who as a monk has renounced the world, has no part in its care and occupations. Caste has no value for him, for everything earthly has ceased to affect his interests, but it never occurs to him to exercise his influence for its abolition or for the mitigation of the severity of its rules for those who live behind in worldly surroundings.[1]

What, then, really hurt the priest caste was a deterioration in their economic conditions. With the near stoppage of the Vedic sacrifices, their fees dwindled almost to zero. With royal patronage going mostly to the Buddhist monasteries, their income from that source decreased markedly. And even the Vysyas, who amassed great fortunes owing to increasing urbanization, leaned heavily toward Buddhism. The priest caste might have put up with a reduced standard of living had it felt that the base on which it had built up over the centuries its social supremacy was not being undermined. That base was Varnashrama Dharma. According to it, a man is born into a caste and his birth fixes unalterably his caste duties. In effect, it makes a large majority of the people virtual slaves for whose food, clothing, and housing the masters, in this case, the upper three castes, have no responsibility whatsoever. Caste slavery is, thus, more callous and inhuman than bond slavery. Barring the Rig-Veda and one or two of the earliest religious scriptures, there are no law codes, no epics, no mythologies, no manuals of family life, indeed, no priestly writings that do not enjoin that the first and foremost duty of a king is to pin down a man for life to the caste in which he was born and to the kind of work that is customarily associated with that caste. This royal duty is stressed even by the secular writings. Though the Buddha did not mount any serious attack on caste and caste duty, the fact was still there, that once a man, however low in the caste hierarchy, turned a monk, he became an equal with the other members of the Sangha. How many from the lower castes were actually being accepted as monks is a different question. Oldenberg was definite that their number was severely limited. And yet he wrote:

> Thus the religious garb of Buddha's disciples makes lords and commons, Brahmans and Sudras equal. The gospel of deliverance is not confined to the high-born alone, but is given "to the welfare of many people, to the joy of many people, to the blessing, welfare, and joy of gods and men."[2]

The priest class rightly sensed that this was the thin end of the wedge. The day, they feared, was not far off when the slave, that is, the Sudra, would become the sire. And their fear proved correct. For the first time ever in India a Sudra dynasty, the Nanda, came to power.[3] It was followed by another Sudra dynasty, the Mauryan. The second had a larger empire and greater power. Its writ ran almost throughout the country. In the northwest it held sway even over Gandhara and beyond. And one of its emperors, Asoka, who embraced Buddhism, dared to introduce *danda samata* (equality of punishment)[4] and *vyavahara samata* (equality in law suits).[5] It was nothing short of dragging the gods on earth down to the level of the low-born Sudras and those subhumans, the Chandalas (the untouchables). To add insult to injury, Asoka, in one of his edicts called the gods on earth the "false gods."[6]

The only way to protect the God-ordained Varnashrama Dharma was to put an end to Sudra rule by some drastic action. That action took the form of the murder of Brihadratha, the descendent of Chandragupta and Asoka, by his "wicked" Brahman commander-in-chief, Pushyamitra, while the emperor was reviewing the troops. By the way, it was Bana, the poet, who described Pushyamitra as "wicked."[7] But a modern historian, the late Niharranjan Ray, thought otherwise. In his view, "The ascription of the term *asura* to the Mauryas by certain epic and Puranic authors cannot be lightly brushed aside on the ground that the writers were Brahmanical and the Mauryas Buddhists."[8] Nor can we lightly brush aside the fact that this Ray was a stout defender of the Emergency in the late seventies. It is a bit ironical on the part of this champion of law and order at any cost to feel pity for the lot of the common people under the tyranny of the Mauryas and to see a great liberator in the person of Pushyamitra! How foxy can a majority of our so-called intellectuals be!

Now to revert to Pushyamitra, having founded the first Brahmanical empire in India, he thought he should give top priority to a double-pronged scheme, the destruction of Buddhism and the revival of Brahmanism. So almost his first move was to kill all good Buddhist monks and to dismantle their monasteries.[9] According to *Divyavadana*, he even issued a proclamation offering a reward of one hundred dinars for each severed head of a *sramana* (Buddhist monk) presented to him.[10] But the next step was not so easy. The times had changed and so did the temper of the people. Brahmanism in its old form cannot be revived; it should therefore be fitted with a new garb. As this would take time, something impressive—really spectacular—had to be done in the meantime. So he performed an *Asvamedha* (horse sacrifice), and after an interval, a second one. At one of these, if not at both, Patanjali seems to have officiated as the principal priest.[11] Other sacrifices like *Agnishtoma, Rajasuya* and *Vajapeya* were also revived.[12] Between them, Pushyamitra and Patanjali initiated by stages what K. P. Jayaswal called the "orthodox counterrevolution."[13] A less caustic name given to it by P. Banerjee is *neo-Brahmanism.* And right from the post-Maurya period, it is, he says, persisting in more or less the same form.[14] As I said on a prior occasion, if Pushyamitra was the sword-arm of the neo-Brahmanism, Patanjali was its guiding brain. Grammar was only a game to him for an idle hour; his real work, indeed, his life's mission, was to preserve the hierarchical structure of the Hindu society and the primacy of the priest caste. And this he achieved so successfully that, as Banerjee has rightly put it, the neo-Brahmanism still retains more or less the same shape and spirit that was given to it by the razor-sharp brain of Patanjali a little more than two thousand years ago.

In his commentary on Panini's grammar, Patanjali alludes to the killing of Kamsa by Krishna and its dramatic representation in *Kamsa-vadha.* He also speaks of Vasudevakas as the worshippers of Vasu-deva.[15] Much earlier, Panini himself referred to the worship of Vasudeva and Arjuna, though the exact degree of worship that each of them received is a matter of dispute among scholars. However that may be, one thing is certain. By the time of Patanjali, that is, the second century BCE, Krishna was being worshipped in some parts of the country by some sections of the people as a personal god. Patanjali was too shrewd a man not to take full advantage of this fact. Though Gautama, the Buddha, neither affirmed nor denied the existence of God, and though never once did he claim to be God himself, his followers raised him to godhead soon after his death. In fact, this was the general trend of the times. As Floyd H. Ross wrote:

In the century following upon the death of Gautama, all of the religious movements of India displayed pronounced popularizing tendencies. It was a period of religious revival, but at a level adapted to the confused emotional life of the masses. Men demanded idealized objects of devotion—personal gods or saviors to whom they could turn, or more vivid symbols to help them in their search for release.

This widespread flight into the derivative forms of the religious life influenced the Buddhist tradition also. Gautama had put emphasis on individual exploration. Within a few years after his death, initiates into the order were reciting, "I take my refuge in the Buddha, I take my refuge in the dharma, I take my refuge in the Sangha." Gautama had asked his friends to take his words experimentally and not uncritically. Many of his followers began to make a cult of him and of his teachings. The Sangha originally was simply the fellowship of seekers gathered around Gautama. It became a church and a missionary society. The strong personal loyalty felt by the early disciples was passed on to succeeding generations of followers. Eventually, Gautama was transformed into a god.[16]

Such a personal god is absent in the Vedas; he is absent in the Upanishads. To please the Vedic gods, you have to perform costly sacrifices. And there is no question of pleasing the Upanishadic god, as he is the neuter Brahman. So when the Buddhists placed the concept of a personal god in whom you could take refuge in good times and bad and receive his grace, millions flocked to Buddhism. To provide the counterattraction of a Hindu personal god, Patanjali should have actively promoted the cult of Vasudeva-Krishna. "The period," says B. N. Puri, "was . . . notable for the evolution of the Vishnu-Vasudeva cult which had originated earlier."[17] While building up Krishna as a personal god, Patanjali, in association with his royal disciple Pushyamitra, took some other effective steps to establish neo-Brahmanism. They were to annul the principles of danda samata and vyavahara samata and to reintroduce the age-old iniquitious system of graded punishments, which in effect meant, for the same offense, nominal punishment for the higher castes and the severest for the lower.[18] Furthermore, Patanjali got some of the old codes revised and some new ones written, his sole purpose being to hold down the Sudra without ever trying to raise his head again. On some of the main aspects of the post-Mauryan neo-Brahmanism, Banerjee is very illuminating. Though somewhat long, it is a passage that I like to quote here:

> Neo-Brahmanism or Hinduism is . . . a multiform structure consisting of polygenous religious ideas. It is a synthesis or a combination of the Vedic and non-Vedic, hierarchical and popular, native and foreign. The orthodox and popular elements are so intimately woven that we can only separate them by an act of abstraction. The process of synthesis, of which neo-Brahmanism is the result, began very early, but it was intensified perhaps from ca. 500 BCE, when dissenting religions like Jainism and Buddhism were spreading fast on Indian soil. Brahmanism showed a great alertness in adjusting itself to existing circumstances. Notwithstanding the zeal with which the Brahmanical teachers threw themselves into popular theosophy and devotional systems of worship, they were careful enough to preserve the old traditions and hierarchical elements. It is true that as time passed, the sectarian and theistic forms of worship gained wider popularity, but the orthodox traditions and ceremonies continued (and in fact are still continuing) in the framework of expanded Brahmanism or neo-Brahmanism, however limited their influence might have been. If the epics and the Puranas were devoted mainly to popularizing the worship of personal gods and deities, the Dharmasutras and Sastras were written to preserve the popularity of the Vedic practices.[19]

What it all boils down to is this: you may be devoted to any god or goddess, worship him or her in any way you like, prefer any of the numerous schools of Yoga, follow any one among the many paths that release you from the cycle of births and deaths, and still you can hope to attain heaven. But you should not forget your caste nor fail to perform your caste duties. However inefficient you may be in discharging them or however demeaning they are to you, you should stick to them; otherwise, you will land right down in hell. It is to sound that grim warning that the Gita was written.

FROM A TRIBAL GOD
TO A NATIONAL GOD

Over the centuries, a nation emerges out of a tribe, and so does a national god out of a tribal chief. This was the case with Krishna. Barth, the French Indologist, suggested that Krishna was "probably at first the *Kuladevata*, the ethnic god, of some powerful confederation of Rajput clans."[1] The Yadavas were never a unified people, and so there could be no question of their forming a "powerful confederation." And if the Yadavas were Rajputs, that is, Kshatriyas, they were, according to many traditional accounts, of a low order in that caste. Indeed, not a few Kshatriyas questioned the social status of Krishna, as is evident from the *Mahabharata*. Moreover, in the Dwaraka itself, where Krishna spent the greater part of his adult life, he received little or no respect from his own folk. In fact, he was disliked, distrusted, denounced. It is on record in the *Mahabharata* that once he spoke bitterly to Narada that "the only enjoyment allowed to me is to listen to their harsh words and constant complaints. The incessant invective I am subjected to by those for whose welfare I am slaving rankles in my heart perpetually." And so there was no question of his having been a Kuladevata even in Dwaraka, not to speak of his being the clannish god of "some powerful Rajput confederation."

All the same, Krishna could very well have been the Kuladevata of

173

the people of Madhura, Brindavan, and the other Surasenas in this particular region. For one thing, Krishna had left the region long ago to distant Dwaraka on the western seacoast. And time and distance must have lent certain celebrity, perhaps even veneration, to his reported heroic deeds at Dwaraka. Second, there were in circulation legends of his colorful childhood, wayward boyhood, and romantic adolescence at the place of his birth and upbringing. Third, the extermination of the Yadava clan at Dwaraka after a drunken orgy, followed by fratricide, should have added a note of sorrow, mingled with nostalgia, for the tragic end of the far-off cousins. Such reasons were enough to elevate Krishna to the status of a Kuladevata in the Madhura-Brindavan region.

In support of my view that Krishna was originally the Kuladevata of the Surasenas I have the testimony of Megasthenes. In the fourth century BCE, he was the ambassador of Seleucus at Chandragupta's court. He held that office, according to some historians, between 304 and 299 BCE. Stationed at Pataliputra, he wrote a full account of the India he came to know, but only stray fragments of it, quoted by others, are now extant. Still they are of considerable historical interest for a country and a people like ours who still lack a historical sense and are incapable of learning from history. Though a digression, it needs to be stated that unless we develop a historical sense, understand the historical processes, and learn to ride historical forces, history will leave us behind as it did during the last one thousand years or more.

Coming back to Megasthenes, it is of interest that he made more than one reference in the surviving fragments of what might be called his "Ambassador's Report" to a popular Hindu god called Herakles, and I give here a small part of one such passage:

> This Herakles is held in especial honor by the Sourasenoi, an Indian tribe who possess two large cities, Methor and Cleisobora, and through whose country flows a navigable river called the Iobares.[2]

It is generally understood, and rightly, that the Herakles referred to here is no other than Krishna, Methor is Madhura, Cleisobora is Krishnapura, and the navigable river Iobares is Yamuna. And so, apart from Panini and Patanjali, we have the testimony of Megasthenes that Krishna was, a few centuries before Christ, a tribal god who was attracting a widening circle of devotees. This goes to show that the case that Lorinser, Weber and Lassan tried to build up to establish the influence of Christianity in the origin and growth of Krishnaism is baseless.[3]

The elevation of Krishna to godhood was, however, a long and tortuous process. As we have seen earlier, at the time of Panini, he was being worshipped along with Arjuna. Later, Arjuna was dropped, and Balarama (also called Sankarsana) was added. Indeed, the earliest image of a Hindu god unearthed so far is not that of Krishna but of Balarama.[4] Still later, even Pradyumna, the profligate, found a place on the pedestal along with his father and uncle.[5] And there was a time when two other members of the family, Samba (Krishna's son by Jambavati) and Aniruddha (Pradyumna's son), climb up the pedestal to receive worship. For the last two facts mentioned here, there is inscriptional evidence at more than one early site.[6] We do not know how long it took Krishna to push down the rest of the members of his family from his pedestal.

But, like the rulers of the post-1947 India, Krishna knew perfectly well that it was hardly possible to prevent the members of his family from claiming a share in his power and glory. And so he found a place for them by his side on a second pedestal, the pedestal of the *vyuhas*.[7] Without going into the theme of the vyuhas, I would like to state that among the different Puranas there is no full agreement about the ten who constitute the ten avataras. Furthermore, in one list there are as many as twenty-two avataras, and it is said in the Bhagavata Purana that "the descents of the Lord are countless and never-ending."[8] This appears to be only too true! For in the India of 1984 alone there are, I believe, not less than a score of avataras, male and female, who through their hold over our ministers, state as well as central, and our officials at every level, are running our secular and socialist government for us!

The concept of the avataras is not found in the Vedic literature, though some scholars manage to see therein the faintest of its outlines.

But A. P. Karmarkar takes a different view. He thinks that "the doctrine of the ten avataras . . . seems not to have come into vogue in the epic period." In proof of this he goes on to say, "It is only in the interpolated sections of the *Mahabharata* that the incarnations are enumerated."⁹ Though the Brahma Sutra is a nonsectarian work, it is significant that it carries no reference at all to avataras.¹⁰ Like the worship of Krishna, the doctrine of avatara, too, should have been vigorously promoted by the Sungas. Of the many redactions of the *Mahabharata* and the *Ramayana*, one of the most reactionary must have been undertaken in the last quarter of the second century BCE, that is, after Brihadradha, the direct descendent of Chandragupta (the Jain), and after Asoka (the Buddhist) was murdered. "While it is quite impossible as yet to say with certainty," writes Farquhar, "that the recasting of the two poems comes immediately following 184 BCE, there can be no doubt that it was about the time that the process of redaction was carried out."¹¹ Hopkins and Macdonell fully share this opinion. For the late start that the avatara theory had, apart from the impediment of the rule of the non-Hindu and non-Brahman dynasty of the Mauryas, there might have been a theological struggle among the Hindus themselves. While the early Upanishads postulate the neuter Brahman, the later, especially the sectarian ones, opt for a personal god. Only after a long time, thinks Farquhar, a compromise was effected between the two schools, and it has taken the form of the Gita.¹² This is quite plausible; it explains quite a few of the many contradictions in the Gita.

Krishna claims again and again in the Gita that he is an avatara; he declares again and again that he descended to earth innumerable times in the past, and in the future, too, he would descend innumerable times. When he suddenly springs up this claim, Arjuna is taken aback and he asks very pertinently, "You state that you taught the Yoga of Knowledge even to Vivasvat (the sun). Is not Vivasvat born aeons earlier to you?" (4.4). As usual, Krishna silences Arjuna with his genius for riddles and paradoxes (4.55 and 7). Furthermore, have we not a Sankaracharya to maintain that only a riddle can explain the supreme reality, only a paradox can express a profound truth? So he tells us in his commentary on the Gita that Krishna is both born and unborn.

How can this be possible? Well, through Krishna's maya (illusion). When you bring in maya there can be no more debate, no further controversy. The advocates of maya eat and drink, they make love and procreate, and the more enterprising among them amass huge fortunes and capture political power; failing that, they make captives of those holding political power, live in luxury, and enjoy the very cream of the earth; but all this is only maya. As Krishna told Arjuna in the Gita on the very first occasion he claimed to be an avatar, if you cannot see all this as maya (here I am quoting Sankaracharya's commentary), "you knowest not the power of vision is obstructed by thy past action, good and bad."[13] Can there be a more clinching argument than that?

From what has been said thus far it should be clear that Krishna's rise from the status of a Kuladevata to that of the incarnation of Vishnu was a long process spread over centuries. Even in the Gita, "the name of Vishnu occurs only three times . . . and the name of Hari twice." Krishna calls himself Vishnu only once, and that as the Vishnu aspect of Aditya, and it is not at all a big claim. He is addressed twice as Vishnu by Arjuna, but in both the cases he seems to have had only the sun in mind. And Sanjaya calls Krishna "Hari" just twice.[14] It is good enough proof for the contention that the total identification of Krishna with Vishnu or Hari came long after the Gita assumed its present form.

Now, Krishna states clearly in the Gita why he descends to the earth again and again. As translated by Radhakrishnan, the relevant verse reads:

> Whenever there is a decline of righteousness and rise of unrighteousness, O Bharata (Arjuna), then I send forth (create incarnate) Myself. (4.7)

If that is the only purpose of the descent of Krishna, that is, of Vishnu, he might, says the pontiff of Pondicherry, as well have remained in his heaven enjoying his *yoganidra* (the sleep of yoga). Here are his exact words:

Avatarhood for the sake of the dharma would be an otiose phenom-
enon, since mere right, mere justice or standards of virtue can
always be upheld by the divine omnipotence through its action.[15]

According to *Webster's New World Dictionary, otiose* means, among
other things, "ineffective," "futile," "sterile," "useless," and "super-
fluous." I cannot, therefore, be accused of having misrepresented the
pronouncement of the pontiff. He often spoke and wrote as though he
was indeed an avatara himself. On that self-assumption, he explains to
us the purpose of an avatara thus:

> The avatar comes as the manifestation of the divine nature in the
> human nature, the apocalypse of its Christhood, Krishnahood, Bud-
> dhahood, in order that the human nature may be molding its prin-
> ciple, thought, feeling, action, being on the lines of that Christhood,
> Krishnahood, Buddhahood transfigure itself into the divine. The
> law, the dharma which the avatar establishes is given for that pur-
> pose chiefly; the Christ, Krishna, Buddha stands in its center as the
> gate, he makes through himself the way men shall follow. That is
> why each incarnation holds before men his own example and
> declares of himself that he is the way and the gate; he declares too
> the oneness of his humanity with the divine being, declares that the
> son of man and the father above from whom he has descended are
> one, that Krishna in the human body, *manusim tanum asritarm,* and
> the supreme Lord and friend of all creatures are but two revelations
> of the same divine Purushottama, revealed there in his own being,
> revealed here in the type of humanity.[16]

What does all this mean? Only one of the oracles of the Auroville
can tell you, and I am not one of them.

Gandhi is no less concerned with God and his descent. Though he
affirms that almost all the religions of the world believe in the concept of
an avatara, he differs from Aurobindo on the purpose of an incarnation.

He explains his own view thus:

> The belief in an avatara, may be belief in God incarnating as man
> and identifying this incarnation with a human being of extraordi-

nary mental and spiritual dimension striking man's mind with amazement at the qualities which make him a savior and deliverer. That attitude is the imaginative attitude. But the same belief rationalized becomes a belief not in God embodied as man, but either in God working out the cosmic purpose through the universal law or in man ascending to the estate of God by wholly divesting himself of all his earthliness and completely spiritualizing himself, or sacrificing himself in God. Having the spark of the divine, we are all incarnations of God.[17]

Gandhi has thus provided ample justification for Rajneeshes and Satya Sai Babas to claim that they are avataras! In one sense, we cannot refute their claim. One of the supreme attributes of an avatara, as Krishna explains repeatedly, is maya. Apart from "illusion," maya has two other meanings; they are "magic" and "trickery." And are not our Sai Babas and Rajneeshes pastmasters of maya in all senses of that word? They know, above all, how to create an illusion in the gullible that they are gods in human form.

Differing both from Aurobindo and Gandhi, Bhagavan Das has postulated a theory of his own with special reference to the descent of Vishnu as Krishna. A friend and colleague of Annie Besant, he was rated a great scholar in his day. A "Bharatratna," his forte was to give a rational look to what is outrageously irrational, to provide a scientific dress suit to what is crassly superstitious. Some of the titles of his books are *The Science of Religion*, *The Science of the Sacred Word*, and *The Science of Emotions*. This "scientist-scholar" is positive about the purpose for which Vishnu descended to earth as Krishna. It was to put down the growing militarism of the day. And so the Bharatratna writes:

> Krishna utilized the bitter personal quarrels between the two groups of cousins, the Pandavas and the Kauravas, with both of whom he and his kinsmen had close matrimonial alliances, for the bringing about of a war on an immense scale in which the militarists would destroy each other, like Sunda and Upa-Sunda.[18]

Now would you like to be enlightened on two of the other great purposes of this avatara? A product of our PhD mills, R. K. Pandey explains them with dazzling brilliance in a monograph of his. It is held against Krishna that he had too many affairs with too many gopis. There can be no sillier or more sacrilegious indictment. "Saints, sages, renowned rishis, and even deities in their former lives," says Pandey, "prayed to Krishna and got a pledge from him he would give them the closest contact." What can be closer than contact in sex play? And so, Krishna asked all of them to become gopis in their next birth; and all of them did. By making love to them en masse he kept his pledge! And, then, why did he steal the clothes of the women bathing naked in the Yamuna? Only people with a dirty mind, feels Pandey, see anything wrong in what he did. What the Lord wanted was "to root out the prevailing evil of naked bath as is usual, strangely enough, in modern swimming and bathing clubs." He had yet another noble aim; it was to give those gopis the promised "closest contact."[19] Surely, this PhD should enable him to be a gopi in his next birth to enjoy "the closest contact" with the Lord!

Literally thousands are the books on one aspect or the other of the life and legend and gospel of Krishna. Most of them compete with Pandey's in silliness. One such is by P. S. Tolani,[20] a second by Kakasaheb Kalelkar,[21] a third by K. G. Warty,[22] a fourth by Hari Prasad Sastri,[23] and a fifth by Chidbhavananda.[24] I admit that I have not read any of them from cover to cover; I just glanced through them, and it was enough to turn my stomach. Slightly better in quality among the heaps of books on the subject that I collected are by W. G. Archer,[25] Milton Singer et al.,[26] Norvin Hein,[27] and Lee Siegel.[28] Of these, Archer's has literary merit. In this context it is highly significant that the largest number of titles on Krishna and the Gita are published by the Bharatiya Vidya Bhavan. Its primary mission, for those who could see through its pretensions, is to hold back India from stepping out of its medieval shell into the broad vistas of the modern age.

Now, I do not know who started the idiotic game, but many of our obscurantists see Darwin's theory of evolution sketched as an allegory in the avatara doctrine. It shows gross ignorance of Darwin's theory.

That revolutionary theory which shook the world when it was first published refutes by its implication all such ideas as an imperishable soul and the migration of that soul from body to body. It falsifies the childish accounts of creation as they are retailed by all religions, major and minor. It refuses to accept the idea of God descending to earth to protect righteousness. It believes in a material basis for all forms of life. It does not belittle the value of the senses as sources of knowledge. It maintains with incontrovertible proof that life has experimented with myriad species and discarded a large number of them when they were found unfit for survival. In contravention to the Christian belief, it does not consider man a fallen angel but an ascending animal. When Darwin's theory knocked the bottom out of the Christian theology, it is rather pitiful on our part to try to bolster up Hindu theology with the aid of the same theory!

The recent discoveries in the realm of biological science have modifed some of the basic postulates of Darwin, but the totality of their drift is not toward God but away from him. One of the latest theories, proposed by two eminent space scientists, Fred Hoyle and N. C. Wickramasinghe, does support the theory of descent. But according to it, the descent was not of God from his heavenly abode but of a life cloud. True, they prefer not to call it "descent" but "invasion." As this is not the proper place to go into the details of their new theory, I quote just one paragraph from their joint book that indicates the basic features of their theory:

> The essential biochemical requirements of life exist in very large quantities within the dense interstellar clouds of gas, the so-called molecular clouds. This material became deposited within the solar system, first in comet-type bodies, and then in the collisions of such bodies with the earth. We might speak of the earth as having become "infected" with life-forming materials, and other planets moving around other stars would be similarly infected. Since other planets probably exist in vast numbers—there may well be ten billion or more stars with planets in our galaxy alone—the prospect for the emergence of life on a galactic scale appears very favorable. The picture is of a vast quantity of the right kind of molecules simply

looking for suitable homes, and of there being very many suitable homes.[29]

I am sure our traditionalists will unearth soon enough the rudiments of this theory, stated as an allegory, from one of our Puranas or an equally fantastic old book of myth or mythology! Indeed, they may go even to the extent of dancing with joy, shouting "well, the prebiotic molecules which, according to Hoyle and Wickramasinghe, fill interstellar space are known to the seers of our Upanishads. What they meant by the neuter Brahman are just these molecules." Leaving them to dance their jig, I pass on to my next point.

In all discussions of avataras, I find a point strictly omitted. It is this: among the ten avataras that are generally listed, we have a fish, a tortoise, a boar, a man-lion, two Brahmans (Vamana and Parasurama) and three Kshatriyas (Rama, Krishna, and Buddha). Of course, the tenth avatara is yet to come, but as its advent is to humble the pride of the Sudras and punish them for their pretensions,[30] it can be presumed that Kalki will also be a Kshatriya who would come riding roughshod on a white charger. The great Vishnu can, when necessary, assume the forms of lower life, such as a fish, tortoise, or boar, or even the weird form of half man and half lion, but never that of a Vysya or Sudra. That, according to his own clear statement in the Gita, would be too degrading. For are not all Vysyas and Sudras born out of the womb of sin?

20

THE TWO BHAGAVANS

There is a longer, tougher, and more tortuous process than elevating a tribal hero into a national god, and that is to provide him with a gospel. In the case of Krishna, the process took almost a thousand years. Even so, there is no unanimity about the nature of that gospel, its scope, its reach, its message, and its meaning. But there is a unanimity among scholars whose critical faculties are not blunted by their devotion to Krishna that this gospel, that is, the Gita, came a long time after his death, and even then, in a halting, groping, tentative form. R. G. Bhandarkar was perfectly right when he said:

> Vasudeva could not have been living when the Bhagavad Gita was composed as a discourse delivered by him, any more than Buddha was living when his discourses were reduced to the form of books. It is worthy of remark that both of them are called Bhagavatas when speaking. Vasudeva must already have been deified before [the] Bhagavad Gita was written.[1]

Essentially, the Gita represents a confrontation between two Bhagavans. The Bhagavan, the Buddha, said about renunciation, *sannyasa*:

183

Full of impediments is the household life, a dusty path (a path of defilement); whereas the life of renunciation is like the open sky (free from hindrances). It is not easy to lead this holy life in all its perfection and purity like a polished conch shell by a person living the household life.[2]

Mahavira, the elder contemporary of the Buddha, had far more rigid views about sannyasa.[3] Mukkhali Gosala, the leader of the Ajivaka school, was also in favor of "going from home into homelessness."[4] And so were Ajita Kesakambali, the materialist; Pakudha Kaccayana, the atomist; Sanjaya Belatthaputta, the agnostic; Purana Kassapa, the fatalist; and a host of other teachers of non-Brahmanic schools of thought. Indeed, in that particular century, that is, the sixth BCE, there were more than sixty wandering teachers,[5] each with his own brand of philosophy, but all of them equally opposed to what has come to be known as Vedanta at a later date.[6] Of these, the most successful was the Buddha, the next was Mahavira, and perhaps the third was Gosala. By the way, that particular century witnessed an unprecedented resurgence of the human spirit. From Greece in the West to China in the East, there was in the whole of the then civilized world a great ferment, a new stirring, a mighty upheaval, in every realm of human life and thought. Some of the leaders of the age were Parmenides, Empedocles, Zarathustra, Mahavira, Buddha, Gosala, Lao Tzu, and Confucius.[7] The next century was in some respects even more creative. For good or bad, these two were among the more decisive centuries in human history. In his major novel, *Creation*, Gore Vidal attempted with great success an imaginative recreation of this refulgent period.

Having deviated far from the point that I started to make at the beginning of the preceeding paragraph, I should go back to it with due apologies. The concept of sannyasa was non-Aryan. When they first entered India, the Aryans were averse to it; their bubbling zest for life would hardly permit them even to think of it. In fact, most of the rishis of the Vedic Age were living with their large families and leading a happy, joyous, and full life. Some of them, like Yajnyavalkya, had two wives. But in the course of time they borrowed the idea of sannyasa from non-Aryans, most probably from the Harappan Dravidians. And they enjoined that only the man of the top three castes can renounce the worldy life, and none else. And that too very late in life. In contravention of this strict rule, Buddha permitted not only the Sudras but also the slaves and Chandalas to opt for sannyasa. He ordained even minors, provided they had the consent of their parents. True, he did all this in a very limited way. True, again, that he debarred lepers and debtors,[8] as well as slaves who failed to obtain their release from their owners.[9] Even so, the pillars of the old order of society based on Varnashrama Dharma saw ominous portents in what the Buddha was doing. Among the more prominent of his disciples were a barber, a cowherd, a fisherman, a deerstalker, a scavenger, a dog eater and some others belonging to equally low castes.[10] What was worse, he allowed a thief to don the saffron robe, permitted some slaves and their womenfolk to take to sannyasa. And the worst of all his transgressions was to admit Amrapali, the courtesan of Vaisali, into his order, Sangha.[11] But the limit was to take into his fold a Chandala woman, despite the protests of King Prasenajit and the Brahmans of Sravasthi.[12] Once this kind of rot started, where would it stop? Is not a former slave, Gosala,[13] already posing as a great philosophical teacher? Next a Chandala may stake such a claim.

Yet to denounce the very concept of sannyasa would be to disown their own Varnashrama Dharma, the last stage of which for the three upper castes was sannyasa. And so, Krishna, the second Bhagavan, came out with a very clever proposition. He said:

Not by abstention from work does a man attain freedom from act; nor by mere renunciation does he attain to his perfection. (3.4)

But he who controls the senses by the mind, O Arjuna, and without attachment engages the organs of action in the path of work, he is superior. (3.7)

Do thou thy allotted work, for action is better than inaction; even the maintenance of thy physical life cannot be effected without action. (3.8)

According to some commentators, this is the very crux of the message of the Gita, and the surest way to attain perfect peace in this world and perfect bliss in the next. As for Radhakrishnan, he sees in this some of the major discoveries of modern psychology![14] But the blunt truth is that it ties down the lower castes for good and forever to their manual labor or menial service and closes to them all avenues to education, enlightenment, and culture. As I have already discussed at some length the diabolical nature of the Varnashrama Dharma, I refrain from covering the same ground again. But I should reiterate that the second Bhagavan said in so many words that even if you happen to be a bad shoemaker, it is in the interests of your life after death to stick to shoemaking, rather than to seek to be a good soldier or scholar. It may be recalled here that for daring to take to *tapas*, that is, a life of religious austerity, Sambuka's head was chopped off with a stroke of his royal sword by Rama, and this outrage had won for him the admiration of Kalidasa.[15]

Though he gave his tacit approval to the caste system outside his Sangha, the first Bhagavan missed no opportunity to stress that the caste of a person depended not on his birth but on his aptitudes, on his qualities and conduct. He stated:

> I do not call a man a Brahman who is born of this parentage, born
> of this mother; one can become a man with a name preceded by "Sir"
> if he happens to be a man of means. I call him a Brahman who owns
> nothing, who receives nothing.[16]

On another occasion, he argued that it was a man's craft, profession, or calling that decided his caste and not his parentage.[17]

The second Bhagavan saw peril to the caste system in this approach. And so, to sanctify the system, he took upon himself full responsibility for its creation. Of course, it is not easy to maintain that one can be high or low in the social scale, without reference to his aptitudes, skills, and character. So he affirmed that he does take them into account, not after their manifestation as men come of age, but on the basis of their good or bad deeds in their past births (4.13). As the postulate of past and future births is based on sheer dogma, you cannot argue against it; you can only accept it or reject it.

The first Bhagavan said that if you strictly follow the path of morality, avoiding falsehood, envy, hate, cruelty, and other evil qualities, you can attain happiness in this life as well as in the next. Indeed, you can escape from the cycle of recurring births and deaths. The emphasis of the second Bhagavan was more on caste and caste duty. If you reconcile yourself to your caste, however lowly, and perform your caste duty, however loathsome, you will attain happiness in your next birth. In other words, what is issued to you is a postdated cheque on a fictitious bank. And the second Bhagavan knew very well how difficult it was to follow the straight and narrow path of morality, and so to attract a far larger circle of devotees than his rival Bhagavan, he said:

Whosoever offers to Me with devotion a leaf, a flower, a fruit, or water, that offering of love, of the pure of heart I accept. (9.26)

As a further inducement to enlist devotees, the second Bhagavan also said:

And whoever, at the time of death, gives up his body and departs, thinking of Me alone, he comes to My status (of being); of that there is no doubt. (8.5)

This means that you might be guilty of every conceivable act of immorality, and yet you can attain heaven in case you die with Krishna's name on your lips. Is this not, so to say, a Magna Carta for immorality?

The first Bhagavan stated this in his very first sermon at Sarnath after his enlightenment under the Bodhi tree! To reach *nirvana*, the best path, if not the only one, to be followed was the noble eightfold path proposed by him. To show that he was by far more liberal, the second Bhagavan proclaimed that whatever be the path followed by a devotee, ultimately it led to him only (4.11). But he immediately remembered that it might impair his precedence over the rest of the gods. Hence he took care to add that those who worship him were his special favorites (12.20), and they would reach the highest heaven, which is his (8.16).

Neither of the Bhagavans was a vegetarian. Though the Buddha discouraged the killing of animals for food, he did not reject a meat dish when it was offered by a lay disciple. In this matter, he acted on the principle "beggers cannot be choosers." In fact, he died after partaking the pork served to him by the smith Chunda.[18] And he was wholly against the consumption of liquor by all, be they monks or not.[19] Krishna, on the other hand, relished meat; he had liquor in moderate dose, quite unlike his half-brother Balarama, a notorious boozer. Of course, the Gita expresses no opinion either for or against liquor, but it advocates killing as a "must" for a man of the Kshtriya caste. In the discharge of his caste duty on a battlefield a Kshtriya should have the least compunction even in killing his nearest kith and kin. The more he kills, the greater his glory in this world and the surer his bliss in the next. Though the Buddha was against causing injury to any living creature— the exception being only fish,[20]—he seems to have never condemned war between states. Perhaps even in this matter, his attitude was identical with the one he adopted toward caste. In his Sangha he did not recognize caste, but he gave it his tacit approval outside the Sangha. I may be wrong, but my fairly wide reading of books on Buddhism has given me the impression that while the Buddha was against violence between individuals, he thought that it could not be avoided altogether between states. It is significant that there are references to wars, war strategies, and war weapons in the Vinaya Pitaka and the Jataka Tales,[21] but no condemnation of war. However that may be, it is really odd that the Gita should plump for ahimsa (nonviolence) and for equality in chapter 10, verse 5. Nonviolence is against the very purpose for which the Gita was taught. And equality is deadly to the caste system, for it is based (to use Ambedkar's phrase) on "graded inequality." This, we should presume, is one of the deliberate interpolations, meant to placate the heterodox sections, which generally favored nonviolence and equality.

Since I have made enough points to convince any open-minded man that the Gita was fabricated to arrest the rapid spread of Buddhism, I will not pursue the subject further. But before I close this chapter I wish to draw the attention of my readers to what N. J. Shende said in his essay entitled "The Authorship of the *Mahabharata*."

> There has been a definite attempt in the whole of the *Mahabharata* to press the majority of the incidents and episodes in the cause of Brahmanic religion. The *Mahabharata* in fact deserves to be called "Encyclopedia Brahmanica."

And Shende concluded his scholarly essay by stressing the point he made earlier that it was the Angirasas and the Bhrugus who gave the *Mahabharata* its present form. He wrote:

> Thus the account of the Angirasas and the Bhrugus certainly favors the conclusion that the Bhrugangirasas were jointly responsible for the final redaction of the *Mahabharata*, for making it a Dharma Sastra, and a Nitisastra, and an encyclopedia of Brahmanical traditions, and for preserving its unity in the midst of its manifold diversity.[22]

All that I wish to add is that if the *Mahabharata* is the "Encyclopedia Brahmanica," the Gita is equally certainly the bible of bondage.

21

ALL THINGS TO ALL MEN

J anus, the Roman god, has only two faces whereas Hari, the Hindu god, has one thousand. And in his avatara as Krishna, Hari speaks with all his thousand tongues. It is for you to pick and choose whichever of the thousand messages his Gita gives. It is also open to you to combine a number of messages that appeal to you. With combinations and permutations, a limitless number of philosophies of the Gita can be made up. That this is not an overstatement is born out by the fact that each season brings its bumper crop of books on the philosophy of the Gita. As for translations and commentaries, it is impossible to keep count. Way back in the eighth century CE, Adi Sankaracharya started the process,[1] and it is still going on. And for each commentary that reaches print, there are at least a hundred that are oral. These take the form of talks, discourses, lectures, and yajnas.

It cannot be repeated too often that the appeal of the Gita is not due to its clarity but to its confusion; not to its logic but to its sophistry; not to its unity but to its heterogeneous nature; and finally, not to its truth but to its verisimilitude. It can indeed mean all things to all men. To the four acharyas of South India—Sankara, Ramanuja, Madhva, and Vallabha—it means four different schools of Vedanta, ranging from absolute monism to outright dualism. It also means to them different paths to salvation. Krishna did, no doubt, say that all paths lead to him ultimately. Nevertheless, Sankara prefers the path of knowledge, Jnana Yoga. For smooth passage through the path, renunciation (sannyasa), he thinks, is essential. The other three acharyas demur, and vote for the path of devotion, Bhakti Yoga, or for a combination of two or more yogas. Though equally opposed to Sankara on all main issues, they differ among themselves on many side issues.

Around each of the four acharyas there has arisen a school of commentators. Of these, the Sankara school is the largest. Its more prominent members are Dhanapati, Hanumat, Madhusudana, Sridhara, Nilakantha, Sadananda, Venkatanatha, and Sankarananda. While they follow Sankara, they do not go with him all the way; every now and then they turn into their own lanes and bylanes. On occasion, they desert him to join forces with his opponents.

Ramanuja, Madhva, and Vallabha have also their separate groups of followers. Ramanuja, for his part, has stout supports in Yamunacharya and a second Venkatanatha, unrelated to the first. Vallabha has his upholders in Purushotham and others. Madhva has by his side Jayatirtha and Raghavendra. Each of these commentators has, in his turn, individual preferences and prejudices.

The southern acharyas and their followers are not the only exponents of the meaning and message of the Gita; there are others, like Kesava and Nimbarka, who belong to no particular group. Each of them insists on his right to interpret the Gita in his own way. In addition, there is a band of Kashmiri scholars, the outstanding members of which are Bhaskara, Abhinavagupta, Anandavardhana, and Ramakanta. Not to be left behind is a bunch of saints, and its outstanding members are Chaitanya of Bengal and Tukaram, Ekanath, and Ramdas of Maharashtra.

Jnanadeva, also of Maharashtra, stands apart. He differs not only from the four South Indian acharyas but also from all the saints and scholars who wrote on the Gita. D. D. Kosambi says that for his radical views he is forced to seek refuge "at the end of the thirteenth century CE from the persecution of his fellow Brahmans at Alandi to write his metrical translation and comment on the Bhagavad Gita."

"This work," he adds, "gave the Maratta language its form and provided inspiration for a long line of successors of all castes."[2] His teaching has pronounced traits of humanism. "The ideal man of Jnandadeva," writes B. P. Bahirat, "is one whose heart overflows with divine love at the sight of any object in the world. . . . The ideal of life is not *moksha* or liberation, but bhakti on this realization of love divine in this very life. Rituals or yogic practices are of no use. Our life is not something sinful or degradation of the absolute but the medium through which divine love experiences itself. To know this, to remember this with longing is the way of intermingling our little self with the divine. This is the highest summum bonum of life which is within the reach of any human being. No barriers of caste or creed, time and space, hinder his way."[3] Only an uncommon man could have deprecated the ideal of moksha and denounced castes and creeds in the thirteenth century. Jnanadeva was indeed a prodigy; in his brief span of life—he died in his twenty-second year—he put his indelible impress on the Marathi language, literature, and thought.

For a detailed study of the Gita by commentators of the earlier age, a useful guide that is at once short and comprehensive is by T. G. Mainkar.[4] Though most people swear by Sankara, Mainkar has a poor opinion of him. He charges Sankara with willfully misinterpreting words; introducing new words in support of his contention; ignoring the Bhakti Yoga, which is central to the Gita, so as to strengthen his own case for Jnana Yoga and sannyasa; and other serious lapses. Mainkar's final verdict on Sankara is this: "He is not a reliable interpreter of the Bhagavad Gita as the spirit of the poem is not faithfully reflected in his comments. It would not be an exaggeration to say that he is the least faithful intepreter of the Bhagavad Gita." I venture to add that to a greater or lesser degree this is true of all traditional commentators on the Gita.

For a comparative study of the commentaries on the Gita, two other useful books are by R. D. Ranade[5] and S. H. Jhabwala.[6] The former is scholarly, whereas the latter is shallow. Both the authors, unlike Mainkar, do not stop short of the medieval dark period, they survey even the modern age. These are, by no means, the only three authors who published such comparative studies; there are hundreds of them in different languages.

Funnily, there are also guides as to how to read the Gita. I have two of them. The first is by Tridandi Swami B. H. Bon[7] and the second by an author who preferred to be anonymous.[8] What the swami attempts is a translation of the Gita, imparting to it a Chaitanyite color. The anonymous author is modest, for he has—to use a witticism of Winston Churchill—"much to be modest about." He quotes with full approval Radhakrishnan's opinion that the Gita "represents not any sect of Hinduism but Hinduism as a whole, not merely Hinduism but religion as such in its universality, without limit of time and space." And yet he writes a guide for the Chaitanyites, a sect, as to how they should study the Gita.

It would have been appropriate if a Muslim has written as to how a Muslim should study the Gita, but that work is undertaken by Sundarlal, a Hindu of Delhi. Its translator, however, is Syed Asadullah, a Muslim of Hyderabad. There are already quite a few Christian guides for reading the Gita; we should now await Buddhist, Jain, Zorastrian, Jewish, Confucian, and Shintoist guides. Maybe some of them are already on their way.

What I now propose to do is to point out briefly that, like the older commentaries, even the newer ones differ in their interpretation of the meaning and message of the Gita. As it is impossible for me to survey all the modern commentaries, I will confine myself to Tilak, Aurobindo, and Gandhi.

Bal Gangadhar Tilak is firm in his opinion that the Gita is a call for action, action for the good of the world, action without seeking any personal benefit (Niskama Karma).[9] R. D. Ranade gives a gist of Tilak's views. It reads:

> Tilak advocates that man has a duty to perform even after the realization of the highest self. In the first place, it is pointed out that action belongs to the body and so long as the body remains, we cannot extricate ourselves from the influence of actions. Then secondly, selfless action or Niskama Karma would alone enable us to

move out of thralldom to actions. Hence a man who performs self-less actions cannot be said to be performing any actions at all. Finally, it is the responsibility of a realized soul to point the way to erring humanity and hence action becomes indispensable even for the realizer. Lokamanaya Tilak has advanced these and other arguments for proving the imperativeness of actions even after the attainment of the highest knowledge.[10]

Tilak's book on the Gita is said to be his magnum opus. He wrote it in Marathi, while undergoing a sentence of six years in Mandalay (Burma) jail. It is translated into English by Balachandra Sitaram Sukthankar. Both Aurobindo and Gandhi disagree with Tilak's interpretation of the Gita, each from his own point of view. Let me first take up Aurobindo. True to his pontifical nature, he dismisses Tilak and his views with a broad sweep of his hand. As if he is laying down the law, he says:

It is a mistake to interpret the Gita from the standpoint of the mentality of today and force it to teach us the disinterested performance of duty as the highest and all-sufficient law. A little consideration of the situation with which the Gita deals will show us that this could not be its meaning. For the whole point of the teaching, that from it arises, that which compels the disciple to seek the teacher, is an inextricable clash of the various related conceptions of duty ending in the collapse of the whole useful intellectual and moral edifice erected by the human mind. In human life some sort of a clash arises fairly often, as for instance, between domestic duties and the call of the country or the cause, or between the claim of the country and the good of humanity or some larger religious or moral principle. An inner situation may even arise, as with the Buddha, in which all duties have to be abandoned, trampled on, flung aside in order to follow the call of the divine within. I cannot think that the Gita would solve such an inner situation by sending Buddha back to his wife and father and the government of the Sakya State, or would direct a Ramakrishna to become a pundit in a vernacular school and disinterestedly teach little boys their lessons, or bind down a Vivekananda to support his family and for that to follow dispassionately the law or medicine or journalism. The Gita does not teach the disinterested performance of duties but the following of the divine life, the abandonment of all dharmas, *sarvadharman*, to take refuge in the supreme alone, and the divine activity of a Buddha, a Rama-krishna, a Vivekananda is perfectly in consonance with this teaching. Nay, although the Gita prefers action to inaction, it does not rule out the renunciation of works but accepts it as one of the ways to the divine. If that can only be attained by renouncing works and life and all duties and the call is strong within us, then into the bonfire they must go, and there is no help for it. The call of God is imperative and cannot be weighed against any other considerations.[11]

To my mind, this is Aurobindo's veiled justification for his sudden withdrawal from active politics and precipitate flight to Pondicherry. He wants us to believe that what he did was not because of his loss of nerve but because of "the call of God." Perhaps he felt subconsciously that the heroic way in which his former colleague, Tilak, stuck to active politics despite a life of many privations and persecutions, was an indictment of his own life of seclusion and security with the patronage of rich disciples!

On which points Tilak and Gandhi differed from each other in their understanding of the Gita is very well brought out by a comparative study of their writings on the subject by D. K. Gosavi. Despite its length, I will quote here a pertinent passage, together with its serial numbers:

(1) Tilak believed in truth, nonviolence, and such other moral virtues as absolutely and invariably binding in a perfect society only; but he recognized, justified, (and held as sanctioned by scriptures) certain exceptions to these high principles of ethical conduct, as might be necessary under the circumstances of each case. He held that these exceptions were necessary in the interest of public good. (Loka Sangraha) Gandhi believed in these ethical principles as absolute and invariable under all circumstances. He did not recognize any exceptions to them; but in case where he failed to observe these principles in their entirety, he pleaded his own imperfection

and weakness, and held that further determined efforts must be made to overcome the weakness with a view to reach the ideal, standard conduct.

(2) Tilak recognized and preached the ethical propriety of "responsive" action for regulating human relations; he would not himself initiate or countenance initiation of any untruthful or violent policy, but certainly would follow and support such a policy, if required, as defensive measure only.

Gandhi recognized solely unilateral obligation for ethical conduct irrespective of the plan and policy the other party might follow; he would in no case initiate or support any untruthful or violent action in retaliation, even in self-defense. He followed and recommended only nonviolent action involving suffering by oneself even unto death.

According to Gandhi, the first, best method of resistance is the nonviolent method only; and as second best he approved the violent method also, in resisting injustice. He never supported cowardice of any kind in the name of nonviolence or otherwise.

(3) Tilak recognized the ethical propriety of retaliation—"tit for tat"—and also recommended expediency if necessary.

Gandhi disapproved retaliation or "tit for tat" policy in toto, and preached and followed the "return good for evil" policy in every case. He disapproved the policy of expediency in its entirety.[12]

I am one of those who believe that if you insist, as Gandhi did, on absolute truth, absolute celibacy, absolute nonviolence, absolute self-sacrifice, and such other absolute ethical values, you will end up with absolute hypocrisy. "The moralist," as Bertrand Russell warned, "is tempted to ignore the claims of human nature, and if he does so, it is likely that human nature will ignore the claims of the moralist."[13] Gandhi, the moralist, did not heed this warning, and in the India of today we are paying a terrible price for his folly. In public as well as in private life, all decencies are thrown to the winds, all moral values are forsaken, and we cover up our nakedness with a thick blanket of hypocrisy.

The roots of this hypocrisy can indeed be traced back to the Gita. Though accepted as the very essence of all earlier scriptures of Hinduism, it is equivocal from first to last. It is, therefore, easy to twist it to suit your purposes. It can be made to lend support to any opinion, belief, dogma, fad, oddity, or eccentricity. It can be used to justify social inequality and economic injustice. What is far more shocking, it can be cited to justify mass murder. The Gita affirms that "one neither slays nor is slain" (2.19). So, when you kill, where is the question of homicide? And when you kill a whole population, where is the question of genocide? Out of ignorance, one thinks that one slays others; in fact, they are already slain by God (10.33). Elaborating the meaning of this sublime truth, Radhakrishnan writes:

> The god of destiny decides and ordains all things and Arjuna is to be the instrument, the flute under the fingers of the Omnipotent One who fullfils his own purpose and is working out a mighty evolution. Arjuna is self-deceived if he believes that he should act according to his own imperfect judgement. No individual soul can encroach on the prerogative of God. In refusing to take up arms, Arjuna is guilty of presumption.[14]

It is really amazing that Radhakrishnan brings "the flute" into this gory business. Surely, a sword that takes life cannot be a flute that pours out the sweetest strains of music! Be that as it may, the point I am trying to make is that in the eyes of the Gita man has no right to a mind of his own or a will of his own; he has no freedom of choice of action; he is just a marionette for God to play with for a while and then to throw away. Vedantists call this *Iswaraleela*, God's sport. And yet a popular peddler of the Gita wants us to believe that the Gita is a treatise on the art of man making! No, it is a manual on the craft of marionette making.

Now, as A. Schweitzer rightly says, "The Bhagavad Gita has a sphinxlike character." The sphinx only smiles enigmatically; the Gita can also talk, argue, cajole, threaten, frown, tempt, attract, repel, impress, and do a hundred and one other things, and do them all enigmatically. And it does not care at all for ethical values. To quote Schweitzer again:

> It contains such marvelous phrases about inner detachment from the world, about the attitude of mind which knows no hatred and is

kind, and about loving self-devotion to God, that we are wont to overlook its nonethical contents. It is not merely the most read but also the most idealized book in world literature.[15]

I agree only with the latter half of what Schweitzer says. Yes, indeed the Gita is undoubtedly a nonethical work. And yet we read it, we treasure it, we venerate it. It is the greatest triumph of the unknown author or authors who fabricated the Gita; it is an equally great tragedy for India and the world.

EPILOGUE

Twelve hundred years ago Sankaracharya picked up the Gita from the dust it was gathering, wrote a commentary on it with his unmatched genius for sophistry, and placed it before the people as the supreme guide to their life and thought and salvation. Since then its influence has been all too pervasive, all too pernicious. It has made our national mind flabby, our national spirit feeble. It has made us callous to human inequality and human suffering. It has made us shameless sycophants and sanctimonious hypocrites. This is the basic theme of a big and bold book by Prem Nath Bazaz. Of its seven hundred fifty pages, nearly five hundred discuss this particular aspect. Next only to the scattered writings on the Gita by Kosambi, the best critique on it is by Bazaz.

As I pointed out once earlier, the emergence of the Gita as a national scripture and the emasculation of the national mind and spirit are closely linked. This is a historical truth that can hardly be challenged. But no devotee of Krishna, nor an admirer of Sankara, would take that statement lying down. They will react strongly and call me all sorts of names. The more violent their tirade against me, the happier will I be. For there can be no surer indication that my writing did have the desired effect. What I desired most was to start a dialogue, to provoke a debate, to stir up a disputation. It is all the same to me whether people agree or disagree with me, whether they praise or abuse me. What I always seek—as I remember to have said elsewhere—is a clash of minds, a flash of ideas. It is the only means for the upsurge of a new spirit, indeed, for the birth of new life.

As I have had my say, it is time for me to wind up. But before doing so, I very much wish to give expression to two of my most ardent wishes. The first is that Krishna, if he is really the greatest god as he claimed to be again and again in the Gita and elsewhere, should not keep his promise to come down again and again to our poor little earth whenever he thinks that righteousness is in jeopardy (9.7). His coming on the last occasion did infinitely more harm than good. In the name of reinstating righteousness, he was primarily instrumental in the outbreak of a terrible war, and if we were to go by the *Mahabharata*, the number of survivors at its end was just nine from among the millions of its active combatants. What is worse, it marked the end of a better age (the Dwapara) and the beginning of a worse age (the Kali). It may also be recalled in this context that Krishna claimed that, of weapons, he was *vajrayudha* or "the thunderbolt," as Radhakrishnan preferred to translate it (10.28). If he were to reappear now, he would claim that he is the latest among the nuclear weapons. And the war that he would actively promote to reestablish righteousness would result in the extermination of all life from the face of our earth.

Now my second wish, no less ardent, is that we as a nation should forget the Gita as Arjuna did. In less than a year or two after it was taught to him by Krishna as a special favor, he told his friend and mentor that it had all "disappeared" from his mind. It will be a great blessing if our nation, too, allows the Gita to disappear completely from its mind. Only then can we awaken from the slumber of ages; only then can we shake off our many illusions and delusions; only then can we know the value of free, daring, and original thought. And only then can we learn to despise the ideal of personal salvation and fix our sights on the future of humanity, indeed, on the time when man can migrate to other, and perhaps better, worlds in our vast cosmos. If only he could reach them, what a great triumph will it be for the ever-questing, ever-soaring, and ever-daring spirit of man! According to Sagan, there may be millions of such worlds in our galaxy alone. Being much older than our earth, some of these worlds may have far surpassed us in arts, science, philosophy, literature, culture, civilization, and the rest of the graces of life.

I will not live to see that happy day when India will forget, like Arjuna, the Gita with all its contradictions and confusions, its equivocations and evasions, its twists, turns, and trickeries. But such a day will come, maybe a long time after my death, but come it will. And when it comes the people of India will begin to live again, vitally, joyously, meaningfully. They would then stop fixing their gaze on the tip of their nose to still the mind and to kill all thought; they would then cease to peer into the so-called empty space within the heart where the soul is believed to have its temporary tenement; they would then scorn the ideal of union with that mirage, the supreme soul (paramatma). With a new awakening, a fresh vision and a burning zeal, they would join the progressive world community in trying to unravel the many mysteries that are still locked inside the microcosm of the atom and the macrocosm of the cosmos.

To hasten that golden dawn on the murky history of India, the first step to be taken is to disown Krishna and to discard the Gita.

NOTES AND REFERENCES

INTRODUCTION

1. Pratap Chandra Roy, *The* Mahabharata *of Krishna-Dwaipayana Vyasa*, 2nd ed., vol. 5 (Calcutta: Oriental Publishing, 1958), pp. 3–4.

This translation appeared originally during the years 1884–96 as the work of K. M. Ganguly while P. C. Roy was its publisher. For some unknown reason Ganguly's name as translator was dropped while printing the second edition. It is good to note that in the latest reprint he is again given credit for his work. All references to the persons and events connected with the *Mahabharata*, here as elsewhere in my present book, unless otherwise acknowledged, are made from this translation only.

2. S. Sorensen, *An Index to the Names in the* Mahabharata, (1904; repr., Delhi: Motilal Banarsidass, 1963), p. 629. Citations are to the 1963 reprint.

This bulky index is an indispensable volume to all those who want to make a serious study of the *Mahabharata*.

3. Pendyala Subrahmanya Sastri, *Mahabharata Charitram*, 2nd ed. (Pithapuram, 1933), pp. 272–86.

For a scholar born in an orthodox family, the intellectual courage that Sastri showed in writing a critical appraisal of the *Mahabharata* in Telugu is really amazing. Though criticized, abused, reviled, and even charged in a criminal court, he stood by his conclusions with his head unbowed and his spirit unshaken.

In the course of his book, Sastri has drawn, among many others, an excellent profile of Karna. To rebut the popular and silly belief that Karna was born to Kunti the moment Surya impregnated her, Sastri has unearthed conclusive evidence to show that Karna was born after the normal gestation period of nine months and that during all this time Kunti had kept her pregnancy a well-guarded secret.

It will be a good thing indeed if this daring and original work of Sastri, long out of print, is reissued at a popular price.

4. Ibid., pp. 329–37.

5. Iravati Karve, *Yuganta: The End of an Epoch* (Poona: Deshmukh Prakashan, 1969), pp. 135–48.

In this book, brilliant in patches, Karve, a leading anthropologist of her day, traces how the enmity between the Pandavas and the Nagas started with the burning down of the Khandava Forest, one of the principal habitats of the Naga people; how they liquidated Parikshit in belated retaliation; and how this led to the genocide of the Nagas for the second time by Janamejaya.

By the way, Karve adduces enough evidence to show that in all probability Yudhishtira was the illegitimate son of Vidura.

6. Sastri, *Mahabharata Charitram*, p. 49.

This, however, is contested by some others. According to them, the life span of Parikshit was sixty years, and having come to the throne at the age of thirty-six, he ruled for only twenty-four years.

7. Sita Nath Pradhan, *Chronology of Ancient India: From the Times of the Rigvedic Divodasa to Chandragupta Maurya, with Glimpses into the Political History of the Period* (Calcutta: Bharatiya Publishing House, 1927), p. 71.

Unlike Karve, Pradhan does not actually use the word *genocide*, but he says that Janamejaya attempted to exterminate the non-Aryan race of Nagas by burning them in a "sacrifice," and that can only mean genocide.

8. Alexander Pope, *The Temple of Fame*, lines 468–72.

CHAPTER 1: A DOUBTFUL WAR

1. E. W. Hopkins, *The Cambridge History of India*, vol. 1, *Ancient India*, ed. E. J. Rapson (Cambridge: Cambridge University Press, 1935), pp. 252–53.

2. V. S. Sukthankar, *On the Meaning of the* Mahabharata (Bombay: Asiatic Society of Bombay, 1957), p. 8.

3. Hopkins, *Cambridge History of India*, p. 253.

4. Max Muller, *A History of Ancient Sanskrit Literature so far as It Illustrates the Primitive Religion of the Brahmans* (Varanasi: Chowkhamba Sanskrit Series Office, 1968), p. 40.

5. V. S. Agrawala, *India as Known to Panini* (Lucknow: University of Lucknow, 1953), pp. 455–75.

Scholars differ widely about the date of Panini. He is placed in all the centuries between the seventh and the fourth BCE. Now the consensus veers to around the middle of the fifth century BCE.

6. A. D. Pusalkar, *History and Culture of the Indian People*, vol. 1, *The Vedic Age*, ed. R. C. Majumdar (London: Bharatiya Vidya Bhavan, 1951), p. 245.

7. Muller, *History of Ancient Sanskrit Literature*, p. 40.

8. D. C. Sirkar, Mahabharata: *Myth and Reality*, ed. S. P. Gupta and K. S. Ramachandran (Delhi: Agam Prakashan, 1976), p. 5.

9. Hopkins, *Cambridge History of India*, p. 252.

10. Ibid., p. 119.

11. Ibid., p. 120–21.

12. R. C. Majumdar, H. C. Raychaudhuri, and K. K. Datta, eds., *An Advanced History of India* (London: Macmillan, 1963), p. 94.

13. V. R. Ramachandra Dikshitar, *War in Ancient India* (Madras: Macmillan, 1944), p. 198.

14. Sirkar, Mahabharata: *Myth and Reality*, p. 6.

15. H. D. Sankalia, Mahabharata: *Myth and Reality*, ed. S. P. Gupta and K. S. Ramachandran (Delhi: Agam Prakashan, 1976), p. 145.

16. Pratap Chandra Roy, *The Mahabharata*, vol. 7, *Stree Parva* (Calcutta, n.d.), pp. 42–43.

17. Sankalia, Mahabharata: *Myth and Reality*, p. 7.

18. Vincent Smith, *The Oxford History of India*, 3rd ed. (Oxford: Oxford University Press, 1958), p. 59.

19. R. G. Bhandarkar, *Collected Works of Shri R. G. Bhandarkar*, 4 vols. (Poona: Bhandarkar Oriental Research Institute, 1933), 1:365.

20. R. C. Dutt, *Civilisation of Ancient India*, vol. 1 (London, 1893), p. 122.

21. Sitanath Tattavabhushan, *Krishna of the Puranas* (Calcutta: T. Roy, 1926), pp. 19–20.

22. M. K. Gandhi, *Gita, My Mother* (Bombay: Bharatiya Vidya Bhavan, 1965), p. 1.

23. Swami Vivekananda, *Thoughts on the Gita* (Calcutta: Advaita Ashrama, 1977), p. 5.

24. D. D. Kosambi, *An Introduction to the Study of Indian History,* rev. 2nd ed. (Bombay: Popular Prakashan,1975), p. 4.

25. D. D. Kosambi, *The Culture and Civilization of Ancient India in Historical Outline* (London: Routledge and Kegan Paul, 1965), p. 92.

26. Published in Delhi in 1976, the incentive for the compilation and publication of this cooperative study was provided by a statement issued by D. C. Sirkar affirming that the nucleus of the *Mahabharata* was only a simple war song of a petty family or tribal feud around which the legend of the epic developed at a much later age.

CHAPTER 2: FALSE SIGNPOSTS

1. Radhakumud Mookerji, ed., *Vikram Volume* (Ujjain: Scindia Oriental Institute, 1948).

This volume deserves the caustic criticism it received at the hands of D. D. Kosambi. In its editorial introduction, a general principle is laid down. It states that a "long-continued tradition must have had its roots in some kind of reality to sustain it." I can hardly imagine a more fatuous statement. The articles in the volume are good examples of the editorial credo.

2. D. D. Kosambi, *An Introduction to the Study of Indian History,* rev. 2nd ed. (Bombay: Popular Prakashan,1975), p. 293.

3. F. E. Pargiter, *The Puranic Text of the Dynasties of the Kali Age* (Varanasi: Chowkhamba Sanskrit Series Office, 1962).

4. F. E. Pargiter, *Ancient Indian Historical Tradition* (Delhi: Motilal Banarsidass, 1962).

5. Plato, *Republic,* trans. Benjamin Jowett (Cleveland: Fine Editions Press, 1946).

6. Frederic Albert Lange, *The History of Materialism* (London: Routledge and Kegan Paul, 1957), pp. 33 and 36.

7. A. L. Basham, *The Wonder That Was India* (London: Sidgwick and Jackson, 1954), p. 39.

8. Sita Nath Pradhan, *Chronology of Ancient India: From the Times of the Rigvedic Divodasa to Chandragupta Maurya, with Glimpses into the Political History of the Period* (Calcutta: Bharatiya, 1927), p. xi.

9. Pargiter, *Ancient Indian Historical Tradition,* p. 130.

10. Ibid., p. 63.

CHAPTER 3: DUEL WITH DATES

1. C. V. Vaidya, Mahabharata: *A Criticism*, 2nd ed. (Bombay: A. J. Combridge, 1929), pp. 55–56.

2. F. E. Pargiter, *Ancient Indian Historical Tradition* (Delhi: Motilal Banarsidass, 1962), p. 175.

3. Abinas Chandra Das, *Rigvedic India* (Calcutta: University of Calcutta, 1927); Abinas Chandra Das, *Rigvedic Culture* (Calcutta: R. Cambray, 1925).

4. A. D. Pusalkar, *History and Culture of the Indian People*, vol. 1, *The Vedic Age*, ed. R. C. Majumdar (London: Bharatiya Vidya Bhavan, 1951), p. 268.

5. Ibid.

6. F. E. Pargiter, *The Puranic Text of the Dynasties of the Kali Age* (Varanasi: Chowkhamba Sanskrit Series Office, 1962), p. vii.

7. Ibid., p. 182.

8. Vaidya, Mahabharata: *A Criticism*, p. 64.

9. A. L. Basham, *Studies in Indian History and Culture* (Calcutta: Sambodhi Publications, 1964), p. 32.

10. P. T. Srinivasa Iyengar, *Advanced History of India* (Madras: Hindi Prachar Press, 1942), p. 54.

11. Vincent Smith, *The Early History of India from 600 BC to the Muhammadan Conquest, Including the Invasion of Alexander the Great*, 3rd ed. (Oxford: Clarendon Press, 1914), p. 45.

12. Pusalkar, *History and Culture of the Indian People*, p. 269.

13. P. L. Bhargava, *India in the Vedic Age*, rev. 2nd ed. (Lucknow: Upper India Publishing, 1971), p. 20.

14. Quoted in Basham, *Studies in Indian History and Culture*, p. 81.

15. A. S. Altekar, quoted in Bimanbehari Majumdar, *Krishna in History and Legend* (Calcutta: University of Calcutta, 1969), p. 9.

16. B. B. Vide Lal, "Mahabharata Archeology," in Mahabharata: *Myth and Reality*, ed. S. P. Gupta and K. S. Ramachandran (Delhi: Agam Prakashan, 1976), p. 57.

17. Pargiter, *Ancient Indian Historical Tradition*, pp. 178–82.

18. R. C. Majumdar, H. C. Raychaudhuri, and K. K. Datta, eds., *An Advanced History of India* (London: Macmillan, 1953), p. 62.

19. See U. N. Ghoshal, *Studies in Indian History and Culture* (Bombay: Orient Longmans, 1957), p. 53.

20. See V. Rangacharya, *Pre-Musalman India*, vol. 2, *Vedic India*, pt. 1 (Madras: Indian Publishing House, 1937), p. 91.

21. H. C. Raychaudhuri, *Political History of Ancient India*, 6th ed. (Calcutta: University of Calcutta, 1953), p. 27.

22. Maurice Winternitz, *A History of Indian Literature*, vol. 1, pt. 2 (Delhi: Motilal Banarsidass, 1963), p. 416.

CHAPTER 4: FEAR OF DISILLUSIONMENT

1. Stuart Piggott, *Pre-Historic India to 1000 BC* (London: Cassell, 1962), p. 265.

2. Mortimer Wheeler, *Civilizations of the Indus Valley and Beyond* (London: Thames and Hudson, 1966), p. 97.

3. Amar Chand, *Hastinapura: The Glory of Ancient India* (Banaras: Jain Cultural Research Society, 1952), pp. 7 and 8.

4. A. Vide Ghosh, *Ancient India*, nos. 11 and 12 (New Delhi: Job Press, 1954 and 1955), p. 3.

5. C. V. Vaidya, Mahabharata: *A Criticism*, 2nd ed. (Bombay: A. J. Combridge, 1929), p. 55.

6. Vincent Smith, *The Oxford History of India*, 3rd ed. (Oxford: Oxford University Press, 1958), p. 95.

7. A. A. Macdonell, *India's Past* (Oxford: Oxford University Press, 1927; Delhi: Motilal Banarsidass, 1956), p. 255. Citations are to the 1956 reprint.

8. See Willard F. H. Libby's piece in the cooperative study entitled *The Frontiers of Knowledge* (New York: Doubleday, 1975), pp. 326–58.

9. Macdonell, *India's Past*, p. 255.

10. Smith, *Oxford History of India*, p. 59.

11. Albrecht Weber, *The History of Indian Literature* (London: Trubner, 1914), p. 187.

12. Romila Thapar, *A History of India*, vol. 1 (Harmondsworth: Penguin, 1968), p. 32.

13. A. L. Basham, *The Wonder That Was India* (London: Sidgwick and Jackson, 1954), p. 39.

14. See V. Rangacharya, *Pre-Musalman India*, vol. 2, *Vedic India*, pt. 1 (Madras: Indian Publishing House, 1937), p. 136.

15. A. D. Pusalkar, *History and Culture of the Indian People*, vol. 1, *The*

Vedic Age, ed. R. C. Majumdar (London: Bharatiya Vidya Bhavan, 1951), p. 269.

16. J. A. C. Brown, *The Evolution of Society* (New York: Hawthorn Books, 1966), p. 73.

17. Vaidya, Mahabharata: *A Criticism*, p. 65.

18. S. B. Roy, *Ancient India: A Chronological Study* (New Delhi: Institute of Chronology, 1975); S. B. Roy, *Date of Mahabharata Battle* (Gurgaon: Academic Press, 1976).

CHAPTER 5: "A FRAUD OF MONSTROUS SIZE"

1. V. R. Narla, *East and West: Myth of Dichotomy* (Nagarjuna: Nagarjuna University, 1981), p. 45.

2. F. E. Pargiter, *The Puranic Text of the Dynasties of the Kali Age* (Varanasi: Chowkhamba Sanskrit Series Office, 1962), pp. 77–83.

3. Iravati Karve, *Yuganta: The End of an Epoch* (Poona: Deshmukh Prakashan, 1969), p. 5.

4. Vemuri Srinivasa Rao, *Poorvagatha Lahari* (Madras, 1952), pp. 327–28.

This is a handy and useful dictionary of Puranic lore in Telugu. I find it more informative than some of its counterparts in English.

5. Hermann Oldenberg, quoted in V. S. Sukthankar, *On the Meaning of the* Mahabharata (Bombay: Asiatic Society, 1957), p. 1.

6. E. W. Hopkins, *The Great Epic of India* (New York: C. Scribner's Sons, 1901; Calcutta: Punthi Pustak, 1969), p. 400. Citations are to the 1969 reprint.

7. Vincent Smith, *The Oxford History of India*, 3rd ed. (Oxford: Oxford University Press, 1958), p. 57.

8. Max Muller, *A History of Ancient Sanskrit Literature so far as It Illustrates the Primitive Religion of the Brahmans* (Varanasi: Chowkhamba Sanskrit Series Office, 1968), p. 40.

9. Radhakumud Mookerji, *Hindu Civilization: From the Earliest Times up to the Establishment of the Maurya Empire* (Bombay: Bharatiya Vidya Bhavan, 1950), p. 141.

10. Albrecht Weber, *The History of Indian Literature* (London: Trubner, 1914), p. 185.

11. V. Rangacharya, *Pre-Musalman India*, vol. 2, *Vedic India*, pt. 1 (Madras: Indian Publishing House, 1937), pp. 69–73.

12. E. J. Rapson, ed., *Ancient India* (Cambridge: Cambridge University Press, 1914), p. 71.

13. L. D. Barnett, *Antiquities of India* (London: P. L. Warner, 1913), p. 11.

14. Hopkins, *Great Epic of India*, p. 385.

15. A. A. Macdonell, *India's Past* (Oxford: Oxford University Press, 1927; Delhi: Motilal Banarsidass, 1956), p. 52.

16. Maurice Winternitz, *A History of Indian Literature*, vol. 1, pt. 2 (Delhi: Motilal Banarsidass, 1963), p. 408.

17. Weber, *History of Indian Literature*, pp. 184–90.

18. C. V. Vaidya, Mahabharata: *A Criticism*, 2nd ed. (Bombay: A. J. Combridge, 1929), pp. 7 and 17.

19. Mookerji, *Hindu Civilization*, p. 141.

20. V. S. Sukthankar, *On the Meaning of the* Mahabharata (Bombay: Asiatic Society of Bombay, 1957), p. 22.

21. Rapson, *Ancient India*, p. 73.

22. T. W. Rhys-Davids, *Buddhist India* (Calcutta: Susil Gupta, 1955), pp. 120–21.

23. D. D. Kosambi, *An Introduction to the Study of Indian History*, rev. 2nd ed. (Bombay: Popular Prakashan,1975), p. 307.

24. Sir Percival Griffiths, *The British Impact on India* (1952; repr., London: MacDonald, 1962), p. 216. Citations are to the 1962 reprint.

CHAPTER 6: OUTER CITADEL AND INNER FORT

1. S. Radhakrishnan, *The Bhagavadgita* (London: Allen and Unwin, 1956), p. 88.

Here, as elsewhere in my book, all English translations of passages from the Gita, unless otherwise acknowledged, are from this version.

2. P. D. Mehta, *Early Indian Religious Thought* (London: Luzac, 1956), p. 246.

3. E. W. Hopkins, *The Great Epic of India* (New York: C. Scribner's Sons, 1901; Calcutta: Punthi Pustak, 1969), p. 402. Citations are to the 1969 reprint.

4. S. Sukthankar, *On the Meaning of the* Mahabharata (Bombay: Asiatic Society of Bombay, 1957), p. 30.

5. Ibid.

6. Ibid., p. 29.

7. C. Rajagopalachari, *Mahabharata*, 11th ed. (Bombay: Bharatiya Vidya Bhavan, 1972).

Rajagopalachari's summary of the *Mahabharata*, originally written in Tamil, has been translated into many languages and has sold more than a million copies so far.

8. K. M. Munshi, *Krishnavatara*, vols. 1–7 (Bombay: Bharatiya Vidya Bhavan, 1961–71).

The first volume appeared in 1961, the sixth in 1971, and the seventh was published posthumously. Munshi could not complete what he considered to be his magnum opus.

9. J. A. C. Brown, *The Evolution of Society* (New York: Hawthorn Books, 1966), p. 23.

10. Bronislaw Malinowski, *Magic, Science and Religion and Other Essays* (New York: Anchor Books, 1954), p. 101.

11. Ibid., p. 125.

12. Ibid., p. 126.

CHAPTER 7: WHO IS KRISHNA?

1. Hermann Oldenberg, quoted in V. S. Sukthankar, *On the Meaning of the* Mahabharata (Bombay: Asiatic Society of Bombay, 1957), p. 24.

2. Incontrovertible evidence to bear out this fact is provided by the Bhilsa columns of the second century BCE. One of these is still in tact at Basnagar, near Bhilsa. I saw it in the early fifties. It is a Garuda pillar erected by "a Greek named Heliodorus, an inhabitant of Taxila and an envoy of King Antialcidas" to the court of the Sunga king, Bhaagabhadia. E. W. Hopkins, *The Cambridge History of India*, vol. 1, *Ancient India*, ed. E. J. Rapson (Cambridge: Cambridge University Press, 1935), pp. 521 and 625.

3. Bepin Chandra Pal, *Sree Krishna*, 2nd ed. (Calcutta: Tagore, 1963).

This was originally published in 1938 with the high-sounding title *Europe Asks Who Is Shri Krishna?*

4. H. H. Wilson, *Rig-Veda*, 6 vols. (Bangalore: Bangalore Printing and Publishing, 1946), 1:190.

5. Vemuri Srinivasa Rao, *Purvagadha Lahari* (Vijayawada, 1952), p. 270.

The episode is from the Bhagavatha Purana.

6. Wilson, *Rig-Veda*, 5:184.

7. H. H. Wilson, *The Vishnu Purana: A System of Hindu Mythology and Tradition* (Calcutta: Punthi Pustak, 1961), pp. 417–20.

8. Robert Ernest Hume, *The Thirteen Principal Upanishads*, 2nd ed. (Oxford: Oxford University Press, 1974), p. 213.

9. Bimanbehari Majumdar, *Krishna in History and Legend* (Calcutta: University of Calcutta, 1969), p. 3.

10. H. C. Raychaudhuri, *Materials for the History of the Vaishnava Sect*, 2nd ed. (New Delhi: South Asia Books, 1975).

11. A. S. P. Ayyar, *Sri Krishna: The Darling of Humanity* (Madras: Madras Law Journal Press, 1957), p. 26.

12. Bepin Chandra Pal, *Sree Krishna*, p. 1.

13. Wilson, *Vishnu Purana*, pp. 423–24.

14. Haridas Bhattacharya, ed., *The Cultural Heritage of India*, 2nd ed. (Calcutta: Ramakrishna Mission Institute of Culture, 1969), p. 257.

15. Manmanatha Nath Dutt, *The Ramayana*, vol. 2 (Calcutta: Girish Chandra Chackravarti, Deva Press, 1892), p. 480.

16. Maurice Winternitz, *A History of Indian Literature*, vol. 1, pt. 2 (Delhi: Motilal Banarsidass, 1963), pp. 487–88.

17. Sitanath Tattavabhushan, *Sitanath Krishna and the Puranas: Essays on the Origin and Development of Vaishnavism* (Calcutta: T. Roy, 1926), p. 68.

18. Nirad C. Chaudhuri, *Hinduism* (New Delhi: Chatto and Windus, 1979), p. 275.

19. Ibid.

20. Ibid.

21. Dhirendra Nath Pal, *Srikrishna: His Life and Teachings*, 3rd ed., 2 vols. (Calcutta: Maunmatha Library, 1904), 1:188.

22. Ibid., p. 190.

23. Mohan Lal Sen, *Lord Sreekrishna: His Life and Teachings*, 2nd ed., 3 vols. (Calcutta: Oriental Publishing, 1954), 1:208.

24. Ibid.

25. Pratap R. Parekh, *Krishna: Myth or Reality* (Bombay: Jaico, 1980), p. 47.

26. Hanuman Prasad Poddar, *Gopis' Love for Sri Krishna*, 4th ed. (Gorakhpur: Gita Press, 1952), p. 36.

27. Ayyar, *Sri Krishna*, p. xiv.

28. Monika Varma, *Lord Krishna: Love Incarnate* (New Delhi: Vikas, 1978).

29. Baba Premanand Bharati, *Sree Krishna: The Lord of Love* (New York: Krishna Samaj, 1904), p. 114.

30. Donald R. Kinsley, *The Sword and the Flute: Kali and Krishna* (New Delhi: Vikas, 1976), p. 55.

CHAPTER 8: KRISHNA AS MAN

1. E. W. Hopkins, *The Great Epic of India* (New York: C. Scribner's Sons, 1901; Calcutta: Punthi Pustak, 1969), p. 374. Citations are to the 1969 reprint.

2. E. W. Hopkins, *The Cambridge History of India*, vol.1, *Ancient India*, ed. E. J. Rapson (Cambridge: Cambridge University Press, 1935), p. 258.

3. Details about the life and work of Winternitz are culled by me from *Winternitz Memorial Number*, Calcutta. My copy gives no date of its publication. But it was in all probability published as a special number of the *Indian Historical Quarterly* in 1938.

4. Maurice Winternitz, *A History of Indian Literature*, rev. 2nd ed., vol. 1, pt. 2 (Delhi: Motilal Banarsidass, 1963), p. 399.

5. Ibid., p. 391.

6. Max Weber, *The Religion of India* (New York: Free Press Paperback, 1967), p. 189.

7. V. S. Sukthankar, *On the Meaning of the* Mahabharata (Bombay: Asiatic Society of Bombay, 1957), p. 24.

8. Ibid., pp. 96–97.

9. Pendyala Subrahmanya Sastri, *Mahabharata Charitram*, 2nd ed. (Pithapuram, 1933), pp. 166–68.

10. Ibid., pp. 168–71.

11. Sukthankar, *On the Meaning of the* Mahabharata, p. 17.

12. John Davies, *The Bhagavad Gita* (Delhi, 1978), p. 11.

13. Manorama Jauhari, *Politics and Ethics in Ancient India* (Varanasi: Bharatiya Vidya Prakashan, 1968), p. 314.

14. Hopkins, *Great Epic of India*, p. 375.

15. The presence of such incidents in the present text of the epic is clear enough proof that the *Mahabharata* was pro-Kuru before it was deliberately tampered with to make it pro-Pandu.

CHAPTER 9: KRISHNA AS STATESMAN

1. Bankim Chandra Chatterji, *Renaissance and Reaction in the Nineteenth-Century Bengal: Bankum Chandra Chatterjee*, trans. M. K. Haldar (Columbia, MO: South Asia Books, 1977), pp. 96–97.

2. Bimanbehari Majumdar, *Krishna in History and Legend* (Calcutta: University of Calcutta, 1969), pp. 248–49.

I have depended almost exclusively on this excellent work for the views of Bankim Chandra Chatterji on Krishna. *Krishnacharitra* was translated decades ago in Telugu; long out of print, its copies have become extremely scarce.

3. K. M. Munshi, *Krishnavatara*, vol. 1, *The Magic Flute* (Bombay: Bharatiya Vidya Bhavan, 1962), p. iii.

4. Niharranjan Ray, foreword to Mahabharata: *Myth and Reality*, ed. S. P. Gupta and K. S. Ramachandran (Delhi: Agam Prakashan, 1976), p. ix.

5. D. C. Sirkar in ibid., p. 141.

6. E. W. Hopkins, *The Great Epic of India* (New York: C. Scribner's Sons, 1901; Calcutta: Punthi Pustak, 1969), p. 396. Citations are to the 1969 reprint.

7. Majumdar, *Krishna in History and Legend*, p. 152.

8. A. D. Pusalkar, *History and Culture of the Indian People*, vol. 1, *The Vedic Age*, ed. R. C. Majumdar (London: Bharatiya Vidya Bhavan, 1951), p. 302.

9. See Manorama Jauhari, *Politics and Ethics in Ancient India* (Varanasi: Bharatiya Vidya Prakashan, 1968), p. 178.

CHAPTER 10: KRISHNA AS GOD

1. Pendyala Subrahmanya Sastri, *Mahabharata Charitram*, 2nd ed. (Pithapuram, 1933), pp. 81–82.

2. Ibid., pp. 84–85.

3. Ibid., pp. 168–70.

4. Sitanath Tattavabhushan, *Krishna and the Gita* (Calcutta, n.d.), pp. 65 and 67.

5. Ibid., p. 74.

6. Bimanbehari Majumdar, *Krishna in History and Legend* (Calcutta: University of Calcutta, 1969), p. 245.

7. Ibid., p. 161.

8. V. S. Sukthankar, *On the Meaning of the* Mahabharata (Bombay: Asiatic Society of Bombay, 1957), p. 100.

9. Majumdar, *Krishna in History and Legend*, p. 164.

10. E. W. Hopkins, *The Great Epic of India* (New York: C. Scribner's Sons, 1901; Calcutta: Punthi Pustak, 1969), p. 395. Citations are to the 1969 reprint.

11. Maurice Winternitz, *A History of Indian Literature*, rev. 2nd ed., vol. 1, pt. 2 (Delhi: Motilal Banarsidass, 1963), p. 401.

12. D. D. Kosambi, *The Culture and Civilization of Ancient India in Historical Outline* (London: Routledge and Kegan Paul, 1965), pp. 114–15.

CHAPTER 11: WHO WROTE THE GITA?

1. C. V. Vaidya, *Epic India; or, India as Described in the* Mahabharata *and* Ramayana (Bombay: Radhabai Atmaram Sagoon, 1907), pp. 419–20.

2. E. W. Hopkins, *The Social and Military Position of the Ruling Caste in Ancient India* (Varanasi: Bharat-Bharati, 1972), p. 198.

3. Sitanath Tattavabhushan, *Krishna and the Gita* (Calcutta, n.d.), p. 81.

4. Weber, quoted in G. S. Khair, *Quest for the Original Gita* (Bombay: Somaiya Publications, 1969), p. 11.

5. M. Monier-Williams, *Hinduism* (Calcutta: Susil Gupta, 1951), pp. 144–45.

6. E. W. Hopkins, *Religions of India*, 2nd ed. (Delhi: Munshiram Manoharlal, 1970), p. 400.

7. K. N. Upadhyaya, *Early Buddhism and the Bhagavadgita* (Delhi: Motilal Banarsidass, 1971), p. 3.

8. Garbe, quoted in S. K. Belvalkar, *The Cultural Heritage of India*, rev. ed., vol. 2 (Calcutta, 1969), p. 137.

9. Rudolf Otto, *The Original Gita* (London: Allen and Unwin, 1939), p. 14.

For those who are curious, according to Otto the original Gita consisted of the whole of chapter 1; verses 1–13, 20, 22, and 29–37 of chapter 2; verses 1–8 of chapter 5; verses 1–6, 8–12, 14, 17, 19–36, and 41–51 of chapter 11; and, finally, verses 58–61, 66, 72, and 73 of chapter 18.

10. Ibid., pp. 13–14.

11. S. C. Roy, quoted in Bimanbehari Majumdar, *Krishna in History and Legend* (Calcutta: University of Calcutta, 1969), p. 45.

According to Roy, if the following interpolated verses were to be removed from the present Gita, it can stand as an independent philosophical work, unrelated in any way with the Kurukshetra War: 1.1–46; 2.1–10, 31–38; 11.26–28, 32–34, 41–42; 18.59–60, 72–78.

12. Surendranath Dasgupta, *A History of Indian Philosophy*, vol. 2 (Cambridge: Cambridge University Press, 1952), p. 552.

13. Franklin Edgerton, quoted in Upadhyaya, *Early Buddhism and the Bhagavadgita*, p. 3.

14. Edgerton, quoted in Majumdar, *Krishna in History and Legend*, p. 36.

15. G. S. Khair, *Quest for the Original Gita* (Bombay: Somaiya Publications, 1969), p. 1.

16. Ibid., p. i.

17. Ibid., p. xi.

18. Ibid., p. xiii.

19. Ibid., p. 159.

According to Khair, the work of the three authors sorts out thus:

1. Chapters 1–6: first and third authors
2. Chapters 8, 13–15, 17, and 18: second and third authors
3. Chapters 7, 9–12, and 17: third author
(quoted from p. 58)

20. Maurice Winternitz, *A History of Indian Literature*, vol. 1, pt. 2 (Delhi: Motilal Banarsidass, 1963), p. 404.

CHAPTER 12: AND WHEN?

1. Bimanbehari Majumdar, *Krishna in History and Legend* (Calcutta: University of Calcutta, 1969), p. 46.

2. Ibid.; for fuller details of the discussion, see pp. 45–46.

3. K. N. Upadhyaya, *Early Buddhism and the Bhagavadgita* (Delhi: Motilal Banarsidass, 1971), p. 1.

4. G. S. Khair, *Quest for the Original Gita* (Bombay: Somaiya Publications, 1969), p. xiii.

5. D. D. Kosambi, *The Culture and Civilization of Ancient India in Historical Outline* (London: Routledge and Kegan Paul, 1965), p. 93.

6. Ibid., p. 266.

7. S. K. Belvalkar, *The Cultural Heritage of India*, rev. ed., vol. 2 (Calcutta, 1969), pp. 136–37.

CHAPTER 13: GITA AS SCRIPTURE

1. S. K. Belvalkar, *The Cultural Heritage of India*, rev. ed., vol. 2 (Calcutta, 1969), p. 138.

2. Surendranath Dasgupta, *A History of Indian Philosophy*, vol. 2 (Cambridge: Cambridge University Press, 1952), pp. 437–43.

3. I have in my personal library a copy of this extremely rare book. But for the last three or four pages of notes, it is a complete copy in fairly good condition. I picked it up from a pavement bookshop in Hyderabad for the fantastic price of, well, three rupees! Book hunting can be far more exciting than the shooting of lions and tigers.

4. P. J. Marshall, ed., *The British Discovery of Hinduism in the Eighteenth Century* (Cambridge: Cambridge University Press, 1979), p. 190.

5. Ibid., p. 5.

6. Ibid., p. 12.

7. D. D. Kosambi, *An Introduction to the Study of Indian History*, rev. 2nd ed. (Bombay: Popular Prakashan, 1975), pp. 283–84.

8. K. N. Upadhyaya, *Early Buddhism and the Bhagavadgita* (Delhi: Motilal Banarsidass, 1971), pp. 106–50.

9. Ibid., pp. 109–10.

10. Ibid., pp. 110–12.

11. Ibid., pp. 112–14.

12. Ibid., p. 114.

CHAPTER 14: HAS THE GITA A PHILOSOPHY?

1. Will Durant, *The Pleasures of Philosophy* (New York: Simon and Schuster, 1953), p. 11.

2. Ibid., p. 8.

3. S. Radhakrishnan, *The Bhagavadgita* (London: Allen and Unwin, 1956), p. 11.

4. E. W. Hopkins, quoted in W. Douglas P. Hill, *The Bhagavadgita*, 2nd abr. ed. (London: Clarendon Press, 1953), pp. 19–20.

5. Arun Shourie, *Hinduism, Essence and Consequence: A Study of the Upanishads, the Gita, and the Brahma-Sutras* (New Delhi: Vikas, 1979), pp. 191–92.

6. Radhakrishnan, *Bhagavadgita*, p. 12.

7. Ibid., p. 13.

8. D. S. Sarma, *Lectures and Essays on the Bhagavad Gita*, 4th ed. (Madras: M. L. J. Press, 1945), p. 19.

9. Arvind Sharma, *Thresholds in Hindu-Buddhist Studies* (Calcutta: Minerva, 1979), pp. 115–16.

10. D. D. Kosambi, *Myth and Reality* (Bombay: Popular Prakashan, 1962), p. 17.

11. K. T. Telang, *The Bhagavadgita with the Sanatsugatiya and Anugita* (Oxford: Oxford University Press, 1908), pp. 12–13.

12. Franklin Edgerton, quoted in Sharma, *Thresholds in Hindu-Buddhist Studies*, p. 113.

13. S. Radhakrishnan, *Indian Philosophy*, vol. 1 (London: Allen and Unwin, 1948), p. 49.

14. Erich Fromm; see Clara Urquhart, ed., *A Matter of Life* (Boston: Little, Brown, 1963), p. 101.

15. "Again and again" is an expression that is used often in the Gita.

16. Fromm; see Urquhart, *Matter of Life*, p. 103.

CHAPTER 15: ETHICS OF THE GITA

1. Bertrand Russell, *Science and Religion* (London: Geoffrey Cumberlege, 1949), pp. 223–24.

2. Bertrand Russell, *An Outline of Philosophy* (London: Allen and Unwin, 1951), p. 241.

3. Sankaracharya, *The Bhagavad Gita with Commentary*, trans. Alladi Mahadeva Sastri (Madras: Samata Books, 1979), p. 341.

4. Ibid.

5. Ibid., p. 392 [emphasis added].

To soften the enormity of the tenet, Sankaracharya adds the comment: "Society of men; of the ordinary, unenlightened and undisciplined people, and not of the enlightened and disciplined men."

6. Swami Ranganathananda; see M. D. Paradkar, ed., *Studies in the Gita* (Bombay: Prakashan, 1970), p. 53.

7. Susruva, *The Esoteric Gospel of Gita* (New Delhi: Affiliated East-West Press, 1978), p. 51.

8. G. W. Kaveeshwar, *The Ethics of the Gita* (Delhi: Motilal Banarsidass, 1971), p. 190.

9. S. S. Sharma, *Ethics of Butler and the Philosophy of Action in Bhagavadgita according to Madhusudana Sarasvati* (Varanasi: Bharatiya Vidya Prakashan, 1967), p. ix.

10. B. S. Gauchhwal, *The Concept of Perfection in the Teachings of Kant and the Gita* (Delhi: Motilal Banarsidass, 1967), p. 178.

11. Maurice Winternitz, *A History of Indian Literature*, vol. 1, pt. 2 (Delhi: Motilal Banarsidass, 1963), p. 11.

12. S. S. Raghavacharya, *Sri Ramanuja on the Gita* (Mangalore: Ramakrishna Ashrama, 1979).

13. P. N. Srinivasachari, *The Ethical Philosophy of the Gita*, 4th ed. (Madras: Sri Ramakrishna Math, 1971).

14. H. V. Divatia, *The Art of Life in the Bhagavad Gita*, 5th ed. (Bombay: Bharatiya Vidya Bhavan, 1970), p. 75.

15. Ibid., p. 106.

16. Will Durant, *The Story of Philosophy* (New York: Pocket Books, 1957), p. 137.

17. Prem Nath Bazaz, *The Role of the Bhagavad Gita in Indian History* (New Delhi: Sterling Publishers, 1975), p. 261.

18. D. D. Kosambi; see Debiprasad Chattopadhyaya, ed., *Studies in the History of Indian Philosophy*, vol. 1 (Calcutta: Sinha Publishing, 1977), pp. 252–53.

19. D. D. Kosambi, *Myth and Reality* (Bombay: Popular Prakashan, 1962), p. 190.

20. Arun Shourie, *Hinduism, Essence and Consequence: A Study of the Upanishads, the Gita, and the Brahma-Sutras* (New Delhi: Vikas, 1979), p. 192.

CHAPTER 16: SOCIOLOGY OF THE GITA

1. M. K. Sharan, *Bhagavad Gita and Hindu Sociology* (Delhi: Bharat Bharati Bhandar, 1977), p. 41.

2. Ibid., p. 28.

3. Ibid., p. 36.

4. Ibid., p. 37.

5. S. Radhakrishnan, *The Bhagavadgita* (London: Allen and Unwin, 1956), p. 160.

6. Sankaracharya, *The Bhagavad Gita with Commentary*, trans. Alladi Mahadeva Sastri (Madras: Samata Books, 1979), p. 125.

7. Ibid., pp. 125–26.

8. John Davies, *The Bhagavad Gita* (Delhi, 1978), p. 36.

9. Sankaracharya, *Bhagavad Gita with Commentary*, p. 275.

10. Swami Chinmayananda, *The Bhagavad Gita* (Madras: Chinmaya Publications Trust, 1979), chapters 7–9 and p. 158.

11. Ibid., p. 160.

12. Radhakrishnan, *Bhagavadgita*, p. 252.

13. Davies, *Bhagavad Gita*, p. 62.

14. Ibid., p. 62n.

15. F. T. Brooks, *The Bhagavad-Gita; or, The Chant of the Blessed One*, translated into rythmical English (Ajmer, undated, probably around 1900), p. 61.

16. Kees Bolle, *The Bhagavadgita: A New Translation* (Berkeley: University of California Press, 1979), p. 111.

For the offending expression his rendering is "no matter how vile their birth."

17. A. J. Bahn, *The Bhagavad Gita* (Bombay, n.d.), p. 27.

For "sinful womb" his rendering is "born in a low station in life."

18. Shakuntala Rao Sastri, *The Bhagavadgita*, 2nd ed. (Bombay: Bharatiya Vidya Bhavan, 1971), p. 275.

Perhaps because she is a woman, she gives the most faithful translation thus: "who are born of the womb of sin, women, Vysyas, and Sudras."

19. Annie Besant and Bhagavan Das, *The Bhagavad Gita, with Sanskrit Text, Free Translation into English, a Word-for-Word Translation, an Introduction to Sanskrit Grammer, and a Complete Word Index* (1905; repr., Madras: Theosophical Publishing House, 1973), p. 172. Citations are to the 1973 reprint.

The rendering is "through of the womb of sin, women, Vysyas, even Sudras." Of the joint translators one was a woman, and the other a Vysya.

20. Annie Besant, *The Bhagavad Gita: The Lord's Song* (Madras: G. A. Natesan, 1922; Madras: Theosophical Publishing House, 1977 repr.), p. 137. Citations to the 1977 reprint.

21. Swami Paramananda, *Srimad Bhagavad-Gita*, 2nd ed. (Madras: Vedanta Centre Publishers, 1982), p. 78.

The expression he preferred is "inferior birth."

22. Swami Vireswarananda, *Srimad Bhagavad Gita with the Gloss of Sridhara Swami* (Madras: Sri Ramakrishna Math, 1980), p. 283.

He preferred "sinful birth" to "sinful womb."

23. Swami Sivananda, *Srimad Bhiagavadgita* (Rishikesh: Yoga-Vedanta Forest Academy, 1959), p. 122.

24. Arthur Osborne and G. V. Kulkarni, *The Bhagavad Gita* (Tiruvannamalai: Sri Ramanasramam, 1973), p. 68.

25. Nehal Chand Vaish, *Musings on the Bhagavad Gita* (Allahabad: S. N. Basu, 1931), p. 342.

Like Radhakrishnan, this gentleman also uses the occasion with little relevance to deliver a sermon on untouchability.

26. P. Lal, *The Bhagavadgita* (New Delhi: Orient Paperbacks, 1965), p. 60.

Lal also opts for the expression "low birth."

27. Sitanath Tattavabhushan, *The Bhagavadgita* (Calcutta, 1929), p. 165.

Srichandra Vidyabhushan Bhagavataratna collaborated with Sitanath in this translation. It shows that two heads cannot always be better than one.

28. Swami Chidbhavananda, *Srimad Bhagavadgita* (Tirupparaitturai: Sri Ramakrishna Tapovananam, 1969), pp. 520–21.

29. Swami Swarupananda, *Srimad Bhagavadgita, with Text, Word-for-Word Translation, English Rendering, Comments, and Index*, 12th rev. ed. (Mayavati: Advaita Ashram, 1976), p. 216.

In his translation he takes the lead from Sankaracharya and adds his own comment: "Of inferior are engaged only in agriculture, etc., and the women and Sudras are debarred from the study of the Vedas." And this Swami was the first president of the Advaita Ashram, Mayavati! Such is Advaita! And such are its Swamis!

30. Sant Keshavadas, *Bhagavad Gita: Thus Sang Lord Krishna* (Bangalore: Saraswathi Press, 1975).

For those born out of "sinful womb," this is Sant's wholly unfaithful translation: "Trading class and laboring class / Women and men of the common mass." Such are the liberties that our Sants take with what they call our most sacred scripture!

31. Swami Prabhavananda and Christopher Isherwood, *The Song of God: Bhagavad-Gita* (New York: Mentor, n.d.), p. 85.

These two luminaries leave out "women" and refer to the rest as the "lower castes." Is truth no part of religion?

32. William Q. Judge, *The Bhagavad-Gita: The Book of Devotion* (Bombay, 1965).

Though he has a kind thought for the Vysyas and the Sudras, this theosophist expresses some surprise at what is said about women, but only for a fleeting moment. He recalls that the Bible was harsher on women and then continues to read in the "Book of Devotion" with serenity. Here is the footnote:

This may seem strange to those who have been born in Christendom, and perhaps appear to be testimony to harsh views on the part of Hindu sages respecting women, but in the Bible the same thing is to be found and even worse, where in 1 Tim. 2, 11–15, it is declared that the woman shall be saved through her husband, and that she must be subservient.

33. Dilip Kumar Roy, *The Bhagavad Gita: A Revelation* (New Delhi: Hind Pocket Books, 1977), pp. 140–41.

In his translation Roy leaps in chapter 9 from verse 31 to 33. He was, I think, a stocky man; yet he did show much agility at this point.

34. Kumar Kishore Mohanty, *Sermon Supernal: Gita in Verse* (Bombay, 1977), p. 66.

With little respect to truth, he translates thus: "Whether they are women or born lowly, whether merchant or servant." Are truth and faith natural enemies?

35. Swami Shri Purohit, *The Gita: The Gospel of Lord Shri Krishna* (London, 1935), p. 57.

This Swami is a law unto himself. And so his translation runs riot thus: "... even the children of sinful parents, and those miscalled the weaker sex, and merchants and laborers." This may be good salesmanship, but hardly anything approaching spiritualism.

36. Edwin Arnold, *The Song Celestial or Bhagavad Gita* (London: Routledge and Kegan Paul, 1955), p. 53.

37. Juan Mascaro, *The Bhagavad Gita* (Harmondsworth: Penguin, 1978), p. 19.

His specialty appears to be to praise all religions and to translate all religious scriptures that have a good market.

38. Swami Prabhupada, *Bhagavad-Gita as It Is* (Los Angeles: Macmillan, 1972), p. 160.

His wholly misleading translation reads, ". . . even a woman, a merchant, or one who is born in a low family."

39. A. S. P. Ayyar, *A Layman's Bhagavad Gita*, vol. 2 (Madras: Madras Law Journal Press, 1956), p. 243.

40. Ibid.

41. Ibid., p. 244.

42. Ibid., p. 198.

43. Sankaracharya, *Bhagavad Gita with Commentary*, p. 113.

44. Sri Aurobindo, *Essays on the Gita* (New York: Sri Aurobindo Library, 1950), p. 455.

CHAPTER 17: THE GITA AND SCIENCE

1. H. V. Divatia, *The Art of Life in the Bhagavad Gita*, 5th ed. (Bombay: Bharatiya Vidya Bhavan, 1970), p. 131.

2. Ibid., p. 120.

3. Ibid.

4. Ibid., p. 128.

5. It was John Gunther who first called Rajagopalachari the "Brahman Savonarola" in his book *Inside Asia* (New York: Harper and Brothers, 1942), p. 458.

6. S. G. Sardesai and Dilip Bose, *Marxism and the Bhagvat Gita* (New Delhi: People's Publishing House, 1982), p. 4.

7. C. Rajagopalachari, *Bhagavad-Gita*, 4th ed. (Bombay: Bharatiya Vidya Bhavan, 1970), p. 30.

8. A. R. Hall, *The Scientific Revolution 1500–1800* (London: Longmans, Green, 1954), p. 244.

9. F. E. Planer, *Superstition* (London: Cassell, 1980), pp. 100–101.

10. James D. Watson, *The Double Helix: A Personal Account of the Discovery of the Structure of DNA* (London: Weidenfeld and Nicolson, 1969), p. 14.

11. Albert Einstein; see Albert Einstein, John Dewey, H. G. Wells, et al.,

Living Philosophies: A Series of Intimate Credos (Cleveland: World Publishing, 1942), p. 6.

12. Frank Crick, *Life Itself: Its Origin and Nature* (New York: Simon and Schuster, 1981), p. 37.

13. Carl Sagan, *The Cosmic Connection* (New York: Anchor, 1980), p. 6.

14. Swami Prabhupada, *Bhagavad-Gita as It Is* (Los Angeles: Macmillan, 1972), p. 229.

15. Jacob Bronowski, *Science and Human Values*, rev. ed. (New York: Harper and Row, 1965), pp. 40–41.

CHAPTER 18: WHY THE GITA?

1. Hermann Oldenberg, *Buddha: His Life, His Doctrine, His Order*, trans. William Hoey (Calcutta: Book, 1927), pp. 153–54.

2. Ibid., p. 153.

3. Bhupendranath Datta, *Studies in Indian Social Polity* (Calcutta: Nababharat Publishers, 1983), p. 189.

For those who may not be aware, I may mention that Datta was the brother of Swami Vivekananda and a leftist intellectual.

4. Romila Thapar, *Asoka and the Decline of the Mauryas* (Oxford: Oxford University Press, 1963), p. 104.

She refers to a pillar edict of Asoka that definitely enjoins danda samata, and yet for some reason of her own wonders whether Asoka really "discontinued the practice of grading punishments according to caste," and graciously adds that had he really done it, that would "certainly have been a daring step."

5. Datta, *Studies in Indian Social Polity*, p. 189.

6. Ibid.

7. Jaganathan; see K. A. Nilakanta Sastri, ed., *A Comprehensive History of India*, vol. 2, *The Mauryas & Satavahanas* (Bombay: Orient Longmans, 1957), p. 94.

8. Niharranjan Ray, *Maurya and Post-Maurya Art: A Study in Social and Formal Contrasts* (New Delhi: Indian Council of Historical Research, 1975), p. 54.

9. K. P. Jayaswal, *An Imperial History of India, in a Sanskrit Text: c. 700 BC–c. 770 AD, with a Special Commentary on Later Gupta Period* (Delhi: Motilal Banarsidass, 1934), p. 18.

10. B. C. Sinha, *History of the Sunga Dynasty* (Delhi: Bharatiya Publishing House, 1977), p. 13.

11. P. Banerjee, *Early Indian Religions* (Delhi: Vikas, 1973), pp. 118–19.

12. B. N. Puri, *India in the Time of Patanjali* (Bombay: Bhartiya Vidya Bhavan, 1968), p. 157.

13. Jayaswal, quoted in Datta, *Studies in Indian Social Polity*, p. 190.

14. Banerjee, *Early Indian Religions*, p. 1.

15. Bimanbehari Majumdar, *Krishna in History and Legend* (Calcutta: University of Calcutta, 1969), p. 11.

16. Floyd H. Ross, *Meaning of Life in Hinduism and Buddhism* (London: Routledge and Kegan Paul, 1952), p. 124.

17. Puri, *India in the Time of Patanjali*, p. 155.

18. For more details of the abominations of the so-called Dharma Shastras, see V. R. Narla, *Indian Culture: Its Caste Complexion* (Hyderabad: Osmania University Press, 1980).

19. Banerjee, *Early Indian Religions*, p. 117.

CHAPTER 19: FROM A TRIBAL GOD TO A NATIONAL GOD

1. A. Barth, *Religions of India* (Delhi: S. Chand, 1969), p. 168.

2. J. W. McCrindle, *Ancient India as Described by Megasthenes and Arrian* (Calcutta: Thacker, Spink, 1877), p. 201.

3. R. D. Ranade, *The Bhagavadgita as a Philosophy of God-Realisation: Being a Clue through the Labyrinth of Modern Interpretations* (Bombay: Bharatiya Vidya Bhavan, 1982), pp. 95–98.

4. Bimanbehari Majumdar, *Krishna in History and Legend* (Calcutta: University of Calcutta, 1969), p. 16.

5. Ibid., p. 17.

6. Ibid., pp. 16–18.

7. T. S. Rukmani, *A Critical Study of the Bhagavata Purana, with Special Reference to Bhakti* (Varanasi: Chowkhamba Sanskrit Series Office, 1970), pp. 210–11.

8. Ibid., p. 209.

9. A. P. Karmarkar, "Religion and Philosophy of the Epics" in S. Rad-

hakrishnan, ed., *The Cultural Heritage of India*, vol. 2 (Calcutta: Ramakrishna Mission Institute of Culture, 1962), pp. 84–85.

10. J. N. Farquhar, *The Crown of Hinduism*, 2nd ed. (New Delhi: Oriental Books Reprint, 1971), p. 243.

11. Ibid., p. 359.

12. Ibid.

13. Sankaracharya, *The Bhagavad Gita with Commentary*, trans. Alladi Mahadeva Sastri (Madras: Samata Books, 1979), pp. 120–21.

14. W. Douglas P. Hill in the introduction to his translation, *The Bhagavadgita*, 2nd abr. ed. (London: Clarendon Press, 1953), p. 33.

15. Sri Aurobindo, *Essays on the Gita* (New York: Sri Aurobindo Library, 1950), p. 133.

16. Ibid.

17. Mahadev Desai, *The Gospel of Selfless Action; or, the Gita according to Gandhi* (Ahmedabad: Navajivan Publishing House, 1946), p. 48.

18. Bhagavan Das, *Krishna: A Study in the Theory of Avataras* (Bombay: Bharatiya Vidya Bhavan, 1962).

19. R. K. Pandey, *The Concept of Avataras, with Special Reference to Gita* (Delhi, 1979), pp. 49–50.

20. P. S. Tolani, *Gita—My Guide: Pearls from the Fathomless Ocean* (Bombay: Bharatiya Vidya Bhavan, 1971).

21. Kakasaheb Kalelkar, *The Gita as Jeevan-Yoga* (Bombay: Bharatiya Vidya Bhavan, 1967).

22. K. G. Warty, *The Geeta Way of Life* (Bombay: Bharatiya Vidya Bhavan, 1971).

23. Hari Prasad Sastri, *Teachings from the Bhagavad Gita* (London: Shanti Sadan, 1949).

24. Swami Chidbhavananda, *Is Bhagavadgita Antiquated?* (Mysore: Prasaranga, 1969).

25. W. G. Archer, *The Loves of Krishna* (London: Allen and Unwin, 1957).

26. Milton Singer, ed., *Krishna: Myths, Rites and Attitudes* (Chicago: University of Chicago Press, 1971).

27. Norvin Hein, *The Miracle Plays of Mathura* (Delhi: Oxford University Press, 1972).

28. Lee Siegel, *Sacred and Profane Dimensions of Love in Indian Traditions as Exemplified in the Gitagovinda of Jayadeva* (Oxford: Oxford University Press, 1978).

29. Fred Hoyle and N. C. Wickramasinghe, *Lifecloud: The Origin of Life in the Universe* (New York: Harper and Row, 1978), p. 157.

30. Pandey, *Concept of Avataras*, p. 30.

CHAPTER 20: THE TWO BHAGAVANS

1. R. G. Bhandarkar, *Collected Works*, vol. 4, *Vaisnavism, Saivism, and Minor Religious Systems* (Poona: Bhandarkar Oriental Research Institute, 1927), p. 42.

2. Quoted from *Digha Nikata* in K. N. Upadhyaya, *Early Buddhism and Bhagavadgita* (Delhi: Motilal Banarsidass, 1971), p. 483.

3. Haripada Chakraborti, *Asceticism in Ancient India* (Calcutta: Punthi Pustak, 1973), p. 476.

4. A. L. Basham, *History and Doctrines of the Ajivikas: A Vanished Indian Religion* (London: Luzac, 1951), pp. 10–18 and 92–93.

5. Bimalacharan Law, *Historical Gleanings* (Calcutta: Thacker, Spink, 1922), pp. 16–20.

6. Edward J. Thomas, *The History of Buddhist Thought* (London: Routledge and Kegan Paul, 1959), pp. 72–73.

7. S. Radhakrishnan, foreword to *2500 Years of Buddhism, A Cooperative Study*, ed. P. V. Bapat (Delhi: Ministry of Information and Broadcasting, Publications Division, 1956), p. v.

8. K. N. Upadhyaya, *Early Buddhism and the Bhagavadgita* (Delhi: Motilal Banarsidass, 1971), p. 208.

9. A. Berriedale Keith, *Buddhist Philosophy in India and Ceylon* (Oxford: Clarendon Press, 1923), p. 121.

10. P. Lakshmi Narasu, *The Essence of Buddhism*, p. 134. (My first edition copy lacks the inner title page.)

11. Hit Narayan Jha, *The Licchavis of Vaisali* (Varanasi: Chowkhamba Sanskrit Series Office, 1970), pp. 42–43.

12. Narasu, *Essence of Buddhism*, p. 126.

13. Chakraborti, *Asceticism in Ancient India*, p. 453.

14. S. Radhakrishnan, *The Bhagavadgita* (London: Allen and Unwin, 1956), p. 132.

15. Chakraborti, *Asceticism in Ancient India*, p. 93.

16. C. Kunhan Raja, *Dhammapada* (Madras: Theosophical Publishing House, 1956), p. 115.

17. Lord Chalmers, *Further Dialogues of the Buddha*, vol. 2 (London: Humphrey Milford, 1926), pp. 43–46.

18. Natalie Rokotoff, *Foundations of Buddhism* (New York: Roerich Museum Press, 1930), pp. 80–81.

19. Ibid., p. 67.

20. E. H. Brewster, *The Life of Gotama, the Buddha* (London: Kegan Paul, Trench, Trubner; Dutton, 1926), p. 157.

21. G. S. P. Misra, *The Age of Vinaya: A Historical and Cultural Study* (New Delhi: Munshiram Manoharlal, 1972), pp. 216–17.

22. N. J. Shende, "The Authorship of the *Mahabharata*," in *Annals of the Bhandarkar Oriental Research Institute*, ed. N. A. Gore (Poona: Bhandarkar Oriental Research Institute, 1942), 24:67–82.

Miss D. Santishree of Madras kindly looked up this quotation for me.

CHAPTER 21: ALL THINGS TO ALL MEN

1. T. G. Mainkar maintains that Sankaracharya was not the first commentator of the Gita and that there were definitely others who preceded him. If true, their work should be taken as stillborn.

2. D. D. Kosambi, *The Culture and Civilization of Ancient India in Historical Outline* (London: Routledge and Kegan Paul, 1965), p. 113.

3. B. P. Bahirat, *The Philosophy of Jnandeva* (Pandharput: Pandharpur Research Society, 1956), pp. 146–47.

4. T. G. Mainkar, *A Comparative Study of the Commentaries on the Bhagavadgita*, 2nd ed. (Delhi: Motilal Banarsidass, 1969).

5. R. D. Ranade, *The Bhagavadgita as a Philosophy of God-Realisation: Being a Clue through the Labyrinth of Modern Interpretations* (Bombay: Bharatiya Vidya Bhavan, 1982).

6. S. H. Jhabwala, *Geeta and Its Commentators* (Bombay: Dhawale Popular, 1960).

7. Tridandi Swami B. H. Bon, *The Gita as a Chaitanyite Reads It* (Bombay: Popular Book Depot, 1938).

8. Anonymous, *Gita Darsan as Bhaki Yoga: As a Chaitanyite Reads It* (Madras, 1938).

9. Bal Gangadhar Tilak, *Om-T at-Sat, Srimad Bhagavadgita-rahasya; or, Karma-Yoga-Sastra, Including an External Examination of the Gita, the Original*

Sanskrit Stanzas, Their English Translation, Commentaries on the Stanzas and a Comparison of Eastern and Western Doctrines (Poona: Tilak, 1975).

10. Ranade, *Bhagavadgita as a Philosophy of God-Realisation*, p. 183.

11. Sri Aurobindo, *Essays on the Gita* (New York: Sri Aurobindo Library, 1950), pp. 30–31.

12. D. K. Gosavi, *Tilak, Gandhi and Gita* (Bombay: Bharatiya Vidya Bhavan, 1983), pp. 46–47.

13. Bertrand Russell, *Human Society in Ethics and Politics* (London: Allen and Unwin, 1963), p. 18.

14. S. Radhakrishnan, *The Bhagavadgita* (London: Allen and Unwin, 1956), p. 280.

15. Albert Schweitzer, *Indian Thought and Its Development* (London: Adams and Charles Black, 1951), p. 195.